Teaching Reading to Adult Second Language Learners: Theoretical Foundations, Pedagogical Applications, and Current Issues

Meena Singhal

The Reading Matrix Inc.

Library of Congress Cataloging-in-Publication Data

Singhal, Meena.
    Teaching Reading to Adult Second Language Learners:
    Theoretical Foundations, Pedagogical Applications, and Current
    Issues
    Includes bibliographical references and index.
    ISBN 0-9763963-0-0
    2006929158

Printed in the United States of America

*Dedicated to my husband Walid Sabbagh -
my source of strength and courage, and my confidante*

Contents

Preface

Audience and Purposes
This book is designed to serve as a teacher resource book for pre- and in-service reading and ESL teachers. It can also serve as a university textbook for courses on L2 reading methods, reading instruction, or in teacher preparation courses which focus on reading.

Overview of the Contents
This text provides an overview of various theoretical frameworks as they apply to reading, the relevant areas of research in the areas of second language and foreign language reading, and the connection of such theories to the teaching and learning of reading. The text aims to provide reading teachers and language instructors with an understanding of the reading process, L2/FL readers, and the ways in which to build reading skills, particularly academic reading skills and comprehension skills. The opening chapters provide teachers and students in reading and language methodology classes with a broad theoretical basis for developing effective classroom methods in the reading class. The remaining chapters provide practical information relating to effective teaching methods, reading assessment, and design and planning of a reading course. The text focuses on both theory and practice leading to a holistic understanding of second language reading and L2/FL readers.

As stated, the concept of the book is essentially information + research + practical application, with equal emphasis on all. It begins with a discussion of reading theories and considers the prominent areas of research in the field of L2/FL reading including reading strategy instruction and computer-assisted reading. It disseminates a wide array of reading research in a very accessible manner. Graduate students and researchers may find those chapters to be of particular interest. The book also considers the factors that affect reading. The pedagogy chapter considers the teaching of reading strategies and skills to improve reading comprehension and provides examples of the types of exercises and reading activities pre, during and post reading. This information is intentionally presented in one chapter so that teachers/methods students acquire a more complete understanding of how the reading process works and how specific strategies can be integrated into reading tasks and activities at each reading stage. There are two separate chapters on literature and vocabulary as both of these topics needed to be discussed in some depth. Numerous examples of types of activities are included providing teachers with a number of activities and ideas to use in the classroom. The chapter on reading assessment defines key terms and provides examples of types of assessment tasks and questions. The chapter on designing a reading course provides an in-depth course outline of a reading course and takes the teacher from beginning to end in terms of course design. The final chapter addresses professional development of reading teachers. The book includes examples of reading activities, charts, sample test questions, reading activity questions and a comprehensive glossary of terms specific to reading. Each chapter also includes a summary and discussion questions. This book has emerged from my own extensive experiences of teaching second language readers in newcomer programs, in adult education programs, and in college level courses, as well from my teaching experiences as a lecturer at the University of California, Irvine where students in the teaching program strongly indicated their desire for a single text which addressed L2 reading specifically, and one which provided them with an overview of the subject matter in a reader-friendly manner.

Acknowledgments

First and foremost, thanks are due to my ESL adult learners both in Canada and the United States who have motivated me to become a better teacher. Their endless enthusiasm and desire to learn is a constant reminder of my role as an educator. I would also like to thank my husband Walid Sabbagh, my sister Rebecca, and my parents Raj and Mona Singhal for their continuous support while writing this book. In addition, I am grateful to my ESL students at Long Beach City College. Finally, I acknowledge my debt to the numerous faculty members and colleagues with whom I have worked over the years, whose ideas infuse this book, whose generosity has allowed me to incorporate some of their ideas, and whose creativity has shown what good teaching can be.

Meena Singhal
March 2006

Chapter 1
Theoretical Perspectives on Reading:
An Overview of Reading Models

This chapter offers a definition of reading in light of the more current theoretical and pedagogical approaches to reading. The chapter begins by providing an overview of the historical perspectives of reading. This is followed by a discussion of the various theoretical models of reading that have been proposed over the years such as bottom-up, top-down and interactive models of reading. The final section of the chapter discusses the main pedagogical approaches to teaching reading emerging from the various theoretical frameworks. This chapter serves as a foundation for the other chapters in the book.

Second Language Reading Pedagogy

Interest in second language acquisition, particularly as it relates to reading in the second language, has burgeoned in the past decade (Aebersold & Field, 1997; Anderson, 1999; Cook 2001; Day 1993; Esky, 2002; Grabe & Stoller, 2002). This has resulted in a growing demand for both effective reading courses as well as high-quality second language reading materials. Sound second language reading pedagogy draws on a variety of sources, including psycholinguistic theories of the nature of second language reading, information about the strategies employed by effective second language readers, and the accumulated knowledge and wisdom acquired from the study of effective teaching practices. Research in this area has demonstrated that in essence, reading in a second language is a dynamic and interactive process in which learners make use of background knowledge, text schema, lexical and grammatical awareness, L1-related knowledge, and real-world knowledge, as well as their own personal purposes and goals, to arrive at an understanding of written material. At the same time, readers' views of the nature of reading are seen to be shaped by their own social, cultural, and personal histories. Before proceeding to a discussion of the various theoretical models, the focus of this chapter, it would be useful to provide a brief historical overview of reading as it relates to reading in a second or foreign language.

Historical Perspectives on Reading

The understanding of what reading is and how reading should best be taught in a second or foreign language context has changed dramatically over the years. One simply has to examine the vast amount of professional literature in the area of L1 and L2 reading (Aebersold & Field, 1997; Anderson, 1999; Barr, Pearson, Mosenthal & Kamil, 1991; Bernhardt, 1991a; Kamil, Mosenthal, Pearson & Barr, 2000; & Pearson, Barr, Kamil, Mosenthal, 1984). During the early decades of this century, reading approaches were very much in line with the Grammar Translation Method which required enormous amounts of memorization and translation. This method was based on the techniques used to learn classical languages such as Latin and Ancient Greek. Learners were required to learn multitudes of grammar rules, do translation exercises, read texts in their original form, and respond to text questions orally and in writing. The result was often a lack of understanding of text and its features. This method was soon replaced by the Audiolingual Approach in the 1950s where the main focus was on speaking and listening. During this period, reading was viewed as a skill to support the acquisition of grammar and vocabulary. In many cases, reading was also viewed as secondary to writing until more recently when many methodologists have pointed out the need to integrate reading and writing (Anderson, 1999; Goodman 1996; Grabe & Stoller, 2002).

The 1960s were followed by an era of researchers who advocated for a much stronger emphasis on reading as a meaning-making process (Goodman, 1967; Smith, 1979). This led to a psycholinguistic model or theory of reading, one which was expanded on by both L1 and L2 researchers alike during the 1980s (see Bernhardt, 1983a, 1983b; 1986; Goodman 1985, 1996; Smith 1982; Swaffer, Arens & Byrnes, 1991). In the 1980s and 1990s numerous publications focused our attention on reading in a second or foreign language (Aebersold & Field, 1997; Alderson & Urquhart, 1994; Anderson, 1999; Bernhardt, 1991a, 1991b; Esky, 2002; Grabe & Stoller, 2002). The extensive amount of literature during the past 20 years suggests the immense desire by both researchers and practitioners alike to better understand the process of reading. For a through review of 25 years of reading instruction see Silberstein, 1987, and for an excellent resource which sheds light on the field of reading over the past twenty years, consult *The Handbook of Reading Research* published in three volumes (Barr, Pearson, Mosenthal & Kamil, 1991; Kamil, Mosenthal, Pearson & Barr, 2000; and Pearson, Barr, Kamil, & Mosenthal, 1984). The first two volumes present reading primarily in terms of one social science: psychology while the third and most recent volume explore a range of issues including reading as a multifaceted discipline, reading research agendas and how they are set, the new definition of literacy, the role of the teacher, and performance standards to name just a few.

Since that time, there has been a strong move to describe the reading process either in terms of skills and knowledge areas within a cognitive process or in terms of metaphors, the most common of which are the bottom-up approaches, the top-down approaches, and the interactive approaches (Anderson, 1999; Bernhardt, 1983a, 1983b, 1991a, 1991b; Grabe, 1991, Rumelhart, 1977; Stanovich, 1980; Swaffar Arens, & Byrnes, 1991). The following section summarizes these processing models as related to the reading process.

Reading Theories, Research and Pedagogy

In the past few decades, there have been profound changes in our understanding of the theory and practice of reading in both the L1 and L2. Various theoretical frameworks have emerged drawing upon works in other related disciplines, e.g. applied linguistics, cognitive psychology, etc. These theories have begun to change L2 reading instruction and have led to fundamental pedagogical shifts in the field. The following discussion considers the different theoretical perspectives related to reading. It must be recognized that while each of these theories has a different focus, the emergence of a new perspective does not necessarily imply the end of an old one. Each of these theoretical perspectives provides rich descriptions of different aspects of reading.

Bottom-Up Models of Reading
Text-Driven Theories of Reading and Related Models

One prevailing past view of reading is that the process of reading begins with letters and sounds. The reading process is therefore termed a text-driven or "bottom-up" model to explain the reading process. Gough (1972) proposed a phonics- based model of the reading process which describes the process of reading as proceeding in a sequential manner from letters, to sounds, to words, and to meaning. According to Gough (1972), graphemic information enters the visual system and is transformed from a letter character to a sound, which is from a graphemic representation to a phonemic representation. The phonemic representation is then converted to a word. The words then undergo meaning processing, and meaning is then assimilated into the knowledge system. The whole process is a data-driven model in which low-level sensory information is transformed to meaning through a series of higher-level encodings.

Similar to those who support a bottom-up view of the reading process, theorists advocating what is termed the discourse comprehension model have also argued that the meaning of a text begins at the word level, then proceeds to the understanding of sentences, and then to overall text meaning. They believe, however, that throughout this process there is movement back and forth between levels, so that word level processing affects the emerging understanding of the overall text, but the emergent overall understanding also affects comprehension of subsequent words (Van Dijk & Kintsch, 1988). This process is often referred to as the bottom-up theory of reading. Van Dijk and Kintsch (1983) point out that although readers process much of the meaning represented in text, they do not remember everything. They tend to remember main ideas and how the main ideas relate to one another. This interrelation of ideas is referred to as the macrostructure. The construction of the macrostructure occurs throughout reading beginning with guesses based on words and a few propositions. Others also emphasize the bottom-up nature of reading (Kintsch, 1988; Weaver & Kintsch, 1991). Words and propositions relate to the reader's prior knowledge, which produces associations to the words and propositions. Words can have a number of different meanings, but the one that is favored in any particular context is the one related to other concepts and text.

Text-driven or data-driven models of reading have come under considerable criticism. The bottom-up model of reading sees processing as proceeding in one direction implying that no higher-level information ever modifies or changes lower-level analysis. However, research has shown that cognitive processing at higher levels does, in fact, influence lower-level processing. Numerous other studies have shown that letters are perceived more accurately when part of a string and when embedded in orthographically regular rather than irregular strings, suggesting that letters are often perceived in clusters. Semantic processing has also shown to influence lower-level processing as readers are able to identify semantically related words faster than those that are unrelated. The theory of discourse comprehension has also been criticized. While proponents of this view of reading do acknowledge that top-down and bottom-up processing occur, their strong emphasis on induction of meaning from text is not consistent with the reports of readers from think-aloud studies who say they make predictions based on prior knowledge and a number of other strategies that are not text-based. This framework, for the most part, is also silent with respect to most other strategies that readers use to comprehend text.

Theorists supporting transactive or interactive models of reading point out that efficient reading does not result solely from the precise perception and identification of letters or words but the skills in selecting the fewest possible, most productive cues to aid comprehension (Goodman 1996). More current theories of reading clearly illustrate that readers use their prior knowledge of text, including semantic and syntactic cues, and knowledge of the text structure and content knowledge, to make possible predictions and to aid in the meaning-making process.

Top-Down Models of Reading
Schema Theory and Related Perspectives

Since the 1970's, a number of schema theories have been proposed by cognitive psychologists who focused on text processing as related to readers' prior knowledge. Despite their slight differences, their common thread is that a number of concepts that commonly co-occur in particular situations are related to one another in orderly systems and expectations. For example, Minsky (1975) proposed frame theory. A frame is a data structure for representing a stereotyped situation. Attached to each frame are several kinds of information, some information of which is about how to use this frame, some is about what one can expect to happen next, and some information is about what to do if expectations are not confirmed. Minsky points out that at the "top levels" of the frames, a network of nodes and relations are fixed, but the lower levels have many terminals or "slots" that must be filled by specific instances or data. On similar lines, Schank and Abelson (1977) proposed that knowledge is represented in scripts. Scripts perform the same function as frames, but more thoroughly. Scripts involve a sequence of events. For example, there is a particular sequence of events or series of steps one goes through for clearly defined or common situations that members in a culture share.

Although these frame and script theories have been important in cognitive psychology, *schema theory*, as developed by Anderson, et al. (1984) has had much more impact in the area of text processing. Schema theory holds that abstract concepts are best understood after a foundation of concrete, relevant information has been established. This knowledge provides a framework into which new knowledge or newly formed structures can be assimilated. According to schema theory, activation of schemata will occur as concepts are encountered in a text. These schemata also permit the reader to make appropriate inferences, and activation of particular schemata would also affect how attention is directed in the passage. Thus readers develop a coherent interpretation of a text through the interactive process of "combining textual information with the information a reader brings to a text" (Grabe, 1988). Over the years, schema theory has had a great impact on understanding reading, and researchers have identified several specific types of schemata. Content schema refers to the systems of factual knowledge, as well as the knowledge of values and cultural conventions readers possess. Formal, or textual schema, refers to the organizational forms and rhetorical structures of written texts (Carrell, 1984). Lastly, linguistic, or language schema, refers to the decoding features used by readers to recognize words and their relationship to each other in a sentence. This would therefore include knowledge about sentence structure, grammatical inflections, vocabulary, and cohesive structures, for example. Schema theory acknowledges the importance of prior knowledge in skilled reading, although it must be recognized that much reading is not so completely knowledge driven, or top-down in nature.

Schema theory has provided numerous benefits to the teaching of reading of L2 reading. For example, in order for readers to comprehend the text, relevant schema must be activated. Schema is activated when readers identify genre, formal structure and topic. Numerous studies discussed in Chapter 4 suggest that recall and comprehension of texts is better when content and form is familiar to learners. Given what schema theory offers, teachers can take the steps to enhance familiarity of content and form through pre-reading activities. There are numerous ways in which schemata may be constructed including demonstrations, visual aids, lectures, discussions, text previewing, discussion of key vocabulary and concepts, and association activities. A more detailed discussion of such activities can be found in Chapter 5.

While schema theory has provided numerous benefits to the teaching of reading, it is not without its limitations. Schema-theoretic applications do not always result in comprehension (Carrell 1988; Hudson, 1982). Top-down models in which efficient readers utilize background knowledge to make predictions and enhance comprehension are misleading as it suggests that providing readers with the right background knowledge and encouraging them simply to use that knowledge will enhance text comprehension. Schema theory also fails to recognize the role of language in L2 reading. The limited vocabulary of L2 readers and limited knowledge of more complex grammatical structures affects both comprehension and fluency. Thus pre-reading activities and other strategies such as encouraging extensive reading are necessary if readers are to develop and improve comprehension skills (Day & Bamford, 2002). It may also be the case that strongly situated schema may make it difficult for learners to assimilate knowledge from other subject areas or domains.

Schema interference, is for example, the activation of dominant or negative schemata, may also affect comprehension. It also appears that transfer of knowledge outside of the context in which it was originally acquired may be difficult and may require that learners are exposed to similar knowledge in numerous different contexts in order to eventually be able to construct less situationally-constricted schema (Price & Driscoll, 1997). Despite these limitations, there is little doubt that schema theory has positively influenced the teaching of reading. Instructional strategies such as pre-reading activities that build up absent schemata and activate existing schemata can significantly improve text comprehension in many different situations.

Metacognitive Theory

    Metacogntive theory is concerned with metacognition - one's knowledge concerning one's own cognitive processes. In simpler terms, metacognition refers to thinking about thinking (Anderson, 1999; Flavell, 1987). The metacognitive theory of reading is one of the more complete models of text processing emanating from cognitive psychology. It argues that metacognitive awareness is essential for skilled reading. The work of Baker and Brown (1984) in particular, highlights the metacognitive process of comprehension monitoring as critical to self-regulation. Comprehension monitoring is the active awareness of whether one is understanding or remembering text being processed. Such monitoring, on the part of the reader, was seen as essential to the planned use of reading strategies, and shifts in strategies during reading, such as when readers change tactics once they are aware that their current approach is not permitting comprehension. The metacognitive theory of reading involves an active evaluation of understanding on the reader's part. Less mature readers are less strategic, largely because they fail to monitor the state of their comprehension as they read. In essence, this theory argues that it is essential for readers to understand and monitor their reading process, and know when and where to use strategies they are aware of (Anderson, 1999; Baker & Brown, 1984). Vandergrift (2002) further states that metacognitive strategies are crucial because they oversee, regulate or direct the language learning task, and involve thinking about the learning process. In general, two fundamental aspects of metacognition are recognized: knowledge and executive control (Brown, 1987). Knowledge can be further divided into person knowledge, which refers to knowledge about the reader him/herself learns and/or process information; task knowledge, which is knowledge about various types of learning tasks; and strategy knowledge, which is knowledge about the effectiveness of various types of strategies. Executive control refers to the control one has over one's own learning process. There are four types of executive control. Predicting, a form of executive control, occurs when the reader predicts such things as how difficult a particular learning task is, or the goal toward which one is working, etc. Planning involves making decisions about what one will do during the learning task, selecting appropriate strategies, etc. Monitoring, the third type of executive control, involves asking what one knows about the material being learned, what is necessary to understand the text, task, or achieve the learning goal, and monitoring the extent to which one is understanding the material being studied. Evaluating, the final type of executive control has to do with one's evaluation of the predicting, planning, and monitoring activities described above.

While metacognitive theory and its place in reading pedagogy has been widely accepted, it is not without it criticisms. Some would argue that it is difficult to distinguish what is "cognitive" from what is "metacognitive". For example, asking a question about the chapter might function either to improve one's knowledge (a cognitive function) or to monitor it (a metacognitive function). Metacognitive theory posits that reading can be understood in terms of the exact information processing activities of the reader, which are operationalized as strategies and monitoring. In terms of metacognitive assessment; however, it may be difficult to employ the data of behavioral protocols as metacognitive activity occurs in the mind and may not be observable. Self-report inventories as well as interviews used to assess metacognitive activity may be limited because different students may interpret the items in different ways, making it difficult to compare responses and participants may be unaware of their mental processing and/or may not be able to accurately articulate them. Because there is no ideal way to assess metacognition, researchers use a combination of methods including observation of strategy use and reading behavior, self-report inventories, interviews and verbal reports. Although these limitations exist, metacognition research in reading has revealed the important place of metacognition and its role in reading comprehension. A number of studies, for example, have demonstrated the beneficial effects of metacognitive strategy instruction (Anderson, 1991; Block, 1986, 1992; Carrell, Pharis & Liberto, 1989; Janzen, 1996; & Knight, Padron, & Waxman, 1985). These studies show that increases in learning and reading comprehension have followed direct instruction in metacognitive strategies. These results suggest that direct teaching of these thinking strategies may be useful - and that gradually students will be able to employ such thinking strategies independently.

Given such findings, it is clear that metacognitive development may be assisted through various approaches focusing on metacognitive strategy instruction (Vandergrift, 2002). This model suggests that it is important to teach the metacognitive strategies in conjunction with the content to which the strategies are applied. Doing so provides concrete experiences with metacognition and applications of skill, which can then be transferred to other contexts. Metacognitive strategy training can include the following types of activities. Teachers can provide explicit instruction in what the task is, what the objectives are, how to assess progress or completion, help students link newly acquired knowledge to previously learned information, think out loud while solving a problem, explain the process of deciding how to attack a problem, issue or task, guide students as they work on tasks, suggesting various strategies for solving or completing a task, and use metacognitive prompts such as asking students what is relevant, identifying what strategies are useful for the task, and identifying the goal of the exercise. Subsequent work in this area has also demonstrated that skillful reading involves complex articulation between strategies, knowledge, and interpretive reactions, not one or the other (Beach & Hynds, 1991; Devine, 1993; Pressley, 1994; Pressley, Borkowski, & Schneider, 1987; Pressley & Ghatala, 1990) and therefore direct instruction and practice can be highly beneficial to students.

Reader Response Theory

Reader response theory was offered as a reaction to the model of literature education that predominated early in the 20th century, which essentially emphasized an objective way of analyzing literature. Louise Rosenblatt (1938), a pioneer of reader response theory, proposed that meanings of text will vary somewhat from reader to reader; readers will vary in their interpretations of the same texts. This occurs because the meaning of a text involves a transaction between a reader, who has particular perspectives and prior knowledge, and a text, which can affect different readers in different ways. The term "transaction" as it applies to literary criticism and the teaching of literature, suggests a "reciprocal, mutually defining relationship between the reader and the literary text" (Rosenblatt, 1990). Transactional theory thus places great emphasis on the role of the reader.

Reader response theory emphasizes that any reader's experience will be unique because of the reader's personal history, their mood at the moment, and the state of the reader's world at the time the text is encountered. Rosenblatt also states that by reflecting on one's responses to literature and various texts portraying different events, and alternative points of view, it is possible to learn much about oneself. Readers can experience the perspective of others through reading, which can stimulate engagement and contemplation of previously unfamiliar ideas. The theory also predicts that readers will attend to text at various levels of analysis, from the word level to the overall meaning of text. Reader-Response theory emphasizes that the reader's individuality must be respected as each reader initially understands a work only on the basis of prior experience. The reader's background, feelings, memories, and associations called forth by the reading serve as the foundation for interpretation and understanding.

Rosenblatt (1994) goes on to point out that what is critical from the perspective of reader response theory, is how the reader experiences and reacts to the text. Sometimes readers respond emotionally to text. They form impressions of characters, for example, and frequently relate their personal and cultural experiences to events encountered in the text. In order to determine what a text means, they may pose questions, or may respond to difficult aspects of text by treating the process of establishing meaning as an exercise in problem-solving requiring probing analysis of text. Rosenblatt states that readers make choices as they read and the choice of stance is crucial to text comprehension. She makes a distinction between two types of reading or choice of stances: efferent stance, in which the reader is primarily concerned with what he will carry away as information from the text, and aesthetic stance, in which the reader focuses on the experience lived through the reading. More specifically, the efferent stance is appropriate when reading for information. Little attention is given to the language, rhythms and images in the text, which may be viewed as possibly obscuring meaning or defects in logic or inadequacies in evidence. The aesthetic stance, on the other hand, involves a reader who is not seeking information or accomplishment of an assigned task, but rather the full emotional, aesthetic, and intellectual experience offered by the text. Such a reader would focus on content but also the feelings, association and memories that are evoked during the act of reading. For such a reader, the process or act of reading becomes an experience itself.

Over the years, reader response theory or the reader-response approach as a teaching method has been actively promoted as the most appropriate method for teaching literary texts. While reader response theory places an emphasis on text interpretation and claims that responses to texts make readers more aware of their overall comprehension and ongoing processing of text, there is little explication as to exactly how such awareness is manifested. Reader response theory is also silent to many of the other kinds of strategies readers employ when constructing meaning from texts. Reader response stresses individual and unique interpretations of text as readers draw upon their own impressions and emotions. However, this may not lead to a complete or full understanding of a literary text. In a class of 30 pupils, it would be unlikely that thirty different responses are possible or even desirable. Purves (1993) suggests that as teachers we try to develop a knowledgeable reader who is taught the ways of knowing a subject area. This may include teaching readers to effectively analyze text. Individual responses to text are still valid and relevant, but these responses must fit within an acceptable set of responses given the text, and furthermore, these responses must be "guided and constrained by the codes and conventions of the subject which the teacher and pupil have to make use of" (Hong, 1997). In other words, teachers must find a balance between drawing out personal responses and instructing readers in focused strategies to help them achieve success in reading and text comprehension. Finally, reader response appears to be more applicable to literary texts such as stories and poetry rather than academic texts, which are less open to personal response.

Despite these criticisms, the reader response approach to the teaching of reading has offered much to reading pedagogy. This approach has direct implications for classroom instruction. Classroom discussions of texts expose students to a range of interpretations which can then lead to significant discussion and writing, as well as build a cooperative classroom atmosphere in which differing opinions about texts are respected. Students are encouraged to examine their own responses and to articulate them and examine their origins, often in light of other literary critiques. While observing features of language and text analysis remain important aspects of reading texts, discussions of their interpretations allow them to expand their own experiences as readers and come to a greater understanding of other world views and themselves. Teachers must, therefore, invite and encourage student responses, allow them time to reflect and verbalize their responses, find points of agreement and contact among students, allow classroom discussions to build, and assist students in connecting their reading with other texts and experiences. In sum, a reader response approach to literature affords students a wide variety of ways and means to personally connect and interact with literature. Those interested in more recent works on reader-response theory may wish to consult Karolides (2000), which promotes Rosenblatt's transactional model and the ideas of reader response by showing its implications and practical means for classroom implementation.

Interactive Models of Reading
Sociotransactional Theory of Reading

Goodman (1992), who falls under the domain of the constructivist perspective of reading, describes the process of reading as being transactive, rather than solely interactive. He states that in a transactional view reading is seen as a receptive written language whereby meaning is constructed through transactions with the text and indirectly through the text with the writer who is the producer of the text. In the transactional view, the writer constructs a text through transactions with the published text and the reader's schemata are also transformed in the process. In other words, both the knower and the known are changed in the process of knowing.

Goodman describes reading as a socio-psycholinguistic transactional process. He states that in order to comprehend a text, readers use language cueing systems, employ cognitive strategies, and proceed through various cycles. Readers select from three cue systems interchangeably. Readers have schemata for the orthography, for the syntax of the language, and for the concepts presupposed by the writer in order to select, use, and supply the cues appropriate to a particular text. There are three language levels providing cues to readers, but their use by readers is simultaneous and integrated. Readers use the graphophonic system, the lexico-grammatical system, and the semantic-pragmatic system as they read. The graphophonic system refers to the relationship between the oral, phonological, symbols for speech and the orthographic symbols for writing. In alphabetically written language there is a set of relationships between the two systems, which we call phonics. Readers may use spelling, sound patterns, or phonic relationships as cues in reading with patterns in one system invoking patterns in the other. Readers also make use of the lexico-grammatical system of the language. Syntactic patterns assign grammatical functions to clauses, phrases, and words, within the sentences. A series of bound morphemes, affixes, form an inflectional system which also indicates person, number, and tense in nouns and verbs. A third system in English grammar is the small set of function words, determiners, auxilliaries, prepositions, etc, which have no lexical meaning but which make it possible to create sentence patterns to express virtually unlimited meanings. Together these syntactic features create the grammatical system of the language. Just as the writer must create a grammatical text to represent meaning, a reader must use the grammatical features of the text to create a grammatical text. A text cannot be comprehensible to a given reader without being grammatical to that reader. Language, therefore, is much more than a string of words. To read the words, readers must first construct a grammar. Lastly, readers make use of the semantic-pragmatic cueing system as they read. The semantic system of a language is not simply a set of definable words. It is the whole system by which language may represent highly complex social and personal meaning. The extent of knowledge shared by reader and writer will very much influence how the text is constructed and how successful the reader's comprehension will be. Ultimately the references and co-references must be furnished by the reader in response to the text. Pragmatic meaning is also a part of the system. This is partly textual and partly contextual. The subtle differences between the straight-forward and the sarcastic, the humorous and the serious, the profane and the profound, etc., are found in cues in both the text and the context of the literacy event. In order to achieve pragmatic comprehension, appropriate schemata in the reader must be evoked.

In addition to employing these three cueing systems, Goodman (1996) suggests that readers use various strategies which he terms "general cognitive strategies." These strategies include initiation or task recognition (making an overt decision to activate a particular strategy, for example, reading the intention of discovering what is new information), sampling and selecting (seeking and selecting information from the textual environment and directing the eyes where to look and what to look for), inferencing (using schemata and knowledge structures to guess on the basis of what is known; inference applies to all aspects of reading and to all cue systems), predicting (anticipating and predicting what will occur in a text; predicting strategies allow the comprehension process to proceed smoothly as the reader constructs text and meaning), confirming and disconfirming (self-monitoring of the inferences and predictions that are made), correcting (revaluing information and making alternate inferences, predictions, and interpretations, and regressing in the text to gather more information), and lastly, termination (deliberately ending the act of reading due to disinterest, inability to comprehend, or because one as reached the end of a text). It is important to point out that these cognitive strategies interact in reading. For example, readers sample on the basis of their predictions and inferences, and predict and infer on the basis of the sampling they are doing; readers also make new inferences and predictions on the same information used to confirm past decisions. These strategies, therefore, interact with one another in various ways and operate in a dynamic search for meaning, a drive to make sense of the text. Though they are continuously available, some are more likely to occur at particular points in reading than others.

Goodman also describes the process of reading as a cyclical psycholinguistic process. The transaction theory of reading which posits that reading is a transaction between the text and the reader, further holds that the transaction depends on visual input. As one reads and perceptual and linguistic processing occurs, it affects the quality of the optical information since the eyes are being directed by the brain in an informed way. The process is cyclical; perceptual processing depends on optical input. Syntactic processing operates on perceptual input and semantic-pragmatic processing depends on syntactic input. Inference and prediction make it possible to leap toward meaning without fully completing the cycles. Yet, although this occurs, once comprehension has been achieved by the reader, the reader has the sense of assigning every syntactic pattern and identifying every word. It is schema theory; however, that explains this phenomenon. During the reading process, the reader is continually assigning the highest level and most inclusive schema available to move toward meaning. Strategies such as inferencing and predicting, for example, allow the reader to read and comprehend the text, rather than simply see the text. As readers engage in the process of reading, information is assimilated into readers' existing schemas. When there is conflict between what we think we know and what we are learning, then accommodation must occur to rebuild our schemas. Readers must be capable of learning through reading in the sense of assimilating new knowledge to established schemas and also in the sense of accommodating existing schemas to new knowledge. But as Goodman (1992) points out, the ability of a reader to comprehend a given text is very much limited by the conceptual and experiential background of the reader. However, since comprehension results from reader-text transactions, involving the use of strategies and cycles, meaning is ultimately created by the reader.

Constructivist Theory of Reading

All of the theoretical models reviewed here have contributed to a better understanding of the reading process. Each perspective, however, emphasizes different aspects of what reading involves and how reading occurs. While all of the theories reviewed in this chapter are on target, none of them go quite far enough. The constructivist view of reading incorporates many of the perspectives presented above. Constructivists, or the interactive school of theorists, argue that both top-down and bottom-up processes are occurring either alternately or at the same time. These theorists describe reading as an interactive process as readers continuously transact with the text to create meaning. While readers are seeking for the overall meaning of text, they are actively searching for information or details that will enhance comprehension. Effective readers continuously reflect on parts of a text, or ideas presented in a text. Effective readers also engage in conscious constructive responses to text by making use of various reading strategies. These strategies include, but are not limited to, the following: Overviewing before reading, looking for important information in text, and paying greater attention to it than other information (ie. adjusting reading speed and concentration depending on the perceived importance of text to reading goals), attempting to relate important points in the text to one another in order to understand the text as a whole, activating and using prior knowledge to interpret text (generating hypotheses about text, predicting text content), relating text content to prior knowledge, especially as part of constructing interpretations of text, reconsidering and/or revising hypotheses about the meaning of text based on text content, reconsidering and/or revising prior knowledge based on text content, attempting to infer information not explicitly stated in the text when the information is critical to comprehension of text, attempting to determine the meaning of words not understood or recognized, especially when a word seems critical to the meaning construction, using strategies to remember text (underlining, repetition, making notes, visualizing, summarizing, paraphrasing, self-questioning, etc.), changing reading strategies when comprehension is perceived not to be proceeding smoothly, reflecting on and processing text additionally after a part of a text has been read or after a reading is completed (reviewing, questioning, summarizing, interpreting, evaluating, considering alternative interpretations, etc.), carrying on responsive conversations with the author, and anticipating or planning for the use of knowledge gained from the reading (Pressley & Afflerbach, 1995).

From the perspective of constructivism, readers also attempt to understand text by relating it to prior knowledge. This prior knowledge includes activation of the various types of schemata discussed previously. Schema activation causes readers to form hypotheses and make predictions about what to expect in a text. As the reader continues to read, hypotheses are either confirmed or revised. Prior knowledge also affects decisions about what is potentially important in a text and worthy of differential attention and what is not so worthy. Inferences are largely based on prior knowledge. Thus, what one knows affects what one is prepared to find in a text. A reader who is high in prior knowledge of a text's domain, is better prepared to spot information in a new text. It is important to recognize that a reader's understanding of a text reflects both his or her prior knowledge and responses to information presented in the text, with many of the responses determined largely by prior knowledge.

Lastly, constructive/interactive theorists embrace the idea of reader response as conceived by Rosenblatt (1938, 1978). A reader's prior knowledge filters information presented in a text, heightening attention to content that is responded to emotionally. The passion is responsive in that it was elicited by particular points in a text. When constructively responsive readers process texts related to their prior understandings and interests, they are less likely either to embrace the messages in text, reject them, or possibly embrace some points and reject others.

Constructive/interactive and transactive theorists have offered a more complete description of what reading involves. In sum, they believe that readers are extremely active in their pursuit of meaning. Readers construct hypotheses about the meaning of new information and test those hypotheses against subsequent input. They filter new information through prior knowledge elaborating the new ideas by relating them to what is already known. Effective readers, as previously described, also employ a range of strategies to enhance text comprehension, and to monitor comprehension and other aspects of reading as part of the strategic planning process that continues throughout the reading, as well as to relate the information in text to prior knowledge, permitting both formation of hypotheses about the meaning of text, and evaluation of the text and the hypotheses.

Main Pedagogical Approaches to the Development of Reading Comprehension Skills

While the above discussion illustrates the key theoretical stances on reading, it must be pointed out that each of these theories contributes to what we know about the reading process and how reading can be taught. In sum, it can be argued quite successfully that positing a solely bottom-up or top-down processing model for reading fails to capture the complex nature of reading. Alternatively, the interactive approach to reading appears to best offer a most complete picture and better explanation of the cognitive processes involved in reading. It is also important to note that many of these models overlap, thus making absolute distinctions difficult to make. Nevertheless, these models of reading allow us to approach the teaching of reading from a number of different perspectives, depending on the purpose and task. In essence, three main pedagogical approaches to the development of reading comprehension skills emerge from the above discussion of theoretical frameworks: The Skills-Driven Approach, Comprehension-Based Approach, and Integrated or Balanced Approach.

Skills-Driven or Bottom-Up Approach

The skills-based approach, sometimes referred to as the bottom-up approach, gives importance to textual decoding which involves lower-level processes such as recognizing letters and words. Teachers who believe the reading process is bottom-up, focus heavily on the skills and abilities needed to accurately and automatically recognize letters and words. These skills are seen as pertinent in that mastery is required before comprehension can occur. The emphasis, therefore, in such an approach would be on the practice of decoding skills until a point of automaticity has been achieved, phonemic awareness training and then increased focus on comprehension. Reading skills are taught in isolation as mastery of each skill itself leads to increased comprehension. Instructional activities that focus on such an approach would include repeated readings of texts to increase accuracy, automaticity of word recognition, and fluency, providing simplified texts if decoding is a problem, and practicing reading skills such as identification of main ideas and supporting details, identification of tone and purpose, inferencing, and so forth. This approach essentially sees reading as a decoding process. The process of decoding texts unravels meaning.

Comprehension-Based, Top-Down, and/or Interactive Approach

The comprehension-based approach is radically different from the skills-driven approach which holds that meaning or comprehension is the driving force of the reading process. Such an approach to reading instruction is more top-down in that the reader's interpretation and prior syntactic and semantic knowledge help in predicting the content of texts and aid in interpretation and comprehension. This approach also emphasizes the interaction between a reader and a text, as does reader response, as well as the interaction of the many component skills that work together simultaneously in the process of reading, as described by the sociotransactional theoretical model. As stated in the aforementioned discussion of the sociotransactional theory, a comprehension-based approach emphasizes that the reading process involves cyclical and cognitive strategy use and synergistic relations between the language cueing systems –the pragmatic, syntactic, semantic, and graphophonic systems. Therefore, breaking down the process of reading into isolated pieces for the purposes of practice does not allow the reader to use all of the cueing systems, nor can the reader engage in full cyclical strategy use in pursuit of meaning. Teachers espousing the comprehension-based approach disagree with isolated skill practice because it interferes with reading as a meaning-making process. Those who adopt this theoretical paradigm are less concerned with accurate reading, but instead encourage their readers to get at meaning and make sense of text. Activities that encourage individual responses to texts such as response journals, book discussions, and literature circles are emphasized as opposed to traditional comprehension questions. Authentic texts, rather than modified or simplified texts are used to expose readers to natural language, while patterned texts are used to encourage readers to employ predicting, selecting, and sampling strategies in order to disconfirm or confirm their hypotheses.

Integrated or Balanced Approach

The integrated approach or balanced approach to reading is one that is most in line with current theories of reading such as the constructivist theory. Teachers who embrace a balanced view of reading would state that reading for meaning is essential, and this is done through practice of both isolated reading skills and the reading skills within the context of authentic texts. In other words, instructional methods might involve pulling out some skills for practice ranging from decoding text structure, to reading and skill strategy practice to text structure and comprehension for more focused work, much of which is discussed in Chapter 5. For example, a teacher might focus students' attention on main ideas and supporting details. Students will practice this skill, which first means understanding the concept and the purpose of main ideas and supporting details. They might practice this skill by attempting to identify main ideas and supporting details in paragraphs, and then do the same with longer texts or within the context of a less structured reading activity involving an authentic text. It must be recognized that although this approach to reading is termed "integrated" or "balanced" teachers who espouse such an approach or methodology, appear all along the reading process continuum from the "skills" end to the "holistic." They may all stress the importance of meaning-making in their instructional activities, some may be more skills-oriented while others will involve their students in reading and writing of authentic texts. In other cases, skill-practice or development is done within the context of authentic text reading. Balance, therefore, does not mean that all skills receive equal emphasis at a given point in time. Rather, balance implies that the overall emphasis accorded to a skill is determined by its importance relative to the task, and students' language and literacy level, and needs.

The integrated approach recognizes that there are "component skills and knowledge areas" involved in reading and that the cognitive processes involved in reading have an influence on comprehension. These skills and areas can be divided into the following: automatic recognition skills, vocabulary knowledge, formal discourse structure knowledge, content knowledge, reading skills and strategies, and metacognitive knowledge and skills monitoring. Automatic recognition skills refer to lower-level processing skills discussed earlier in this chapter. This includes recognizing letters, characters and words. Vocabulary knowledge, discussed in more detail in Chapter 7 is essential as readers try to match written words with their mental representation and construct the meaning of whole sentences. Lack of vocabulary knowledge can hinder comprehension and therefore vocabulary development and strategies for deciphering word meanings are an essential part of any reading program. Formal discourse structure knowledge is the reader's knowledge of the genre, which helps to predict the organization of the text. This might be termed formal or textual schemata, which is knowledge of typical structures of text. Content knowledge as discussed earlier refers to knowledge about the world, concepts, and topics of readings. Next, reading skills and strategies allow readers to read more efficiently and effectively. Students develop reading skills and learn reading strategies by being exposed to texts written for different purposes and audiences and those that range in difficulty level, genre, and topic. Chapters 5 to 7 address how such strategies can be taught and learned within the context of meaningful activities. Finally, metacognitive knowledge and skills monitoring, which can be both conscious and subconscious, is essential as it allows readers to monitor their own reading process, evaluating and examining the correctness of the comprehension process, and making adjustments where necessary (Anderson, 2002). Figure 1 illustrates how such an approach views the process of reading and the various component skills or areas of knowledge that make up the act of reading, and that readers must develop to enhance text comprehension.

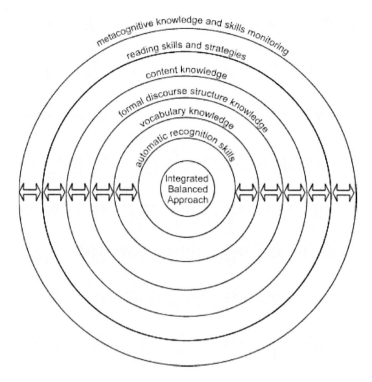

Figure 1 The Reading Process: Interaction of Component Skills and Areas of Knowledge

It is essential for teachers to identify their assumptions and beliefs about reading, the reading process, and how reading is best taught and learned. While many different theoretical paradigms and pedagogical approaches have been presented in this chapter, research and experience clearly illustrate that the development of integration of component skills and knowledge areas in reading lead to greater efficiency and comprehension. While teachers may differ in the emphasis they place on skills-oriented activities or more holistic experiences, the goal of reading instruction, is to facilitate text processing and to motivate students to read in quantity. Figure 2 presents a general list of suggestions to help teachers provide a balanced reading program incorporating multiple methods.

- Always keep meaning as the major focus when reading.
- Assist students in building background knowledge and schemata.
- Assist students in expanding their vocabulary.
- Maintain a balance between teacher-directed and student-initiated reading.

- Embed skills and strategy practice within meaningful activities.
- Transform deliberate strategies for word recognition and comprehension into automatic skills.
- Use both direct instruction and independent practice to further and foster reading.
- Promote basic skills as well as higher-order reasoning tasks and critical thinking skills.
- Incorporate tasks and activities that encourage and promote critical thinking.
- Provide students with a wealth of materials differing in topic and genre.
- Provide students with opportunities that immerse them in real reading for real purposes.
- Provide students frequent opportunities to read.

Figure 2 Elements of a Balanced Reading Program

Teachers dealing with the second language student must recognize that each student will have his or her own prior literacy experiences and reading histories, ranging from not reading in their native languages to reading a great deal but having little knowledge of the texts they will have to read, or may want to read in the second language. Thus, a large part of a teacher's job is to introduce students to the kinds of texts commonly encountered in the language. This would include authentic texts often read for pleasure as well as academic texts. Teachers should also encourage extensive reading, in turn leading to the development of reading skills and strategies, enhanced comprehension, speed and fluency, accuracy and an interest in reading. Given these goals, teachers must be aware of the many factors and problems specific to second language learners such as language problems, lack of background knowledge, and unfamiliarity with texts and their uses. Chapter 4 examines some of these factors while several other chapters in this book suggest activities and instructional procedures that serve to further the development of reading comprehension skills.

Summary

The focus of this chapter was on the theoretical models of reading. While several models discussed in the chapter have contributed to a better understanding of the reading process, the constructivist view of reading provides a more holistic and complete picture of the reading process. This theoretical model suggests that both bottom-up and top-down processes are occurring either alternately or simultaneously depending on the task.

Readers also engage in conscious constructive responses to texts by using a vast range of comprehension strategies, prior knowledge, and metacognitive knowledge to enhance their understanding. In sum, constructivist theorists posit that readers are extremely active in their pursuit of meaning. Theoretical models have also led to pedagogical approaches to the development of reading comprehension skills. The integrated or balanced approach to reading is most in line with current theories of reading, which recognize that there are component skill and knowledge areas involved in reading and each of these areas needs to be developed through skill development and practice using a variety of tasks and activities, and authentic materials.

Discussion Questions and Activities

1. Based on the theories discussed in this chapter, what is your own theoretical stance on how reading is best taught and learned. Share your responses with your peers.

2. Individually or in a small group, design and prepare a set of interview questions for an ESL Reading Teacher Position.

3. Describe what you believe about the process of reading in a second/foreign language. Why do you believe what you do? How do you think your beliefs affect the instructional methods you select and use in the classroom?

4. Write a short reading lesson which illustrates a balanced approach to teaching reading. Share your lesson with your peers and discuss your ideas.

Chapter 2
Prominent Areas of Research in L2 Reading: Past, Present and Future Directions

> This chapter covers the main areas of empirical research in second and foreign language reading over the last two decades. It includes a discussion of reading strategy and reading proficiency studies, studies investigating the role of metacognition in reading and effects on comprehension, strategy training studies, schema research studies, and orthographic differences and reading. The chapter ends with a discussion of the implications of reading research for second language reading instruction.

Prominent Areas of Research in Second Language Reading
Research in Reading Strategies and Reading Comprehension

The current explosion of research in second language reading has begun to focus on readers' strategies in both print text and online environments (Anderson, 2003; Janzen 1996; Macaro, 2001; Sheorey & Mokhtari, 2001). Reading strategies are of interest for what they reveal about the way readers manage their interaction with written text and how these strategies are related to text comprehension. Research in second language reading suggests that learners use a variety of strategies to assist them with the acquisition, storage, and retrieval of information (Rigney, 1978). Strategies are defined as learning techniques, behaviors, problem-solving or study skills which make learning more effective and efficient (Oxford, 2001; Oxford & Crookall, 1989). In the context of second language learning, a distinction can be made between strategies that make learning more effective, versus strategies that improve comprehension. The former are generally referred to as learning strategies in the second language literature. Comprehension or reading strategies, on the other hand, indicate how readers conceive of a task, how they make sense of what they read, and what they do when they don't understand. In short, such strategies are processes used by the learner to enhance reading comprehension and overcome comprehension failures.

Since the early 1970s, for the most part, research in this area has concentrated on teaching second language students to use a variety of language strategies in order to improve their reading skills and use of strategies. These consist of a whole range of strategies including skimming and scanning, contextual guessing, reading for meaning, utilizing background knowledge, recognizing text structure, predicting content, word identification strategies, and so forth. In developing principles for the teaching of L2 reading, it has been recognized, as a result of both research and teaching practices, that effective teaching strategies should address both top-down and bottom-up dimensions of reading, should help learners identify appropriate attitudes toward texts and purposes for reading, and develop readers' awareness of appropriate reading skills and strategies, and at the same time should be meaningful and engaging for learners.

Reading Strategies of Successful and Unsuccessful Learners

Since much of the research in the area of reading strategies has stemmed from first language studies in reading, a review of both the major research in first language and second language learning is included. In many first language studies, the use of various strategies has been found to be effective in improving students' reading comprehension (Baker & Brown, 1984; Brown, 1981; Palinscar & Brown, 1984). Some studies have also investigated the reading strategies used by successful and unsuccessful language learners. In a second-language study, Hosenfeld (1977) used a think-aloud procedure to identify relations between certain types of reading strategies and successful or unsuccessful second language reading. The successful reader, for example, kept the meaning of the passage in mind while reading, read in broad phrases, skipped inconsequential or less important words, and had a positive self-concept as a reader. The unsuccessful reader, on the other hand, lost the meaning of the sentences when decoded, read in short phrases, pondered over inconsequential words, seldom skipped words as unimportant, and had a negative self-concept.

Block (1986) also used a think-aloud procedure in her study of non-proficient readers from which she was able to obtain information about four characteristics, namely integration, recognition of aspects of text structure, use of general knowledge, personal experiences and associations, and response in extensive versus reflexive modes which differentiated successful from less successful, non-proficient readers. In the reflexive mode, readers related affectively and personally, directed their attention away from the text and toward themselves, and focused on their own thoughts and feelings, rather than on information from the text. In addition, they tended to respond in the first or second person. In the extensive mode, the reader's focus was on understanding the ideas of the author, not on relating the text to themselves. They tended to respond in the third person. Among the non-proficient readers Block investigated, one group which she designated as "integrators", integrated information, were generally aware of text structure, responded in an extensive mode by dealing with the message conveyed by the author, and monitored their understanding consistently. The "non-integrators" on the other hand, failed to integrate, did not recognize text structure, and were more reflexive in that they relied much more on personal experiences. Overall, the "non-integrators" made less progress in developing their reading skills and demonstrated less success after one semester in college.

In another study, Block (1992) investigated the comprehension-monitoring process used by first and second language readers of English. The subjects were 25 college freshmen, and consisted of proficient and non-proficient readers of English. The results of a standardized test (Descriptive Test of Linguistic Skills) determined the proficiency levels of the students. There were 16 proficient readers (8 L1 and 8 L2 readers) and nine non-proficient readers (3 L1 and 6 L2 readers). While reading an expository text, the participants were asked to think aloud, or more specifically, to "say everything they understood and everything they were thinking as they read each sentence" (Block, 1992, p. 323). The results indicated that when facing a vocabulary problem, proficient ESL readers used background knowledge, decided on whether the word contributes to the overall meaning of the passage, reread the sentence, and used syntactic clues. These meaning-based strategies are classified as global behaviors. On the other hand, non-proficient ESL readers focused on identifying lexical problems and did little to figure out the meaning of words, both signs of processing.

Strategy Use and Individual Differences

Knight, Padron and Waxman (1985) conducted a study to determine whether there were differences in either the type or frequency of cognitive strategies reported by ESL and monolingual students. Individual interviews which were audiotaped for analysis were conducted with 23 Spanish-speaking ESL students and 15 monolingual students from the third and fifth grades of an inner-city public school. The San Diego Quick Assessment was used to determine their reading levels. A matched passage from the Ekwall Reading Inventory Manual (Ekwall, 1979) was used to identify the strategies the students were using during a reading task. Spanish-speaking students were permitted to speak in their native language in order to clearly explain the strategies being used. Using an adapted version of a structured interview format from Chou Hare and Smith (1982), the students' strategies were categorized as follows: 1. Rereading, 2. Selectively reading, 3. Imaging, 4. Changing Speed, 5. Assimilating with personal experiences, 6. Concentrating, 7. Assimilating with passage events or thinking about previous events, 8. Noting/searching for salient details, 9. Summarizing, 10. Predicting outcomes, 11. Self-generated questions, 12. Student perceptions of teacher expectations, and 13. Rehearsal. It was found that English monolinguals cited the strategy of Concentrating the most, while the strategy of Student's Perceptions of Teacher's Expectations was least cited. ESL students, on the other hand, cited this strategy the most. The categories of Imaging, Noting Details and Predicting outcomes were not cited by any bilingual students during the interviews. The use of three strategies, Concentrating, Noting Details, and Self-Generated Questions was reported significantly more often by monolinguals than ESL students and overall, English-speaking subjects used more strategies than ESL students. One explanation that the authors offered for these results was that ESL students may not have had enough time to develop these strategies in their first language and were transferred to English texts too quickly.

Differences in strategy use were also examined by Anderson (1991). He carried out a study to investigate the individual differences in strategy use by adult second language learners while engaged in two reading tasks: taking a standardized reading comprehension test and reading academic texts. The subjects consisted of 28 Spanish-speaking students enrolled at a university level intensive ESL program in the Southwestern United States. Their English proficiency level as determined by a placement test ranged from beginning to advanced level. Students were administered two forms of the Descriptive Test of Language Skills (DTLS) and The Textbook Reading Profile (TRP). The questions on the DTLS were grouped into clusters according to the type of reading skill being measured. The TRP questions asked the subjects to use think aloud protocols as they responded to comprehension questions at the end of the passage. Analysis of both quantitative and qualitative data revealed that there was no single set of processing strategies that significantly contributed to success on these two reading measures. Both high and low scoring readers appeared to be using the same kinds of strategies while answering the comprehension questions on both measures; however, high scoring students seemed to be applying strategies more effectively and appropriately. Anderson's (1991) study seems to indicate that strategic reading is not only a matter of knowing which strategies to use, but in addition, the reader must know how to apply strategies successfully. This may be one factor contributing to the relationship between proficiency levels and reading strategies used by readers.

Olshavsky's (1977) study was designed to identify reader strategies and to relate their usage to three factors: interest, proficiency and writing style. A 2x2x2 design was used with two types of reader interest, high and low; two types of reader proficiency, good and poor; and two types of writing styles, abstract and concrete. The subjects included 15 boys and 9 girls enrolled in a tenth grade English class. Each subject was asked to read a short story and to stop at various points in order to answer questions. At predetermined stopping points in the story, they were asked to talk about what happened in the story and about what they were doing and thinking as they read it. Despite a number of limitations in this study, Olshavsky's (1977) study showed that readers do use strategies. While this is a well-known fact today, the types of strategies that were identified lent support to the theoretical position that reading is a problem-solving process. This study seemed to indicate that a reader identifies problems and applies strategies to solve those problems. Although the types of strategies do not change with the situation, the frequency of use of strategies does change. As stated, most strategies were applied when readers were interested in the material, with readers that were proficient, and when they were faced with abstract material.

Reading Strategies and Younger Learners

Various other studies in the area of reading strategies have found that younger and less proficient students use fewer strategies and use them less effectively in their reading comprehension (Garner, 1987; Waxman & Padron, 1987). Waxman and Padron's (1987) study involved 82 Hispanic ESL students in the third, fourth, and fifth grades of a public elementary school. The reading comprehension section of the Stanford Diagnostic Reading Test (Karleson, Madden & Gardner, 1966) was administered twice in a four month period to determine the relationship between the strategies cited by students and gains in reading comprehension. The Reading Strategy Questionnaire, a 14 item Likert-type questionnaire (Waxman & Padron, 1987) was administered to the subjects so that students could indicate the extent to which they used a particular strategy. A score of 3 meant that the student perceived using the strategy all the time, a score of 2 meant it was used some of the time, whereas a score of 1 indicated that the student perceived using the strategy none of the time. The results showed that the most cited strategies were asking questions about the parts of the story that weren't understood, checking through the story to see if the student remembers all of it, imaging or picturing the story, and looking up words in the dictionary. The least cited strategies were reading as fast as one could, thinking about something else while reading, writing down every word, and skipping parts in the story that were not understood. Results of the questionnaire were compared to results on the task which indicated that student's perceptions of the strategies they use have predictive validity for their reading comprehension. These findings support previous metacognitive research conducted with monolinguals which has found that lower achieving students use less sophisticated and inappropriate reading strategies during reading (Brown, Armbruster, & Baker, 1983). This study also suggests that the use of negative strategies by Hispanic students, specifically strategies that are ineffectively applied, may be another factor other than English proficiency that interferes with their reading comprehension and hence reading achievement. Both studies indicated that there is indeed a relationship between the types of reading strategies readers use and proficiency level. Overall, these studies suggest that high proficient students seem to use different strategies than low proficient students, and also appear to apply them more effectively.

Other studies have shown that students who use metacognitive strategies, such as those who monitor their reading comprehension, adjust their reading rates, consider the objectives and so on, tend to be better readers. A two-part first language study by Paris and Meyers (1981) was carried out to examine comprehension monitoring and study of strategies good and poor readers. The initial part of their study investigated the differences in comprehension monitoring between good and poor fourth grade readers during an oral reading of a story. Their ability to monitor comprehension of difficult anomalous information was measured by spontaneous self-corrections during oral reading, by directed underlining of incomprehensible words and phrases, and by study behaviors. Their study demonstrated that poor readers do not engage in accurate monitoring as frequently as good readers. Furthermore, poor readers also demonstrated less accurate comprehension and recall of the stories than good readers. The second phase of their study was conducted to provide additional information about the differences between good and poor readers' comprehension skills. The researchers paid particular attention to children's strategies for deriving meaning for difficult vocabulary words. It was found that good readers used comprehension strategies far more frequently than poor readers. For example, good readers wrote notes and summaries related to the text. The children were also asked to define specific vocabulary words. Most good readers reported using strategies of asking questions or referring to the dictionary to determine word meaning, while none of the poor readers did so. Poor readers were more concerned with the pronunciation of words rather than meanings. Overall, poor readers engaged in a few spontaneous study behaviors, failed to ask questions, take notes or use a dictionary as often as good readers. High proficient readers, on the other hand, used cognitive, memory, metacognitive, compensation, and social strategies to a far greater extent than low proficient readers. Although the above discussion pertaining to reading strategies and second language learning is by no means exhaustive, it does provide one with an overview of the kinds of investigations and range of studies that have been carried out by researchers in this area.

From the above findings of research in reading strategies, it becomes clear that there are indeed differences between successful or good readers, and less successful or poor readers in terms of strategy use. There is also a strong relationship between reading strategies used by readers and proficiency level. Overall, successful readers or high proficient readers appear to be using a wider range of strategies. Moreover, these readers also appear to use strategies more frequently than less successful or poor readers. Results of some studies have also shown that successful readers know when and how to apply reading strategies on a given task. A pertinent point to note, however, is that while many of these studies have examined strategy use by different types of readers, (successful vs. less successful, good vs. poor, and so forth), such simplistic dichotomies can tend to be limiting in nature. While descriptions are needed to identify different types of readers, such broad categories may also overlook subtle and important differences between learners and strategy use. One must use caution in employing descriptions as mere labels. These differences must be examined closely in order to assist learners in improving their reading abilities, and skills.

Metacognitive Awareness and Comprehension Research Studies

Research in the area of reading has also begun to focus on the role of metacognition. While previous research has focused on strategy use, researchers are examining readers' awareness of strategies during the reading process – their metacognitive awareness. Metacognition is a relatively new label for a body of theory and research that addresses learners' knowledge and use of their own cognitive resources (Garner, 1987). Metacognitive knowledge or awareness is knowledge about ourselves, the tasks we face, and the strategies we employ (Baker & Brown, 1984). Knowledge about ourselves may include knowledge about how well we perform on certain types of tasks or our proficiency levels. Knowledge about tasks may include knowledge about task difficulty level. For example, in the area of reading, we may know that familiar-topic material is easier to understand than unfamiliar material; explicit sentences assist us in tasks that require reduction of texts to their gists. About strategies, we may know that verbal rehearsal and elaboration of material assist in retrieval, or that prediction of article content based on titles improves comprehension, and so forth. Therefore, metacognitive awareness also involves the awareness of whether or not comprehension is occurring, and the conscious application of one or more strategies to correct comprehension (Baumann, Jones, & Seifert-Kessel, 1993). This body of work has enormous explanatory power for description of the reading process in both the L1 and L2 contexts. First language reading researchers, most notably Baker and Brown (1984) have investigated several different aspects of the relationship between metacognitive ability and effective reading. Two dimensions of metacognitive ability have been recognized: 1) knowledge of cognition or metacognitive awareness; and 2) regulation of cognition which as stated includes the reader's knowledge about his or her own cognitive resources, and the compatibility between the reader and the reading situation. For example, if a reader is aware of what is needed to perform effectively, then it is possible to take steps to meet the demands of a reading situation more effectively. If, however, the reader is not aware of his or her own limitations as a reader or of the complexity of the task at hand, then the reader can hardly be expected to take actions to anticipate or recover from difficulties (Carrell, 1989).

Related to this is the reader's conceptualization of the reading process. Devine (1983) has investigated L2 readers' conceptualizations about their reading in a second language. Analysis of transcripts of reading interviews provided information on beginning ESL readers' theoretical orientations toward reading in their second language. Devine's results are reminiscent of first language reading research which has generally shown that younger and less proficient readers tend to focus on reading as a decoding process rather than as a meaning-making process (Myers & Paris, 1978; Garner & Krauss, 1982). Some of these first language studies using self-report data have also found a lack of correlation between what readers say they do and what they actually do when reading. While at other times, a reader does not describe how to use a particular strategy but in fact does use it when reading. To explain this, Baker and Brown (1984) point out that "knowing that" (declarative knowledge) is different from "knowing how" (procedural knowledge), and that knowledge that a particular strategy is useful (awareness) precedes its routine use, which in turn precedes the ability to describe how it is used.

Some studies have shown that better readers are also better strategy users. Carrell (1989) for example, conducted a study to investigate the metacognitive awareness of second language readers about reading strategies in both their first and second language, and the relationship between their metacognitive awareness and comprehension in both first and second language reading. Two groups of subjects of varying proficiency levels including 45 native speakers of Spanish enrolled in an ESL intensive program at a university, and 75 native speakers of English studying Spanish were involved in the study. A metacognitive questionnaire was developed to elicit relevant information from subjects to tap their metacognitive awareness and judgments about silent reading in their first and second language. Subjects were also tested in both their first and second languages by reading a text in each language and then answering comprehension questions pertaining to the text. The findings of the study yielded some interesting results. For reading in the L1, local reading strategies such as focusing on grammatical structures, sound-letter, word meaning, and text details tended to be negatively correlated with reading performance. For reading in the L2, there were some differences between the Spanish L1 and the English L1 groups. The ESL group, of more advanced proficiency levels, tended to be more global (used background knowledge, text gist, and textual organization) or top-down in their perceptions of effective and difficulty-causing reading strategies, while the Spanish-as-a-foreign language group, at lower proficiency levels, tended to be more local or bottom-up, perhaps because they may have been more dependent on bottom-up decoding skills. Carrell (1989) cautions these results are to be taken as suggestive as further research in this area is needed.

In another study of L2 reading involving 278 French language students, Barnett (1988a) investigated the relationships among reading strategies and perceived strategy use on reading comprehension. The initial part of the study required students to read an unfamiliar passage and write in English what they remembered. The second part of the study asked the students to answer a series of background knowledge questions before reading a text, and the third part of the study required students to continue the ending of a text. The final part required the subjects to answer a 17-item questionnaire in English about the types of reading strategies they thought best described the way they read. "Background knowledge scores," "comprehension scores" and "strategy-use scores" were used for analysis, which revealed that students who effectively consider and remember context as they read, (i.e. strategy use) understand more of what they read than students who employ this strategy less or less well. Moreover, students who think they use those strategies considered most productive (ie. perceived strategy use) actually do read through context better and understand more than do those who do not think they use such strategies" (Barnett, 1988a, p. 156).

More recently, Sheorey and Mokhtari (2001) and Mokhtari and Sheorey (2002) are conducting research on the identification of metacognitive reading strategies of L2 learners. They have developed a new instrument named the Survey of Reading Strategies (SORS) designed to measure the metacognitive reading strategies of L2 readers engaged in reading academic material. The first study investigated the differences between ESL and US students in their perceived strategy use while reading academic texts and whether there was a relationship between reported strategy use and self-rated reading ability. Results showed that the ESL students reported a higher use of strategies, which seems logical because they are more likely to need more support strategies. The results also showed that students who had a higher self-reported rating of reading ability reported using a higher frequency of strategies than those who gave themselves a lower rating. Sheorey and Mokhtari (2001) report that skilled readers could better reflect on and monitor their cognitive processes and could also regulate their use of strategies while reading.

Given the above discussion, there appears to be a strong relationship between reading strategies used by readers, metacognitive awareness, and reading proficiency. In essence, successful readers appear to use more strategies than less successful readers and also appear to use them more frequently. Better readers also have an enhanced metacognitive awareness of their own use of strategies and what they know, which in turn leads to greater reading ability and proficiency (Baker & Brown, 1984; Garner, 1987; Pressley & Afflerbach, 1995; Sheorey & Mokhtari, 2001). In essence, researchers in this area have found that more proficient readers are more aware readers, and therefore, they tend to exhibit the following types of reading behaviors:

- Overview text before reading
- Employ context clues such as titles, subheading, and diagrams
- Look for important information while reading and pay greater attention to it than other information
- Attempt to relate important points in text to one another in order to understand the text as a whole
- Activate and use prior knowledge to interpret text

- Reconsider and revise hypotheses about the meaning of text based on text content
- Attempt to infer information from the text
- Attempt to determine the meaning of words not understood or recognized
- Monitor text comprehension
- Identify or infer main ideas
- Use strategies to remember text (paraphrasing, repetition, making notes, summarizing, self-questioning, etc.)
- Understand relationships between parts of text
- Recognize text structure
- Change reading strategies when comprehension is perceived not be proceeding smoothly
- Evaluate the qualities of text
- Reflect on and process additionally after a part has been read
- Anticipate or plan for the use of knowledge gained from the reading (Aebersold & Field, 1997; Pressley & Afflerbach, 1995).

While this list is not prioritized or complete, it does provide one with a description of the characteristics of successful readers, and continues to grow as more research into reading and metacognition is conducted.

Methodological Concerns in Reading Strategy and Metacognition Research

Protocol analysis is the main methodology through which the reading comprehension is investigated. In most of these studies, interviews or think-aloud procedures are used. Interviews may occur during or after the task, while in the think-aloud method, the researcher provides a task and asks subjects to say aloud "everything they think and everything that occurs to them while performing the task" (Garner, 1987). Think-alouds require a reader to stop periodically, reflect on how a text is being processed and understood, and relate orally what reading strategies are being employed. In other words, think-alouds involve the overt, verbal expression of the normally covert mental processes readers engage in when constructing meaning from texts. Investigations of reading have used protocol analysis both as an exploratory methodology (inductively) and as a means of testing hypothesis about reading that emanate from initial explorations (ie. deductively). Protocol analysis has been used to investigate the range of reading strategies and behaviors as subjects read, and to better understand the cognitive processes during reading (see

Afflerbach & Johnston, 1986; Ericsson & Simon, 1980; Pressley & Afflerbach, 1995; Wade, 1990).

While protocol analysis based on verbal interviews and think-aloud data continues to be used in reading research, it is not without its problems. The most basic concern expressed in the literature is that we may not be able to observe the workings of our own minds with any accuracy. In other words, we may be unaware of the operations of memory, attention, comprehension processes, and the like – perhaps because many of these processes are so automatic. Ericsson & Simon (1980) point out that as processes become more automated, and hence unconscious, only the final products are left in memory available for reporting to an interviewer. Subjects may draw inferences about what probably occurred in processing and report these events rather than what actually occurs. Memory failure can also be a particularly serious problem for verbal-report data. Reports taken at a great distance from processes they are intended to tap may reveal little about the reading comprehension process and strategies used by the reader. Such methodology has also shown that while students may report using a particular strategy, it is not used at all, and by the same token, strategies that are used by readers, are not reported. Therefore, the discrepancy between knowledge versus use should be recognized when using think-aloud report data. Lastly, verbal facility of the reader may affect the outcome of the interviews. Learners, especially younger children can fail to provide a full response for a number of reasons other than lack of knowledge. One reason is limited language skills. Even in instances in which cognitions are generally accessible and remembered, it is possible that they cannot be verbalized. It must also be recognized that considerable differences exist in the tendency to speak aloud.

Despite the criticisms of verbal report data, most researchers do believe that a great deal can be learned about the reading comprehension process and the psychology of thinking by making subjects think aloud about definite problems. Ericsson and Simon (1993) and Garner (1987) offer the following methodological recommendations and conclusions about how verbal-reports should be collected.

- Avoid asking about processes that are engaged in automatically and which are therefore inaccessible upon reflection. Complex, difficult, and novel tasks may provide more information than much-practiced simple tasks.
- Reduce the interval between processing and reporting.

- Use multiple methods to assess knowledge and use of strategies (interview questions, questionnaires, data from verbal-reports and think-alouds).
- Avoid general questions asking subjects to provide a generalized description of their processing as this may fail to reflect processing accurately.
- Emphasize that reporting should reflect exactly what is being thought.
- Provide directions to subjects that encourage intermediate and final products of processing rather than descriptions of explanations of processing.
- Use reliable categories to code verbal and think-aloud reports.
- Recognize that there are individual differences in the ability to provide think-aloud reports and in thinking.

In sum, verbal protocol and metacognitive research have made important contributions to our understanding of reading which provide rich descriptions of ways in which younger and less successful readers differ from older and more proficient readers. We can conclude that less effective readers often have misconceptions about the reading process, fail to monitor their comprehension, underutilize effective reading strategies, and employ fewer reading strategies when reading. Skilled readers, on the other hand, know and use many different strategies in coming to terms with text. They employ both "bottom-up" and "top-down" reading strategies, use a wider range of strategies and use them more frequently, and employ metacognitive knowledge, that is knowledge of when and how comprehension and monitoring processes apply.

Strategy Training Studies

A number of first language training studies have been carried out which have shown that comprehension abilities of students have improved with training in reading and comprehension strategies (Brown, Armbruster, & Baker, 1983; Miller, 1985; Palincsar & Brown, 1984; Pressley et al. 1989). Such research has sought to better understand the contexts in which reading strategies improve comprehension, the training procedures which are most effective, and the variables which influence strategy instruction. Fewer strategy training studies have been carried out in an L2 context which have been directed at improving the reader's use of strategies through training. The following discussion; however, will consider research in both L1 and L2 contexts.

Carrell, Pharis and Liberto (1989) showed that strategy training with semantic mapping and with the ETR (experience, text, relationship) method both improved reading comprehension scores. Their study specifically examined if strategy training enhances L2 reading. The study involved a heterogeneous group of 26 ESL students in a level four intensive ESL program at a university. Two experimental groups were formed of which one received the semantic mapping training and the other received the ETR training. A control group simply received the pre and posttest. During a four day training session, the first group was given a series of reading passages. Questions were used to stimulate discussion and semantic maps were created. The ETR group received the same passages; however, group activities included note-taking, discussion, comprehension questions and vocabulary activities that related to the texts. Subjects received a pretest prior to the onset of training and a posttest nine days after the training. The tests included questions in varied formats and two out of three passages on the test required the subjects to complete semantic maps. Scoring was done according to predetermined criteria. The results indicated that the control group did not have significant gains in scores between their pre- and posttests on any of four dependent measures which were multiple-choice questions, open-ended questions, cloze semantic mapping, and open-ended semantic mapping questions. Each training group, however, showed significant gain scores on the open-ended questions. Carrell, Pharis and Liberto (1989) do caution, however, that such results need to be supported by further research in this area.

Kern (1989) conducted a study involving fifty three students enrolled in a French class to determine the effect of strategy training on reading. One treatment group received explicit instruction in reading strategy use in addition to the normal course content and the control group received no instruction in reading strategy use but covered the same material. Subjects were presented with a passage in French and were asked to report what they were thinking as they read each sentence, what they understood, what they did not understand, how they went about determining the meaning of unfamiliar words, whether they made predictions or inferences, and whether they translated into English. Both a comprehension and word inference measure were derived from the reading task. Data analysis revealed that reading strategy training had a strong positive effect on L2 readers' comprehension gain scores. Those who had the most difficulty reading appeared to benefit the most from reading strategy instruction which suggests that mid and high ability readers may have already transferred more of their effective L1 reading strategies to the second language reading task. In terms of the effects of such strategy training on word inference ability, the results were less clear. Overall, Kern (1989) reported significant improvement with FL readers of French over a semester of training with emphasis placed on word, sentence, and discourse analysis strategies. Similar strategy studies performed with L1 readers have yielded similar results (Geva, 1983; Singer & Donlan, 1982). Barnett (1988b) also reported improvement in reading comprehension from a year-long strategy training experiment in reading. In a related experiment over one semester, however, she did not see significant improvement in the training group.

Strategy instruction was also found to be beneficial to low-level readers as illustrated in a year-long case study conducted by Jimenez and Gamez (1996). During a two week period in a middle school, three Spanish/English bilingual students were taught how to engage in think-alouds while reading, and explicit metacognitive and cognitive reading strategies in order to improve their poor reading skills. Use of culturally relevant texts, student-generated discourse, and instruction designed to promote comprehension was found to have a strong potential for promoting and fostering the reading ability of such students who were performing at low levels of literacy in the middle school grades. In another study involving third grade Spanish/English bilingual students, Kucer (1995) spent one year in a classroom teaching students a repertoire of strategies to help children become more effective and efficient readers. Through collaboration with the students, the teacher developed a series of strategy wall charts. Students were encouraged to use these charts whenever they encountered difficulties in reading. "Problem-Solution" and "Response Conferences" allowed students to share their difficulties in reading. Over the year, students became much more aware of how to both talk about strategies, and how to use strategies which was reflected in both their reading and writing activities. In another investigation of reading strategies involving younger learners, sixty-seven fifth and sixth grade students participated in a study by Dole, Brown, and Trathen (1996). The authors compared a teacher-directed strategy in which teachers read prepared scripts designed to activate prior knowledge with interactive instruction in which students and teachers together activated and discussed students' prior knowledge before reading. Results indicated that at risk readers who received strategy instruction made superior gains in comprehension performance over their peers who received story content or traditional basal instruction.

Hansen (1981) carried out a study to investigate the effects of two experimental methods intended to improve inferential reading comprehension of 24 second grade children. The children were grouped into three experimental conditions. The Strategy Group had practice in pre-reading strategies and focused on integrating text information and prior knowledge before reading; the Question Group received practice in answering questions which required inferencing practice between the text and prior knowledge; and the Control Group received traditional story instruction and the typical mix of literal inferential probes. The instruction was applied to ten basal-reader stories. Results of comprehension questions revealed that the performance of the children in both experimental groups surpassed that of the control group. Standardized test scores and scores on an experimenter-designed test also favored the experimental groups. In a similar study, the inferential comprehension of good and poor fourth grade readers was investigated by Hansen and Pearson (1983). Forty fourth grade students were assigned to one of four instructional groups, two groups of good readers (an experimental and a control group), and two groups of poor readers (an experimental and a control group). The experimental treatment consisted of three parts: a) making students aware of the importance of drawing inferences between new information and prior knowledge structures; b) getting students to discuss some of their own experiences that were similar to events in the text; c) and providing students with many inferential questions to discuss after reading the texts. The results showed that poor readers benefited significantly from the instruction, but good readers did not, indicating that instructional procedures in reading do have positive effects on reading comprehension.

Brown and Palincsar (1985) report the results of another line of research using a successful technique of instruction, reciprocal teaching, which is an example of explicit comprehension instruction. Subjects in this study were taught to use four key strategies: summarizing the main content, formulating potential test questions, clarifying difficult parts of the text, and predicting future content. An expert worked with the students to model how the strategies were to be used until gradually the students assumed responsibility for using them on their own. Using such a technique, the independent test scores of poor readers improved dramatically going from below 40% correct to over 75% correct. This study led further evidence that comprehension can in fact be taught. This study also suggested that current instructional paradigms need to include teacher modeling of specific reading strategies for learning how to improve reading comprehension.

Various other studies examining reading strategy instruction have focused on specific strategies such as comprehension monitoring. Miller, Giovenco, & Rentiers (1987) examined the benefits of self-instruction training on performances of below average and above average readers. Forty-eight fourth and fifth grade students were tested on their ability to detect between-sentence contradictions in short expository texts after receiving either three sessions of self-instruction or equivalent didactic instruction. The 24 children in the self-instruction group were taught a series of self-statements designed to define the task, to designate an approach to complete the task, to evaluate the approach taken, to reinforce the learners' efforts, and to check on the completion of the task. The tasks closely resembled metacognitive and monitoring reading strategies. Subjects in the control group were not exposed to the self-verbalization strategies. Results of think aloud protocols and post reading questions on nine passages indicated that self-regulatory remediation strategy in reading was successful in enhancing students' regulatory process while reading.

A similar study was carried out by Loranger (1997) to determine whether students who were taught specific research-based strategies using a transactional strategies instruction (TSI) approach would a) improve in comprehension achievement, and b) would be more engaged during reading groups. The TSI refers to an approach that involves teaching readers to use comprehension strategies as they jointly construct interpretations of text. Vocabulary instruction occurs as needed when students encounter difficulty while reading and extended discussion of text replaces comprehension check questions. The emphasis is on grasping meaning of the text, which is codetermined by teachers and students in "transaction" with the text. The participants in this study were 32 fourth grade students between the ages of 8-10. The treatment group was taught four comprehension strategies - predicting, questioning, clarifying, and summarizing, following the TSI approach. The comparison group was conducted as a traditional reading group. The study was conducted over eight weeks for a total of three hours of instruction per week. The reading sessions were videotaped, and pre- and post interviews to determine knowledge of strategies were conducted with the students. Students were also required to write response journals about their reading sessions. The findings favor the strategies treatment and include observations of greater focus and engagement during reading sessions, improved knowledge and use of strategies, and improved achievement in comprehension.

Given such findings, it is clear that reading strategy instruction improves readers' comprehension of specific texts, specifically texts that are less familiar or somewhat challenging to readers. A growing body of research suggests that strategy instruction is indeed beneficial and should be a requirement in all areas of literacy learning. In general, these studies support the notion that students can be taught to use strategies, and that strategy use increases students' awareness of their own performance as they read. Overall, comprehension could be improved by teaching students to monitor the process of comprehending - that is by helping students become more aware of where they get information to answer questions in a text (Garner, 1987; Pressley et al., 1989; Pressley et al., 1992).

Schema Research Studies
Background Knowledge and Reading Comprehension

Numerous studies have investigated the role of schemata in reading comprehension. Many of these studies were variations on Carrell's (1987) paradigm. This study involved 28 Muslim Arabs and 24 Catholic Hispanic ESL students of high-intermediate proficiency enrolled in an intensive English program at a midwestern university. Each student read two texts, one with Muslim-oriented content and the other with Catholic-oriented content. Each text was presented in either a well-organized rhetorical format or an unfamiliar, altered rhetorical format. After reading each text, the subjects answered a series of multiple-choice comprehension questions and were asked to recall the text in writing. Analysis of the recall protocols and scores on the comprehension questions suggested that schemata affected the ESL readers' comprehension and recall. Participants better comprehended and remembered passages that were similar in some way to their native cultures, or that were deemed more familiar to them. Other studies have shown similar effects in that participants better comprehended and/or remembered passages that were more familiar to them (Ammon, 1987; Carrell, 1981; Johnson, 1981, 1982; Langer, Barolome, Vasquez, & Lucas, 1990; Shimoda, 1989). Further evidence from such studies also suggested that readers' schemata for content affected comprehension and the ability to remember more than their formal schemata for text organization. For example, in Carrell's (1987) study described above, subjects remembered the most when both the content and rhetorical form was familiar to them. However, when only content or only form was unfamiliar, unfamiliar content caused more difficulty for the readers than did unfamiliar form.

Steffensen and Joag-Dev (1984) conducted a study using two descriptions of weddings both written in English. One was a description of an American wedding, while the other was of an Indian (subcontinent) wedding. Both the Indian students, for whom English was an L2, and the American students, for whom English was the L1, read the descriptions and were asked to recall the descriptions. It was found that readers comprehended texts about their own cultures more accurately than the other. While the readers indicated that the words were easy to understand, the unfamiliar cultural protocol of an Indian wedding made the passage more difficult to remember.

Johnson's (1981) study investigated the effects of the cultural origin of prose on the reading comprehension of 46 Iranian intermediate advanced ESL students at the university level. Half of the subjects read the unadapted English texts of two stories, one from Iranian folklore and one from American folklore, while the other half read the same stories in adapted English. The subjects' reading comprehension was tested through the use of multiple-choice questions. The recall questions and the texts were also given to 19 American subjects for comparison purposes. Results revealed that the cultural origin of the story had a greater effect on comprehension than syntactic or semantic complexity of the text. In another study, Johnson (1982) compared ESL students' recall of a reading passage on Halloween. Seventy-two ESL students at the university level read a passage on the topic of Halloween. The passage contained both unfamiliar and familiar information based on the subjects' recent experience of the custom. Some subjects studied the meanings for unfamiliar words in the text. Results of recall protocols suggested that prior cultural experience prepared readers for comprehension of the familiar information about Halloween on the passage. However, exposure to the unfamiliar words did not seem to have a significant effect on their reading comprehension.

Pritchard (1990) also utilized two different reading passages: a culturally familiar and culturally unfamiliar passage to examine the process of how a reader activates and utilizes the relevant schema to facilitate comprehension. More specifically, his study aimed to identify "the strategies proficient readers report employing to develop their understanding of culturally familiar and culturally unfamiliar passages, and to examine those strategies in relation to the cultural backgrounds of the readers and those strategies in relation to the cultural backgrounds of the readers and the cultural perspectives of the reading materials" (Pritchard, 1990, p. 276). Participants in the study were American and Palauan students, and the two passages used were a letter from a woman to her sister describing the events surrounding a typical funeral in each of the two cultures. Pritchard found that the American students used a wider variety of strategies than the Palauans, and they also reported using the strategies more often. Pritchard proposed that the strategy use results were related to cross-cultural differences. In both cultural groups, significantly more idea units were recalled from the culturally familiar text. There were also a greater number of distortions reported in the subjects' retellings of the unfamiliar text, and subjects made more appropriate elaborations when recalling the familiar text. Pritchard's findings suggested that "reading is a content-specific activity; that is, when the content of reading materials changes, processing behavior changes as well" (p. 291).

An interesting study was carried out by Kang (1992). Kang's study examined how second language readers filter information from second language texts through culture specific background knowledge. Korean graduate students with advanced English read stories and answered questions. A think-aloud protocol assessing their understanding and inferences indicated an effect of culture specific schemata and inferences upon text comprehension. Although all the variables and factors surrounding the issues of how culture shapes background knowledge and influences reading are not fully understood, there is agreement that background knowledge is important, and that content schema plays an integral role in reading comprehension. Overall, readers appeared to have a higher level of comprehension when the content was familiar to them. Given this, second language readers do not possess the same degree of content schema as first language readers, and hence, this can result in comprehension difficulties.

Formal and Linguistic Schema and Text Comprehension

Many studies have also examined the role of text schemata in relation to readers' comprehension. Most of these studies employed similar methodologies in that participants read texts and then recalled information, for the most part in writing. The structures inherent in the texts (e.g., compare-contrast, problem-solving structures in expository text, and standard versus structurally interweaved versions of stories) were identified. Recalled information was analyzed for specific variables such as the number of propositions recalled, and temporal sequence of story components. For the most part, these studies suggested that different types of text structure affected comprehension and recall (Bean, Potter, & Clark, 1980; Carrell, 1984). Some studies also showed that there may have been differences among language groups as to which text structures facilitated recall better (Carrell, 1984). For example, Carrell's (1984) study showed that Arabs remembered best from expository texts with comparison structures, next best from problem-solution structures and collections of descriptions, and least well from causation structures. Asians, however, recalled best from texts with either problem-solution or causation structures, and least well from either comparison structures or collections of descriptions. These results; however, must be taken as suggestive as further studies examining the interaction of language background with text structure are needed. Regardless of these findings, as previously stated, it is important to recognize that organizational structures in text will differ across cultures.

Stone's (1985) study examined whether language patterns found in English, which differed from those in Spanish, would have a significant effect on ESL learners' comprehension while reading English text. Average fifth grade readers were randomly assigned to either an initial Spanish-speaking group or an initial English speaking group. Nine stories were developed for the study, three for each of three different language patterns categories: similar, moderately similar, and dissimilar. Measures included a retelling and comprehension questions. Results showed that on the retelling measures, the lowest scores were found on stories that were most dissimilar from the students' initial language, and oral reading errors increased as language pattern similarity decreased. The results support the contention that texts violating readers' expectations about language patterns can have disruptive effects.

The field of contrastive rhetoric initiated by the work of Kaplan (1966) has also shed some light on the relationship of textual structure, textual schemata, and reading comprehension. Its areas of focus are the role of the first language conventions of discourse and rhetorical structure on L2 usage, as well as cognitive and cultural dimensions of transfer, particularly in relation to writing. For the most part, contrastive rhetoric identifies problems in composition encountered by L2 writers and by referring to rhetorical strategies of the first language, attempts to explain them. It is clear that such differences in text structure can lead to difficulties in reading. Mauranen (1992) examined cohesion in both Finnish and English economic texts and found that Finnish writers employed relatively little metalanguage for organizing text and orienting the reader. In contrast, native English speakers used plenty of devices for orienting the reader in terms of what is to follow in the text and how the reader should understand the different sections of the text. This pattern was found in their writing as well. Finnish writers used less demonstrative references than native English writers. Lindeberg (1988), in her examination of text linguistic features, found differences between Finnish and English writers in terms of topic development and the functions of verbs. Numerous differences have also been found in terms of writing styles between American-English and other languages. American students, for example, will often comment on the more theoretical and abstract essays of French writers whose essays lack the details and rhetorical patterns found in the American essay tradition. Chinese writing is often described as being verbose, ornamental, and lacking in coherence from a Western point of view, while Japanese writing has been noted for differences in text organization. It appears that they prefer a specific-to-general pattern placing the general statement at the end of paragraphs (Connor, 1996).

Lastly, it is important to point out that the differences between the writing systems and rhetorical structures of the native language and the target language may be another factor that influences reading. Orthographic systems, as discussed in the following section, vary widely and while some languages may contain many numbers of symbols, other languages contain a limited number. For example, Chinese calligraphy is a writing system with numerous symbols and one that has strong aesthetic elements thereby differing from English. Arabic also has a unique writing system in that it is written and read from right to left. These kinds of differences in writing systems can pose difficulties for second language readers. Undoubtedly, students reading in a second language will encounter such difficulties not faced by first language readers. In summary, teachers must, therefore, be explicit about the structures of the materials the students are reading in the L2 class through which students can become aware of culturally shaped expectations about text and language. Connor (1996) provides an extensive survey on contrastive rhetoric and offers a comprehensive discussion of CR encompassing theories of such divergent fields as applied linguistics, linguistic relativity, rhetoric, text linguistics, discourse analysis, genre analysis, literacy theories, and translation. She also considers the types of differences between the native and target language that can interfere with text comprehensibility, and teaching and research implications are also discussed.

Local Text Processes, Orthographic Knowledge, and Reading

Orthographic knowledge plays a critical role in L2 reading, particularly in the area of lexical processing. Numerous L2 vocabulary studies, for example, consistently show that the ability to utilize context in inferring the meaning of unknown words is highly correlated with reading proficiency. Even more important, the failure to use context for lexical inference is, in many cases, attributable to word misidentification. Many identification errors also result from insufficient information derived from orthographic processing, which in turn leads to poor comprehension.

There are three major orthographic systems – logography, syllabary, and alphabet which differ in two critical dimensions: 1) the basic unit of representation and 2) the regularity in symbol-to sound correspondence (Koda, 1997). Both of these dimensions not only differentiate orthographic systems, but also determine their phonological recodability in each system. This phonological recodability, in turn, is responsible for the procedural variations in the phonological processing of the orthographies. The same kinds of variations are also evident in L2. Word recognition research shows that qualitatively different processing procedures are used in the visual scanning and phonological recoding of L2 readers with different L1 orthographic backgrounds. Differences in these L2 word recognitions patters are linked with specific properties in the learner's L1 orthographic system. The following section considers some of the research that has been carried out in this area.

Research in reading has also focused on local text processes, specifically letter and word recognition and how this affects L2 reading. For many L2 learners, learning to read in a second language involves learning a new script. Reading in a native language itself is somewhat of a challenging task as it takes time for children to be able to differentiate between graphic symbols after years of exposure. Research has also shown that children's knowledge of the letters of the alphabet is a strong predictor of current and future reading achievement (Adams, 1990). More recently, studies have been carried out to determine whether readers apply the knowledge or procedures that they use to visually recognize words in their native language to the process of L2 reading. The following discussion briefly examines some of the research examining this question when the L1 and L2 share a writing system, that is they have similar scripts, and when the L1 and L2 have different writing systems.

In syllabaries, such as the Japanese Kana, the written characters are represented or map onto speech syllables. In Japanese for example, the syllables are in some cases represented by arbitrary characters and in others, the syllable is represented by a pictorial symbol (Rayer & Pollatsek, 1989). The pictorial symbol might not even be related to the meaning of the word as whole. The characters in phonemic or alphabetic writing systems generally represent phonemes. Languages can have shallow orthographies characterized by a regular grapheme-phoneme correspondence in that a phoneme generally represents a single letter, or deep orthographies where the one letter represents more than one phoneme. These kinds of differences have led researchers to question whether there are processing differences based on different writing systems. Beiderman and Tsao (1979) used the Stroop task to investigate this question. Skilled English and Chinese readers were presented with a color name (e.g. blue) printed in a different ink color. The reader was asked to name the color and ignore the meaning of the word. Under this condition, readers took longer to name the color than when the ink color appears on the color patch. This has been interpreted as evidence that skilled readers are unable to refrain from processing the meaning of a word, presumably because their processing skills of words have become automated. They also confirmed predictions that if meaning were more closely related to the appearance of the stimulus in the logographic characters, then Stroop interference would be greater for Chinese readers than English readers since they associate the graphic stimulus to meaning by application of sound-spelling rules. Chinese readers did in fact experience more interference than English readers when completing the Stroop task. Tzeng and Wang (1983) conducted a study using a modified version of the Stroop task. English-speaking readers were asked to identify numbers on a screen. When a number of smaller values appeared in larger font, the interference occurred. When the same numbers were presented as words, there was no interference. With Chinese speakers, the interference occurred in both situations and did not disappear when the numbers were printed as Chinese characters. Other studies have provided similar evidence supporting the claim that logographic characters are processed differently than alphabetic scripts (Perfetti & Bell, 1991; Perfetti & Zhang, 1991).

Researchers have also investigated the impact of the native language on the processing of the second language that uses the same writing system, more specifically how knowledge of one language influences visual processing in another language when both are based on the same script. These studies have mostly dealt with the way in which bilinguals, whose two languages share a script, decide what lexicon to search when they are presented with a visual stimulus. Most of these studies have been with bilingual learners and have shown that learners use their knowledge of the orthographic patterns found in their two languages when identifying words. The ability to exploit such information may even speed up the rate of processing of words during reading in either language (Beauvillain 1992; Grainger & Beauvillain, 1987; Grainger & Djikstra, 1992).

Other studies have been carried out in the area of second language learners' eye movements and reading. Oller and Tullius (1973) carried out a study involving a group of ESL college students of 21 different language backgrounds who were compared to native English speakers in terms of number of fixations (the number of times the eyes fixate on words); and the fixation duration; number of regressions (the number of times the eyes returned to a previously fixated word on the same line), the average word span (the average number of words recognized during a fixation), and the number of words per minute. Results showed that for those readers who read the text with 70% comprehension or more were no different in average number of regressions. Results also showed that average fixation duration for the ESL learners was significantly longer than that for native speakers. In other study involving German L2 learners, Bernhardt's (1987) found that as proficiency increased, the fixation durations approximated those of native German readers. It was also found that despite the high fluency level of some German learners, the average fixation duration was still longer than native speakers. Lastly, a study by Osaka (1989) involving English and Japanese bilingual readers showed that fixation durations for these readers were longer for the English (L2) texts than for the Japanese texts. Given the results of these studies, it appears that L2 readers spend more time processing individual words in the second language. Longer fixation durations may reflect the addition time needed to access word meanings, or may reflect the additional processing due to the orthographic structure of the two languages.

The empirical data presented here suggests that there is a strong relationship between the L1 orthographic systems and the L2 processing procedures. Research findings have also shown that L2 learners' multiple sets of linguistic knowledge and processing skills interact during L2 comprehension, and that prior orthographic experience impacts L2 processing skills and strategies. Koda (1997) provides an extensive literature review of the studies related to orthography and reading.

Given the findings of such studies, teachers can employ various steps in the reading class to facilitate instruction. In the area of vocabulary instruction, given that L2 readers use their L1-based strategies, and that some languages relate more closely in orthographic properties to the target language than others, we can logically assume that beginning L2 readers, because of their varying orthographic backgrounds, develop processing skills and different rates. If teachers become more aware of the similarities and differences between the students' L1 and L2, they can anticipate the difficulties their students might face in learning to read a new language. Teachers can also then provide guidance in dealing with various processing problems. Additional practice through individualized instruction now made available through new technologies such as CALL can further facilitate the processing difficulties, including rate and recognition difficulties students may have.

In addition to the above, since diverse L1 reading experiences engender qualitatively different processing mechanisms among L2 readers, direct strategy instruction would be extremely beneficial in helping learners develop effective verbal processing skills. Strategy instruction which is in line with or related to a learner's L1-based strategies can result in enhanced reading performance (Gairns, 1992). It must be noted; however, that L2 learners often select various strategies based on what they perceive as being effective, when in fact, this may not be the case. Students may, therefore, be resistant to strategies introduced by the teacher so teachers should carefully monitor the changes in student progress and make modifications in their instruction as they become necessary.

Finally, explicit instruction on L2-specific orthographic and other linguistic functions may help students develop a cognitive grasp of the ways such features facilitate the reading. Koda (1993), for example, reports that L2 learners of Japanese from non-logographic backgrounds are reluctant to use Kanji in written composition because they are unclear about the system. Enhanced awareness of the relationship between symbols and sounds in a language and the underlying system of spelling in that language can be utilized to facilitate text recognition. Explicit instruction in these areas can lead to an increased conceptual understanding and organization of the linguistic system of the target language, in turn promoting its mastery and improving language skills.

Implications of Reading Research for L2 Reading Instruction

The studies reviewed in this section suggest that there are differences in the strategies used by more and less proficient L2 readers and those used by native and L2 readers. Several studies suggest that less proficient readers focus on lower-level processing strategies while more proficient readers engage in meaning-building strategies. Strategy-training studies have also shown that training readers in strategy use and application can improve comprehension. In addition, research on metacognitive strategy training and reading suggests that explicit instruction in this area is also necessary. Clearly readers need to know of strategies, have experience using those strategies, and have opportunities to apply those strategies in a variety of contexts. The results of the studies reviewed here suggest that instruction promoting awareness and experience with reading strategies may facilitate the application of strategies in L2 reading.

The research on prior knowledge clearly provides evidence to support the conclusion that prior knowledge can affect the reader's ability to comprehend texts in a second language. Readers are more likely to read faster and remember the content of text containing culturally familiar topics and those that are structurally familiar. An implication of such research is that teachers need to provide readers with the background knowledge they need to better understand texts. This means building their vocabulary and syntactic knowledge, world and content knowledge and knowledge of text structures. Specific training emphasizing different rhetorical modes and text structures can also help learners to improve comprehension of L2 texts. The use of authentic materials, as opposed to modified texts, can expose readers to a range of syntactic patterns and rhetorical modes thereby improving familiarity. Another implication of this research relates to the diagnosis L2 reading problems. Given that prior knowledge affects comprehension, a distinction between reading difficulties arising from lack of prior knowledge or those that arise from the execution of cognitive skills that support meaning-construction and reading needs to be made. Teachers may choose to use listening and reading comprehension tests on the same topic to determine whether poor reading comprehension performance is due to a reading problem or prior-knowledge problem. It is imperative that teachers take the time to accurately identify readers' areas of difficulty and the causes of those difficulties. One can easily infer an inability to read with comprehension when in fact, the problem for a learner may be lack of prior knowledge, more specifically content, textual, and or linguistic knowledge.

Finally, the research related to orthography or letter/word level processing indicates that L2 readers need to develop fast and accurate decoding skills. Fluent reading in an L2 is associated with efficient and effective decoding strategies and knowledge of the orthographic patterns of a language. Therefore, teachers must provide students with direct instruction that develops knowledge of the sound-symbol relationships and that provides enough practice to develop automatic decoding skills.

Given what we know about reading through the extensive research that has been carried out over the years, it is clear that readers must be provided with the kind of support that makes them more aware of their reading process and the various strategies they can use to facilitate that process, in turn improving text comprehension. As discussed in Chapter 1, a balanced or integrated method or approach to teaching reading integrates strategy and phonics instruction wherever needed into a meaning-based reading curricula. Several chapters in this book focus more specifically on the nuts and bolts of teaching reading describing how reader awareness and a wider variety of skills and strategies can be developed.

Recommendations for Future Research

While extensive research in the area of second language reading has been carried out, especially over the last two decades, much more about the nature of L2 reading remains to be uncovered.

Liontas (1999, p. 543) and Singhal (1999) offer several recommendations for future research. These take the form of possible research questions.

- Is the process of reading acquisition the same or different in naturalistic or classroom settings?

- Does successful reading result from comprehensible input? Can we presume that modified texts are of pedagogical value to second language learners?

- Does the nature of a task or text type have a marked influence on learners' choice of cognitive and metacognitive strategies, i.e., does it predispose learners to use a particular strategy or combination of strategies?

- Should certain text types or structures be used before others when building reading skills and strategies?

- What are the linguistic and cognitive mechanisms that are at work in understanding figurative and literary language used in literary texts?

- What are the linguistic and cognitive mechanisms that are at work in understanding academic language used in academic texts?

- Can strategy training of specific features of specific texts lead to enhanced comprehension? Can we presume that second language learners can comprehend figurative language and textual features found in literary and academic texts by way of demonstration, practice, and feedback?

- How do individual learner factors such as age, sex, social class, ethnic background and motivation, and psychological factors such as language aptitude, learning style, and learners' attitudes and beliefs influence learning outcomes and the level of reading proficiency achieved?

- What are the optimal interactional conditions that aid the development of reading? To what extent can an adult SL learner achieve a high-level of reading proficiency and develop higher-order thinking skills without having the above in the L1?

- How is reading online or the reading of hypertext documents different than reading traditional printed materials? Does reading online influence use of specific reading strategies?

- What skills are needed to effectively read online material? What pedagogical methods can be used to facilitate reading of online texts?

Second and foreign language learners can become effective readers if comprehension strategies and skill development is properly cultivated and given the proper focus and attention in meaningful contextualized language instruction. As Liontas (1999) points out, the goal of reading teachers and researchers is to better understand the reading process itself, the complex factors affecting the process, and the optimal combination of factors that will result in efficient and effective readers.

Summary

Research in second language reading has investigated a number of different areas. Much of the research in the 1970s and 1980s focused on teaching second language students to use a variety of language strategies in order to improve their reading skills and use of strategies. Research has shown that there is a strong relationship between reading strategies used by readers and proficiency level. Successful readers tend to use a wider range of comprehension strategies and use them more frequently. Other studies have shown that readers who employ metacognitive and monitoring strategies tend to be better readers as they know when and how to apply strategies. Strategy instruction training studies have demonstrated that explicit instruction improves reading comprehension and that effective application of strategies can be taught. Numerous studies have also investigated the role of schemata in reading comprehension and have found that when content, text format and linguistic structure is more familiar to readers, comprehension increases. Finally, research in the area of orthography and reading has shown that different writing systems can affect word recognition and reading rate. These prominent areas of research clearly illustrate the need for teachers to better understand the obstacles facing many second language readers and to realize that they must provide their students with the kind of support that will make them more aware of their own reading process and the various strategies they can use to facilitate that process, thereby improving comprehension of texts across a variety of subject areas and disciplines.

Discussion Questions and Activities

1. Select a recent research-based article on reading to present to your peers. Compile the list of articles into an annotated bibliography to be shared by everyone.

2. In what ways does research inform theory and theory inform research?

3. In small groups, brainstorm a list of three-four questions related to reading that you would like to find out more about. Use the library and the Internet to find out if any research has been carried out in these areas.

4. Write a one-page journal entry describing what you learned in this chapter.

5. Select one of the articles cited in this chapter and write a one page summary of it.

Chapter 3
Computer-Assisted Instruction and Reading

Though computers are being used to a greater extent now than before in educational contexts, the research on computer-assisted instruction and reading is somewhat limited. This chapter discusses the body of research in that area and its implications for classroom practice. The chapter also provides specific examples of the various types of web-based reading activities and reading software currently available. Also discussed are instructional considerations and future applications.

Brief History of Computer-Assisted Language Learning and Computer-Assisted Instruction and Reading

Interest in using computers to enhance learning began in the mid 1960s (Warschauer, 1999). In the beginning, mainframe computers were hooked through telephone lines to terminals which were connected to computers located in other rooms. In the 1970s, computers continued to be made use of for educational purposes. The first well-known study to develop these programs was the Stanford Computer Assisted Instruction project. This was an on-going study to develop programs capable of individualized reading instruction for kindergarten through third grade. The first institutions to launch the project concerning the use of computers in foreign language learning were the University of Illinois, Harvard, and Pennsylvania State University. In 1975, the first commercial program PLATO to teach basic skills was released. Simultaneously, other projects began to emerge and develop computer-based strategies for learning to read. In 1979 Dr. Frank Otto began the development of the idea of an "English as a Second Language Course" with the help of a computer. His search for federal funding led him to contacts which resulted in the creation of CALICO in 1982, a significant organization today. Since that time, we have seen numerous important developments in the area of computer-assisted language learning including journals and conferences devoted solely to these issues, graduate and specialized courses in CALL focusing on email and web for language learning, software writing, concordancing, data-driven learning, and the development of materials offering possibilities for skill development and authentic interaction. The latter portion of this chapter considers some of these materials in more detail.

As far as the pedagogical approaches to computer assisted language learning are concerned, the history of CALL can be divided into three main stages: behavioristic CALL, communicative CALL, and integrative CALL (Hanson-Smith, 2002; Warschauer & Healey, 1998). The 1960s and 1970s were dominated by behavioristic approaches which focused mainly on language drills constituting the so called "drill-and-practice" exercises where the computer was essentially a "mechanical tutor" (Warschauer & Healey, 1998; Warschauer, 1999; Warschauer, 2000). The next stage was introduced in the late 1970s and early 1980s and it emphasized the importance of using forms. Many activities such as text-reconstruction exercises in which words were mixed and students had to arrange them into meaningful text, dominated software design. This period focused on the assumption that learning was a process of discovery and expression. The third stage, integrative CALL emphasized the integration of the four skill areas: reading, writing, speaking and listening and therefore programs were task-based and strived to place language learners in an authentic context. As hardware and software continues to become more sophisticated, more exciting possibilities for learners and teachers will emerge. The movement towards web-based instruction and web-based software is also opening up new ways of teaching and learning as will be explored further in the chapter.

Overview of Research in Computer-Assisted Instruction and Reading
Computer-Assisted Instruction and Reading Skill Development

Before proceeding to a discussion of computer-assisted instruction and reading, it would be useful to consider a brief overview of the research conducted in this area to better understand how the field has progressed, the focus of the various research studies that have been carried out in this area, and the implications of this research. For the most part, these studies were conducted to determine how specific computer programs affected students' reading ability. Fletcher and Atkinson (1972) conducted one of the earlier studies in which children of an experimental group received eight to ten minutes of computer assisted instruction per day for five months; the remainder of the day was the same for all children. Results of post-test gain scores showed that most students who received CAI performed better than those who did not.

In a similar study, Fletcher and Suppes (1972) used the Computer Curriculum Corporation reading curriculum for grades four to six with 162 students, ten minutes a day for the entire school year. They found that students learned twice as many new words as students using traditional basal texts only. A number of other studies conducted in the 1970s were research projects that addressed major issues related to student achievement with computer assisted instruction.

In the 1980s and 1990s, many studies involved the implementation of courses, which combined the teaching of reading skills with computer aids that provided various types of support. One such study was carried out at Duquesne University in Pennsylvania (Orndorff, 1987). The rationale behind the development of such a program was that it was believed many college students lacked the ability to read and think critically. Generally, those students who achieved high marks in university were those that were better readers. The researchers employed two computer programs in the sequence of two courses in critical reading and thinking. The program "Abstract" was designed to teach students how to analyze a work for literary genre and structure, and was designed to be used with a book. The program "Interlocutor" allowed teachers to create tutorials, which featured various kinds of question and answer formats, screen manipulations, and the ability to have an on-line dictionary of words and concepts. Various activities included summary writing, short essay questions, sections which focused on form of the texts, and quizzes. The author points out that because of such programs, both student achievement and retention levels increased.

Krasilnikov (1989) describes a course developed in Russia using computer assisted instruction for the development of second language reading skills. Nine computer programs consisting of learning modules were developed to address specific reading skills not likely to have been attained by students at that level of second language literacy. The modules provided practice in word recognition and word comprehension, recognition of word boundaries and sentence structures, recognition of the devices used to create textual cohesion, sentence completion, vocabulary development, skimming skills, scanning, and practice in reading for global understanding, and reading for total comprehension. While the effects of this particular program are not discussed as this was merely a description of a computer program created to teach specific reading skills, the creators of these modules do emphasize the teaching of particular skills, although this list is not comprehensive by any means. In addition, the activities described appear to provide practice in both top-down and bottom-up reading comprehension strategies.

Computer-Assisted Instruction and Effects on Reading Comprehension

Various studies in the area of reading and CAI have investigated how reading intervention programs or training affects comprehension. Carrasquillo and Nunez (1988) investigated the effectiveness of two computer-assisted metacognitive strategies, the Tutorial-Direct Monitoring Strategy (TDMS) and the Schema-Direct Monitoring Strategy (SDMS), on the reading skills and reading comprehension of 68 ESL fourth grade students. Both treatment conditions used computer-mediated texts as the instructional materials. The Tutorial-Direct Monitoring Strategy consisted of monitoring techniques including summarizing, clarifying and questioning, skill modeling reading texts, and comprehension exercises, whereas the Schema-Direct Monitoring Strategy used reading texts, comprehension exercises, and a monitoring strategy in flowchart form. In the TDMS program, reminders of monitoring comprehension strategies were available throughout, however, in the SDMS program, this option was not available and students had to refer to the flowchart each time a comprehension failure occurred. The results of the study demonstrated significant differences in favor of the TDMS illustrating that training in metacognitive strategies can enhance reading comprehension performance, as well as reading comprehension skills.

A study by Arroyo (1992) examined the effect of extended use of computers on reading achievement. The subjects consisted of 75 grade seven students attending an elementary school located in a predominantly low income socio-economic neighborhood of South Chicago. Of this total, 15 students were subjected to an intensive computer assisted instruction program for the entire school year, while 15 others, randomly selected from the remaining group of 60 received no computer training and served as a control group. Results of the Iowa Tests of Basic Skills indicated a statistically significant increase in reading achievement of the students who used computers. In addition to an improvement in reading scores, Arroyo also points out that use of the computer also appeared to increase student motivation to learn.

Another interesting study in the area of reading and CAI was carried out by Pederson (1986) to determine if passage availability (making the reading passage available on a computer screen while answering comprehension questions) affected reading comprehension. Eight class sections of French students participated in the study. Subjects answered questions related to the texts from French periodicals; the subjects were either in the "passage available" condition or "passage unavailable" condition in which the passage was removed from the computer display when the subject pressed the return key to view a question. Data indicated that subjects consistently answered questions about a passage when it was unavailable for re-inspection. Regardless of the students' level of verbal ability or difficulty level of the question, the "passage unavailable" treatment always resulted in a comparatively higher comprehension rate. This may have been because the demands of the "passage unavailable" condition required subjects to read very carefully and this condition may have induced the use of specific types of reading strategies. Computer instruction or intervention has also been used to improve reading rate and efficiency. Wepner, Feeley, and Wilde (1989) conducted a study to assess whether a commercially prepared reading package, *Speed Reader*, could be utilized as effectively as traditionally printed paper text with college students over time to improve reading efficiency, namely, rate and comprehension. Two of four sections of a second-level basic skills course were randomly designated as the experimental group and the other two were control groups. All sections read a novel and spent one period a week using *Speed Reader II* materials. The only difference was in the mode of delivery as the experimental group used the materials in the computer lab and read passages on a computer screen. At the end of eight weeks, all students were tested using the Fast Reading Section of the Stanford Diagnostic Reading Test. While no significant differences in rate gain were found, different reading efficiency patterns were found for the experimental group. The authors conclude that computers can be used as effectively as traditional approaches in delivering timed, whole text readings with comprehension checks to improve the reading efficiency of college students. In addition, motivation benefits were also observed for the computer-displayed group.

Adler-Kassner and Reynolds (1996) also implemented computer use in basic composition classes at the University of Minnesota's General College. Although specific computer assisted instruction packages were not utilized, the computer was used as a reading tool in order to help students become more aware of their reading processes. Real-time conferencing was used so that students could engage in real-time discussions about texts and various questions they had about their readings. Students also had opportunities to enter into dialogic readings with one another or with an instructor through electronic mail. Overall, the researchers found that students tended to disclose more about their interaction with readings over email than they did in the classroom. The authors also point out that the feedback students received in terms of email responses also strengthened confidence about their encounters with unfamiliar academic texts.

In addition to these types of uses, students were also shown how to use web browsers and electronic library databases in order to locate other sources and make connections to their texts and readings. The main goal was to show students how to read widely across several documents or screens, with the purpose of enhancing their responses to texts. In effect, these efforts were intended to help students make links from their individual texts to authoritative academic texts.

Multimedia Reading Software, Reading Comprehension and Vocabulary Acquisition

In addition to the studies described above, more recent studies in the area of computers and reading have examined the effects of multimedia reading software on reading comprehension. Lomicka's (1998) study explored how multimedia annotations influence the level of comprehension. Twelve college students enrolled in a second semester French course were instructed to think aloud during the reading of text on the computer screen. Participants read the text under one of three conditions: full glossing, limited glossing, or no glossing. In addition, a tracker was set up in the software to record the amount and type of glosses and length of time that each was consulted. The data indicated an increase in the number of causal inferences generated for students who had access to full glossing. She concluded that computerized reading with full glossing may promote a deeper level of text comprehension.

Lyman-Hager and Davis (1996) also examined vocabulary acquisition and student glossing choices for intermediate level students studying French. Two conditions were used in this study: computerized reading and non-computerized reading of an excerpt from the story by F. Oyono, *Une Vie de Boy.* Both groups had access to glosses; the computer group had access to multimedia annotations, while the text group could consult printed text with the same glosses. Subjects were asked to perform a written recall protocol immediately after reading the text. A week later, an in-class vocabulary quiz of "critical" words in the story was distributed following a class discussion. Lyman-Hager et al. (1996) concluded that students who worked with the multimedia program were better able to retain vocabulary words than students who worked with non-computerized text.

In an article exploring multimedia annotations and vocabulary acquisition, Chun and Plass (1996) present the results of three studies with students in their second year of German who used *CyberBuch*, a multimedia application offering annotations through pictures, text, and video. Specifically, the goals of their investigation include exploring incidental vocabulary learning, examining the effectiveness of multimedia annotations, and investigating the relationship between look-up behavior and vocabulary test performance. Students were introduced to the program and watched a video which provided an overview of the story before working with the multimedia application. After reading the story and using the multimedia annotations, students took a vocabulary test and wrote a recall protocol. Chun and Plass (1996) report that the recall protocol for visual annotations (i.e., words annotated with text and pictures, text, and video) was higher than for words annotated with text alone. While both Lyman-Hager and Davis (1996) and Chun and Plass (1996) investigated vocabulary learning through the use of recall protocols, some researchers point out that recall or post-reading measures may be more representative of a memory test used to simply "recall" knowledge.

A more comprehensive endeavor in the area of computers and reading involves the R-WISE project - Reading and Writing in a Supportive Environment (Carlson & Larralde, 1995). R-WISE is a software program which teaches the use of language as a vehicle for critical thinking. The developers of this program have designed a battery of "procedural facilitators" staged so as to promote progressively sophisticated forms of reading comprehension. Specifically, R-WISE promotes three qualitatively different types of activities and models each for the student: 1) identifying concepts and units of meaning in a text, 2) formulating interpretations and making inferences, and 3) metacognitive control over performative skills.

At the beginning of each new lesson, the student is asked to go through a preliminary activity that helps to 1) delineate the requirements of the task, 2) identify features of the text, such as level of difficulty, structure, and aim of the discourse, 3) identify strengths (such as prior knowledge) and weaknesses (such as limited experience with the type of discourse) the reader brings to the situation. This introductory section of the program is designed to increase metacognitive awareness and encourages the student to formulate a loose plan for the cognitive task about to take place.

The second way R-WISE encourages the active construction of meaning during reading fits in with the current emphasis on "visual referents" for teaching abstract concepts. The interface of R-WISE represents visual organizers for specific intellectual processes. R-WISE contains a "concept mapper" - the workspace that encourages the deconstruction of linear prose into more symbolic on semantic networks. Similar to "webbing" or "schematicizing" paper and pencil techniques used in the traditional classroom, this technique encourages the student to formulate a "meta-view" in a more visible language. The student can consult the text in one section of the screen or window, but the main focus of the activity is in the workspace on the opposite side of the screen where the student builds a model of the knowledge structure of the text passage. The student can click on an icon representing one of four aspects of comprehension: 1) identify the main idea, 2) locate a major support statement, 3) identify a supporting detail, 4) draw an inference from the text. Multiple occurrences of icons are acceptable and icons are movable, meaning that students can use placement of the tokens to construct a visual illustration of verbal statements. The process of mapping allows readers to see things as a synoptic overview. However, an even deeper processing of the concepts of the text is encouraged by having the student elaborate on the meaning for each icon.

The program also contains what is termed "four strategic elements" which include nodes (main ideas, key concepts, details, and inferences), author's purpose (to explain, inform, persuade, entertain), text type (genre, form), and reader's purpose (to obtain information, leisure reading, etc). In addition, 600 advice statements consisting of prompt questions related to reach of the four main areas are included. These statements offer additional information to students and also prompt them to consider questions related to the text content and textual characteristics. The prompts operate as a form of embedded instruction and students can have the flexibility of moving from one area of the program to another. All written observations the students make on icons in the elaboration interface are transferred to the notebook section of the program where they are available for review. These observations can be modified at anytime based on any new information the students may have obtained through the question and information prompts.

While the program appears to be highly segmented in nature, it does seem to contain some important elements relevant to text processing and comprehension. For example, the elaboration segment encourages students to examine and link their previous knowledge with the new knowledge presented in the text. Second, the object-oriented nature of the tutor provides visualization for obscure mental operations. By mapping and elaborating, the process becomes more explicit so that the student can become both an observer and a participant in these higher-order thinking skills. Third, while many reading software programs have visual representations or simulations of texts, this program combines the manipulations of constructing a model with guidance. R-WISE's interactive feedback provides functions of self-appraisal, gives knowledge about one's own knowledge, and initiates self-management of cognitive activity. Lastly, the inclusion of the adaptive advice statements which serve as embedded cueing, represent the monitoring process of text processing. These activities enable the reader to modify or abandon a particular strategy, if necessary, and provide students with additional information, which may further facilitate their comprehension of texts.

Reading Behavior Tracking Studies

Other studies in the area of second language reading have also made use of a tracking tool for keeping a record of reading behaviors that students engage in which cannot be made available for study through print-based media (Blake, 1992; Chun & Plass, 1996; Davis & Lyman-Hager, 1997). Blake (1992) created a Spanish Hypercard program consisting of several components including the main text, cultural notes and background information, grammar tutorials, and a dictionary. While reading, students had the option of clicking on any of the above. A log record showed every card that opened, every button clicked, every word searched, every question answered, and the time when each action was taken. Overall, Blake found that first semester students relied more on native-language glossing of words than more advanced students. Less advanced students were also not able to take advantage of the vast number of cognates that exist between English and Spanish across all lexical categories. While Blake's study was not designed to advocate the computer as a methodological advancement over other traditional formats, he was advocating the use of the computer as a unique means of tracking second language reading behaviors and strategies.

Summary of Computer-Assisted Instruction and Reading Research

It is clear from the earlier discussion that various efforts have been made to include the computer in the reading classroom as an instructional tool. Research has also been carried out to determine and assess the effectiveness of various kinds of computer uses, programs, and interventions in terms of improvement in reading achievement and comprehension. However, despite these efforts, some of these programs have failed to include a sound pedagogical foundation or theoretical base in terms of how reading should be taught, and what should be emphasized in a reading program or curriculum.

It is important to recognize that many studies that show benefits of CAI in relation to reading involved short-term instruction and then measured gains in reading achievement. One would expect an immediate improvement after a few hours or days of instruction, even due to memory effects, but there is often no follow-up in these studies to ensure whether students have in fact learned specific reading strategies and skills in order to effectively and efficiently apply them to future tasks. Other projects have instituted various computer instructional programs in their existing curriculum, but again little information is provided as to how students have in fact benefited from such instruction. While the goals of the program are clear, the results are less straightforward because some of the studies described above do not provide such information. Furthermore, those studies that do emphasize the teaching of specific skills and strategies (Krasilnikov, 1989; Orndorff, 1987) via the computer do not seem to present information within a context. For the most part, the exercises are isolated drill and practice type activities. Numerous studies have also focused on reading speed and accuracy of decoding, rather than on meaning-making and overall comprehension (Fletcher & Atkinson, 1972; Warren & Rosebery, 1988; Wepner, Feeley, & Wilde, 1989). In such studies, the process of reading is viewed solely as a bottom-up process in which students are focused on aspects of the text itself such as individual words and sentence structure. Many studies to date in this area have been concerned with gains in reading achievement based on pre- and posttest scores. Finally, the more recent studies (Chun & Plass, 1996; Lomicka, 1998) examining effects of multimedia reading software on reading comprehension, and the research on glossing and multimedia annotations, have concentrated primarily on vocabulary learning, acquisition, and retention, and have only scratched the surface of research involving computer-assisted reading comprehension and multimedia annotations. Few studies have been longitudinal and many have not implemented programs that teach students a range of reading strategies and skills to become more aware of their own reading processes, and to use strategies effectively in different reading contexts in order to make sense of what they read. Without a doubt, this is an area that will continue to receive much attention in the years to come.

Examples of Computer-Based Reading Activities and Exercises
Online Activities
Numerous reading exercises currently exist on the Internet. The Reading Matrix has compiled an online database or collection of reading exercises available on the Internet <http://www.readingmatrix.com/directory/pages/>. The list continues to grow as users can make additions at any time. Figure 1, a screen shot of

their interactive database, shows the various categories of exercises. This discussion focuses on a select few to demonstrate the range of activities and practice exercises currently available online. In order to better explain some of the features of each of these websites which include reading activities, screen shots have been included here. At the time of publication, these sites were freely available to Internet users.

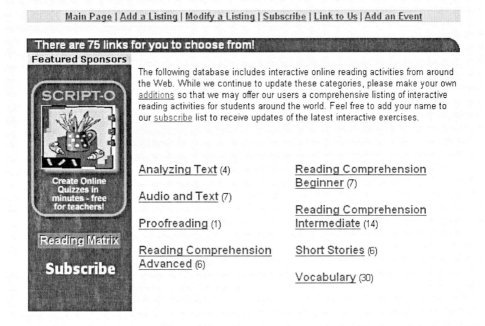

Figure 1 Screen Shot of The Reading Matrix Interactive Database of Online Reading Exercises <http://www.readingmatrix.com/directory/pages/>.

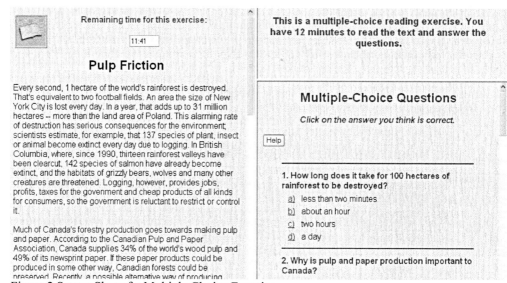

Figure 2 Screen Shot of a Multiple Choice Exercise
<http://web2.uvcs.uvic.ca/elc/studyzone/570/pulp/index.htm>

The English Language Centre website (University of Victoria) includes a range of reading exercises such as timed skimming and scanning exercises, pre-reading exercises in which students answer multiple-choice questions about a topic, reading comprehension exercises which usually involves a timed reading, that is students are given twelve minutes to read the passage as it disappears once the time is up, and then they answer a series of multiple-choice questions on the text. As the student works on each question, they are given feedback about their answers and in the end, a final score is provided. Vocabulary exercises related to the readings are also included, and most of the questions require students to identify the meaning of words as used in context (in the reading). Gap fill exercises and sentence ordering exercises are also included. In each of these cases, students are told whether their answers are correct or incorrect. Finally, the last exercise is called "Scavenger Hunt." The user has to answer a series of questions related to a topic. In order to do so, the user has to read other information which is provided through links and other valuable resources. The last two exercises focus on critical thinking. One such exercise presents the students with quotations from number of quotations from different interest groups or lobbies. Based on the information given, they are to determine whose position is represented. Once again students are given feedback on their responses in the form of a scores and comments. At time of publication, this site was available to Internet users.

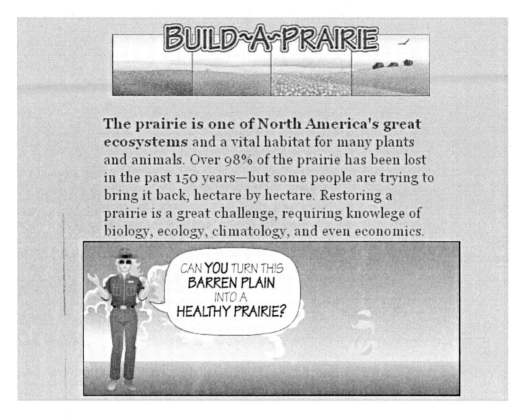

Figure 3 Screen Shot of Reading Comprehension Exercise
<http://www.bellmuseum.org/distancelearning/prairie/index.html>

The Bell Museum of Natural History website is one of the most interesting on the web in terms of reading comprehension exercises. It consists of a series of web adventures or mazes. The user can select from many different choices including "Build a Prairie" or an "Interactive Watershed Game." The user has to take the necessary steps to restore the landscape and this is done by making appropriate choices about which types of plants and animals should be grown and brought to the area. In order to make the right decisions, users are presented with additional information which is obtained by clicking a button under each photo. If students make an incorrect decision, they are prompted to try again but if their decision is correct, they are shown a short video clip with the results of their decisions. The pages also include a link to an online dictionary so that if students cannot understand words in the description, they can easily obtain meanings while the task window is still open. This site is also freely available to Internet users.

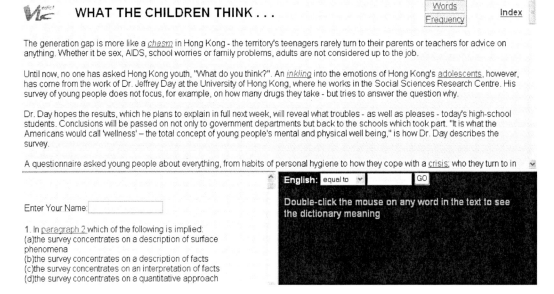

Figure 4 Screen Shot of Reading Comprehension Exercise with Questions
<http://www.edict.com.hk/vlc/comp/readcomp.htm>

The Edict Virtual Language Centre website provides a number of reading comprehension exercises for students and Internet users. Some are password protected but some are not. Students are presented with a story or article and answer a series of related multiple-choice questions. The questions are designed to cover a range of reading strategies and focus on higher-order thinking skills. The screen is divided into three sections, one for the story, one for questions, and for an online monolingual English dictionary. Difficult words are highlighted in the reading and students can obtain meanings by clicking on the word. If the student needs to look up any of the other words, the online dictionary can be used, which in addition to providing definitions, provides the part of speech and sentence examples. Students can obtain a final score with explanations of responses.

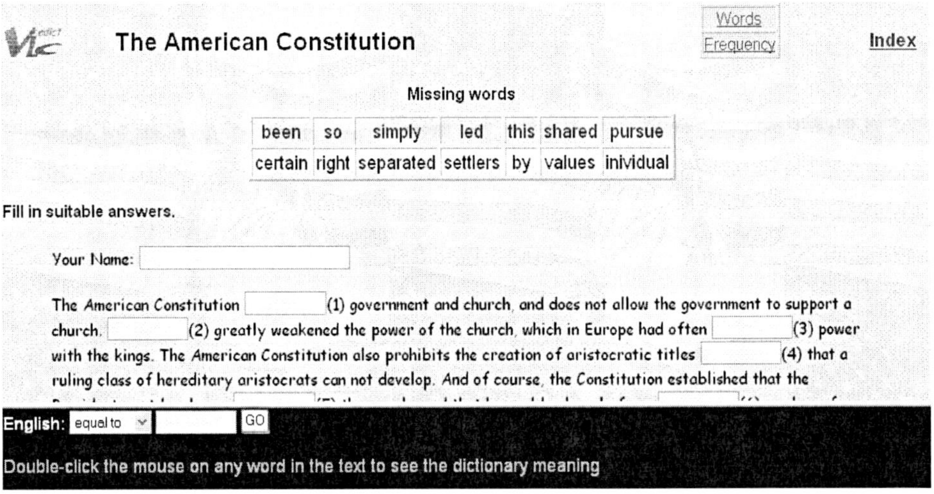

Figure 5 Screen Shot of Cloze Exercise <http://www.edict.com.hk/vlc/cloze/cloze.htm>

The Edict Virtual Language Centre also includes a series of cloze exercises in which students are given both a list of missing words and the gapped reading passage. An online dictionary is provided to aid in the completion of the exercise. In the past, these exercises have been accessible to all Internet users.

Figure 6 Screen Shot of CNN SF News Article Reading Comprehension Exercises Page <http://literacynet.org/cnnsf/archives.html>

The CNN-Western Pacific Literary Network includes story modules and comprehension activities. Stories are provided by CNN (San Francisco) and are intended for adults with moderate reading and speaking comprehension skills and advanced ESL or non-native English speakers. Overall, it is an excellent site. An abridged story version is also available in which the text has been modified to simplify complex ideas and sentences, exchanging advanced words with less difficult ones, and changing difficult concepts into precise terms. Abridged stories can, therefore, be used for with readers who have low reading comprehension skills including beginning ESL or non-native English speakers. Each story also includes a story outline which provides a summary of basic edited story elements. A range of comprehension activities designed to interactively test learner comprehension of the story are included. These exercises include word selection, multiple choice, vocabulary, and sequencing activities. After answering a modules question, learners can check their responses by clicking the "Review Answers" button at the end of each lesson. A "report card" of correct and incorrect answers is quickly transmitted back. The activities were created using Half-Baked Software. Along with the text, most story modules contain full streaming video of the broadcast, and text of the story read by Greg Lefevre, CNN SF Bureau Chief and Correspondent.

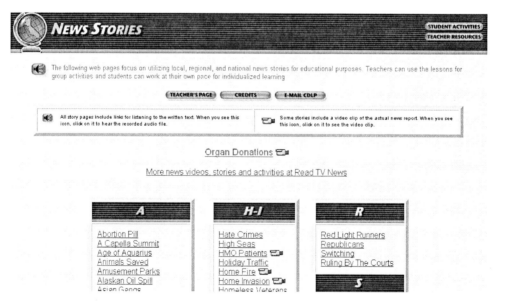

Figure 7 Screen Shot of California Distance Learning Project Website.
<http://www.cdlponline.org/news.html>

The Internet also includes numerous vocabulary practice exercises. Some sites are devoted to practice of words commonly found on the SAT, GRE, or TOEFL tests. Others are cloze-type or fill-in-the-blank exercises, some provide practice in Latin and Greek roots, while others are vocabulary exercises related to reading passages. As mentioned earlier in the chapter, The Reading Matrix has compiled these vocabulary exercises and activities so that many of them are available in one place and can easily be accessed by web users.

Match the words and sentences. A word can only be used once. When you have finished, type your name, your email address if you have one, and your teacher's email address. Press "Submit".

1. We drove through the _____, rocky landscape.   select one ▾
2. I think we should _____ capital punishment. It does not solve our problems.   select one ▾
3. After the war this town was a _____.   select one ▾
4. The town is busy now but in the winter it is completely _____.   select one ▾
5. The area has been _____ by war.   select one ▾
6. She was _____ so I was unable to recognize her.   select one ▾
7. It is important to have someone to _____ on. We all need help sometimes.   select one ▾
8. _____ erupted when the local tax was increased.   select one ▾
9. The original house had servants' _____ on the top floor.   select one ▾
10. The table was _____ with all sorts of food.   select one ▾
11. There was a _____ of anger in what she said.   select one ▾
12. Be careful when you hold that cactus plant. It is very _____.   select one ▾

Figure 8 Screen Shot of Vocabulary Quiz
<http://www.readingmatrix.com/cgi-bin/ezmatch/main.cgi?q=chapter8esl63>

The site also contains links to short story exercises, pages where audio and text are both available, exercises focusing on literature and literary elements, and proofreading exercises. The exercises are grouped according to difficulty level and are categorized into beginner, intermediate, and advanced levels. While the pages come from a variety of sources and web sites, they have been placed together in this database to make it easier for reading teachers and students. For more details, consult <http://www.readingmatrix.com/directory/pages/>.

Another kind of reading activity is concordancing. A concordance essentially consists of a list of the words in the text with a short section of the context that precedes and follows each word. The computer software searches for all examples of a word, phrase, or word ending and then arranges all examples found as a list on the screen, usually with the found items in the middle of the screen so that a sentence context of about 10 words surrounds each one. *Conc,* a beta test version as freeware can be downloaded at:<http://www.sil.org/computing/conc/conc.html>. Grammar Safari (Mills & Salzman, 2002) is an online activity very similar to concordancing, but on a less automated level. One can use the Find function on any Internet browser to search an electronic text. By paying attention to the list of the words in context, students can devise rules, or check their own usage of a structure in their essays against the authentic examples. This technique is an inductive approach to understanding vocabulary and grammar and can be very effective for intermediate to advanced level students.

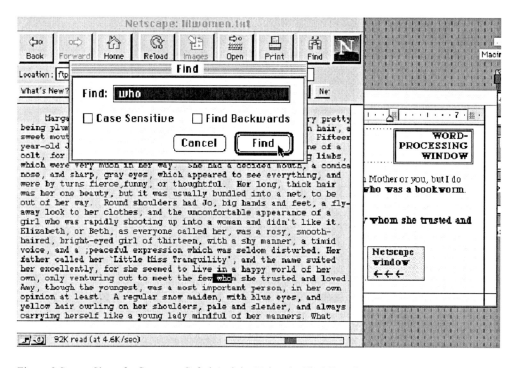

Figure 9 Screen Shot of a Grammar Safari Activity Using the Find Function

Other programs now make it possible for teachers to gloss vocabulary in a text to facilitate comprehension. Previous research, in fact, has shown that glossing expands the amount of information available to the student and individualizes the learning experience by hiding the glossing until the student feels the need to access it. In addition, students working with multimedia programs and glossed texts were better able to retain vocabulary words than students who worked with the non-computerized text (Davis & Lyman-Hager, 1997; Martinez-Lage & Herren, 1998; Lomicka, 1998; Lyman-Hager & Davis, 1996). Two glossing tools which are available as freeware can be found at <http://www.voycabulary.com> and <http://lang.swarthmore.edu/gloss/glossmaker.htm>. *VoyCabulary* makes the words on any web page into links so users can look them up in a dictionary or other word-reference-site of your choice, by simply clicking on the words. This tool appears to work much more effectively when the text is simply copied and pasted into the scroll box rather than typing in the URL of the web page as suggested. Teachers can also select which online dictionary meanings will be provided to the learners. *Glossmaker* requires slightly more input on the part of the teacher as one has to identify and mark the sections of the text to be glossed, and type in the definitions beforehand.

Finally, many publishers of assessment materials and standardized tests are now producing computerized versions of their tests. The Test of English as a Foreign Language (TOEFL) has also now computerized their test. The TOEFL measures the ability of nonnative speakers of English to use and understand North American English as it is used in college and university settings. Scores on the test are required by more than 4,300 two- and four-year colleges and universities, professional schools, and sponsoring institutions. The reading section measures the ability to read and understand short passages similar in topic and style to those that students are likely to encounter in North American universities and colleges. In most exercises, the learner is asked to click on the paragraph describing a particular situation, event, or object. The task is designed to assess comprehension of the text. Scores are counted automatically and reported to the Educational Testing Service (ETS).

Sample Passage and Questions

> The railroad was not the first institution to impose
> regularity on society, or to draw attention to the
> importance of precise timekeeping. For as long as
> *Line* merchants have set out their wares at daybreak and
> (5) communal festivities have been celebrated, people have
> been in rough agreement with their neighbors as to the
> time of day. The value of this tradition is today more
> apparent than ever. Were it not for public acceptance of
> a single yardstick of time, social life would be unbearably
> (10) chaotic: the massive daily transfers of goods, services,
> and information would proceed in fits and starts; the
> very fabric of modern society would begin to unravel.

Example I   **Sample Answer**

Ⓐ Ⓑ ● Ⓓ

What is the main idea of the passage?

    A. In modern society we must make more time for our neighbors.

    B. The traditions of society are timeless.

    C. An accepted way of measuring time is essential for the smooth functioning of society.

    D. Society judges people by the times at which they conduct certain activities.

The main idea of the passage is that societies need to agree about how time is measured in order to function smoothly. Therefore, you should choose answer C.

Figure 10 Screen Shot of Reading Passage on TOEFL Sample Test <http://www.toefl.org>-Available on the Internet at time of publication.

TOEFL has also launched what they call the *Next Generation TOEFL*. In this TOEFL version, students are asked to demonstrate how well they can use English to communicate by reading, writing, listening, and speaking. The test includes questions that involve integrated skills. For example, a student may be asked to read a passage and write about it, or listen to a lecture and speak about it. This provides more and better information about the student's ability to use English. The new TOEFL test will be delivered via the Internet. As stated on the website, Internet-based testing (iBT) allows ETS to capture speech and score responses in a standardized manner. Multiple full-length forms of the test along with an array of practice and learning materials will also be available at the site. Students and English language teachers will be able to use the site to familiarize themselves with the format and content of the test, as well as to practice and strengthen their language skills for this new communicative competency-based assessment. Scores on the full-length timed test will be reported to students only. No scores will be reported to designated institutions. TOEFL iBT was introduced in the United States, Canada, France, Germany, Italy, and Puerto Rico in 2005. The second phase of the rollout began in March 2006 when test centers in selected cities in Africa, the Americas, Europe, Eurasia, the Middle East, and North Africa offered TOEFL iBT for the first time. For updates, readers may wish to consult the TOEFL website.

Reading Comprehension Software

Numerous reading comprehension packages are now available through publishers who are becoming more aware of ESL and adult students' needs. Merit Software for example, has developed a series of reading programs such as Developing Critical Thinking Skills for Effective Reading, Literature-Based Reading, Reading Critically: Non-Fiction; and Reading Critically: Non-Fiction for College Prep, and Real World Reading Skills. Developing Critical Thinking Skills is discussed in more detail here. This program is designed to evaluate the learner's comprehension skills. The students must sign in at the beginning which allows the instructor to view student scores. The learner is presented with a text in a small window and next to the window various kinds of comprehension questions are displayed. Four different tasks are presented. The learner is asked to choose the best replacement word for highlighted words in the text, the learner answers questions designed to test higher-order thinking and critical thinking skills, the learner is asked to select the best title for a given paragraph, and finally, the learner is asked to choose the two best answers that describe what the paragraph is about. If an incorrect answer is selected, the computer tries to prompt the learner and reasons for the incorrect answer are also given. At the end of each exercise, the computer displays a crossword containing words from the text the student has worked with. The text is also available on screen while the student works on the crossword. A "Hint" button can be used to provide clues to the words in the crossword puzzle. Final scores on each section are provided once all the exercises have been completed. Students can track their improvement through progress-to-date and last session scores are automatically kept in a record management system allowing teachers to print detailed reports.

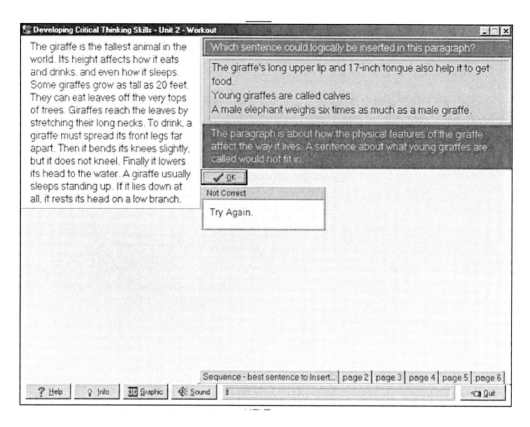

Figure 11 Screen Shot of a Reading Comprehension Question and Student Feedback
<http://meritsoftware.com/>

Other programs on the market today focus on specific types of activities. For example, Camsoft has produced a number of gap-fill or cloze-type programs. One such program is *GapKit* which consists of a series of gapped texts. The learner has to complete the text given a set of words. In each case, the learner has a choice to see the list or can opt to complete the text without the wordlist. *Fun With Text, Copywrite,* and *Prediction* also by Camsoft are similar types of programs.

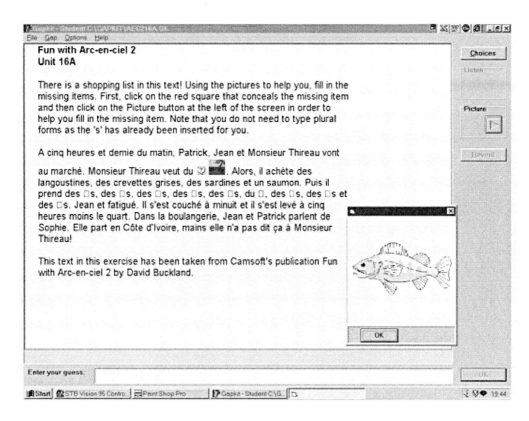

Figure 12 Screen Shot of an Exercise from GapKit <http://www.camsoftpartners.co.uk/>

Other programs focus on both skill development and reading speed. AceReader Pro Deluxe developed by StepWare Inc. is designed to improve reading comprehension and speed. Rather than seeing the entire text, the user sees words presented one at a time on the screen, a technique referred to as Rapid Serial Visual Presentation. In this type of activity, the reader has to make sense of text by focusing on the structure and meaning of the text and therefore it is not enough to activate lower-level processing, that is recognize characters and words. The focus of this exercise is to activate the reader's vocabulary, activate content, formal, and linguistic schemata, encourage the application of synthesis, evaluation, and monitoring skills. AceReader also uses the Tachistoscopic technique which displays the words forcing the reader's eyes to move just as they would when reading normally. The aim of this technique is to build speed as the speed can be set by the reader. Readers can also move back or forward by clicking the appropriate buttons and can also select the difficulty level of the text.

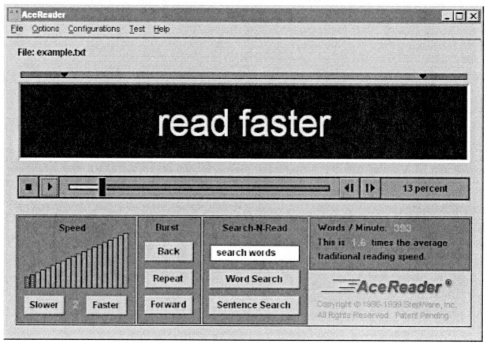

Figure 13 Screen Shot of Speed Reading Exercise by AceReader
<http://www.acereader.com/acereader.html>

The Internet and software applications described above are only a few examples of reading comprehension activities. While it was not possible to discuss the many programs suited for upper level reading courses and academic reading instruction, Figure 14 does provide a general list of some of the more common programs designed to improve reading skills. Teachers may also wish to consult the Agora Language Marketplace <http://agoralang.com/> for a list of available language software or the TESOL CALL Interest Section Software List <http://oregonstate.edu/dept/eli/softlist/> which provides a publisher list and descriptions of available programs.

Software/Program	Publisher/Producer
FReader (Efficient Reader)	ReadingSoft <http://www.readingsoft.com>
Developing Critical Thinking Skills for Effective Reading Literature-Based Reading Reading Critically: Non-Fiction Reading Critically: Non-Fiction Reading Critically: Non-Fiction for College Prep	Merit Software <http://www.meritsoftware.com>

Vocabulary Fitness and Vocabulary Stretch Accu-Reading	
Advancing Vocabulary Skills Building Vocabulary Skills Improving Vocabulary Skills Ten Steps to Advancing College Reading Skills Ten Steps to Building College Reading Skills	Townsend Press <http://www.townsendpress.com>
Compass Reading	ACT <http://www.act.org/>
Comprehension Power	Milliken <http://www.millikenpub.com>
Cloze Encounters in English ESL TOEFL Prep	Lingo Fun <http://www.lingofun.com>
I Speak English - Advanced Reading Comprehension (TOEFL)	Intechnica International <http:www.intechnica.com>
Imagination Express: Destinations	Edmark Corporation <http://www.edmark.com>
College Level Reading Comprehension	Queue Inc. <http://www.queueinc.com>
Core Reading and Vocabulary Development Diascriptive Cloze and Writing Practice Activities Diascriptive Reading I, II, III, IV Diascriptive Reading in Social Studies and Science How to Read for Everyday Living Reading in the Workplace	Educational Activities Software <http://www.ea-software.com>
Ultimate Speed Reader	Davidson & Associates <http://www.knowledgeadventure.com/>
Academy of Reading	Autoskill International <http://www.autoskill.com>
Ace Detective	Mindplay <http://www.mindplay.com>
Alexis, the Encomium TOEIC Test Preparation System	Encomium Publications <http://www.encomium.com>
Alphabetizing	Computers for Education <http://www.geocities.com/ehansonsmi/>
Amazon Trail II The Art Lesson Inside the SAT/ACT	The Learning Company <http://www.learningco.com>

New Reader	Hyperbole Software (Athens, Ohio)
Amnesty Interactive	Amnesty International <http://www.amnesty.org>
Basic Skills for the Real World	Wasatch Education Systems <http://www.wasatchnet.com>
Bilingual Graph Club	Tom Snyder Productions <http://www.teachtsp.com>
Business Territory I and II	Lingonet Oy <http://www.linetti.com>
CALLEAP Eurocentres CALL Library GapMaster	Wida Software <http://www.wido.co.uk/>
Click into English Read It! Study Skills	Clarity Language Consultants <http://www.clarity.com.hk>
REAL Reading in English	TELL Consortium <http://www.hull.ac.uk/cti/tell.htm>
Graffiti One	SpeakWare <http://www.speakware.com>
SuperCloze, Hangman in Context, and Hangword	Vance Stevens and Steve Millmore
Stor-E-Book	The Reading Matrix Inc. <http://www.readingmatrix.com/ebook/ebookonline/>
High Steps to Comprehension	Knowledge Adventure <http://www.KnowledgeAventure.com
Road to Citizenship	Trinity Software Email: trsoft@worldpath.net

Figure 14 List of Reading Programs Suitable for Adult/College Learners and Publishers

From the above overview of online reading activities and reading software, it becomes apparent that there are numerous advantages to using computerized reading programs for both educators and learners. Some of these advantages are discussed in the following section.

Advantages of Computer-Assisted Reading Instruction

One of the main advantages of using CALL in the development of reading comprehension skills is the individualized instruction offered by the computer (Hanson-Smith, 2002; Warschauer, 2002). Pace of learning and learning styles can vary considerably so it is imperative that students be able to work at their own pace and at the skills that require practice and improvement. Slower learners can catch up while more advanced students can be engaged in more challenging activities. Learners at different proficiency levels can work on exercises suited to their skill level. Many software programs today include tools to record student work and areas of difficulty. Adaptive testing whereby examinee questions are quickly matched to the examinee's ability level based on performance is an integral part of many new software programs (Chalhoub-Deville 1999; Chalhoub-Deville, 2001; Chalhoub-Deville & Deville, 1999). Students can also select the reading activities they want to work on and are not limited to text-based exercises which cannot be manipulated. Because the computer allows users to work individually, it also offers privacy. The learner no longer has to fear making mistakes in front of others which might inhibit learning or motivation. Instead the computer frees learners to focus on the development of their reading skills without worrying about outside factors.

Computer software and computerized reading activities are also ideal for their ability to present texts as timed or paced readings (the latter with scrolling text). The teacher or student can set a target reading time, presumably increasing it with each text to encourage students to read fast enough while still obtaining global meanings. Timed readings are a possibility on both web-based activities and stand-alone programs.

Computerized activities also include multimedia components and features which can enhance learning. Animation and sound can make a text more interesting and appealing. It can also be accompanied by direct references to a dictionary. Al-Seghayer (2003) discusses the numerous benefits of electronic dictionaries and the various forms they might take. By clicking a word, the students can obtain the definition of the word enhancing student comprehension. The feature included in a dictionary will depend on what has been included but the student will often have access to the definition, part of speech, and sentence examples showing the word in context. Today numerous vocabulary practice activities exist on the Internet. Vocabulary games attempt to give additional language exposure and practice in order to build the automatic recognition needed to read fluently (See Hanson-Smith (2003) for information on numerous links to reading activities on the Internet). In addition, online and stand-alone reading programs often include glosses. The student simply has to point at the word with a mouse to receive the meaning or translation. Glosses might be explanations in the target and in the native language or can be visual or audio representations of the meaning of the words. Lomicka (1998) who has done much work in the area of text glossing and comprehension states, "Through hypermedia-annotated text, readers will be able to approach the text more globally, rather than linearly. To achieve a more global understanding of the text, other multimedia annotations such as images, sounds, cultural, historical and geographical references, and guiding questions could enhance comprehension" (p. 42). Research has also shown that readers who have access to multimedia-annotated text performed better than groups who had access to printed texts and glossaries (Lomicka, 1998, Chun & Plass, 1997). Because less time is spent accessing a dictionary, students may also be more motivated to read more thereby facilitating the development of reading skills. Multimedia tasks have also been shown to be more attractive and motivating for learners than traditional books and tapes (Brett, 1996; Hanson-Smith, 2003).

Computers can also provide immediate feedback unlike traditional exercises or text-based activities. Computers can provide hints to answers simply by clicking a help or hint button. If a student selects an incorrect answer, an explanation of why the response is incorrect is often provided. Some applications also allow for feedback while students are working on questions, which can be in the form of explanations and comments or in the form of a percentage score. Other applications provide an overall score so that students have an idea of their performance and improvement as they work on a series of activities. Online activities can also provide feedback in similar ways to students. Script-O!, a freeware program, is an online quiz-making tool often used for matching, cloze, or multiple-choice questions, which allows the teacher to obtain student scores and then download them into an Excel worksheet (<http://www.readingmatrix.com/scripto/index.html>). A comprehensive listing of other quiz-making tools can be found at: <http://eleaston.com/quizzes.html>.

Finally, the computer, especially the Internet can provide access to authentic materials for both teaching and learning. The Internet provides an abundance of reading material for learners. Learners can search the web for articles on specific topics accessing newspapers, journals, databases, and up-to-date websites (See Hanson-Smith, 2003; Krajka, 2000 for a list of Internet resources). Some of these websites such as The New York Times Learning Network (<http://www.nytimes.com/learning/students/pop/>) include glossed texts encouraging learners to read materials they otherwise might not read. For example, learners can click the "Vocabulary On" button and words in the text are glossed or they can click on the "Geography On" button and hyperlinks appear on the country names so students can obtain more information about each country and location. Linguistic and content knowledge of students is improved. Using authentic materials for reading instruction also allows learners to acquire "usable skills in real life situations" (Kramsch, et. al, 2000, p. 78). For example, the web can also be used for research purposes to build background knowledge or to acquire new knowledge. The act of searching for materials itself requires the use of reading skills such as skimming web search results to decide which sites or links are relevant or useful for their research topic. Critical reading skills such as evaluation and analysis are then used to read texts and make decisions about whether they can be used or discarded. Such skills are also used when reading these texts more closely to identify bias, point of view, and the underlying values of writers. Designers of language learning software now also include links to relevant and related Internet sites just as hyperlinks on the web allowing students to interact with the text in different ways and to obtain additional information when necessary. In sum, the Internet fosters the development of reading skills and teachers must explore the numerous possibilities it offers in the reading classroom.

Instructional Considerations and Future Applications

The introduction of reading instructional technology requires several considerations. Teachers must select programs and tools that are inline with current theories of reading and activities that most effectively foster the development of reading skills. Some students may also not be proficient in computer skills and therefore some instructional time must be devoted to these aspects. Learners may also need explicit instruction in hypertext reading and navigation strategies. Preliminary findings in the area of strategy use in computerized environments suggest that some learners may benefit from working with multimedia texts and instruction which facilitates use of strategies to better comprehend hyperlinked and multimedia documents including visual and text components (Anderson 2003; Coiro, 2003; Hanson-Smith, 2003; Leu 2002). Future research in this area will need to focus on more interactive learning assistance when reading texts and when answering questions, as well as instruction in navigation and locating relevant and salient information in texts. *The Reading Matrix* is currently developing a program called *Interactive Reader* which is part of a larger web-based program called *Script-O Pro*. (See <http://www.scriptopro.com> for more details. This program is designed to improve the reading comprehension, text analysis, and critical reading skills of readers by making readers more aware of text features. It is a text analysis tool to be used by students in academic reading and English/ESL courses. It imports text material from a text file and provides all the tools needed to identify textual features, and mark and annotate the text. Once the student has finished, the marked text can be printed or saved for retrieval at any time. Earlier Cummins (1998) developed the

E-lective Learning System approach to computer-supported language learning that uses target language text as input for learning. The text is made comprehensible to learners as a result of dictionary and learning strategy supports built into a multimedia CD-ROM. The dictionary supports can be provided in learners' first and second languages (L1 and L2) and learning strategy supports include graphic organizers to facilitate comprehension of content as well as a variety of vocabulary building and grammar learning supports. These supports represent scaffolding that enables the reader to process the meaning of texts that otherwise would have been inaccessible. The benefit of the two programs described above is that any text in electronic form can be imported into the system and used as authentic input for target language learning. Computer programs designed for classroom use should also have such built-in features allowing teachers to incorporate the specific electronic texts students may be using in class rather than pre-selected texts chosen by the software creator or publisher.

Future research should begin to examine the differences among the same readers in online reading contexts and hard-copy contexts to determine if there are any significant differences or if there is any carryover in terms of strategy use and reading behaviors. Another important area for further research is the role of reading rate and online reading. Research on L1 reading indicates that reading rates drop 10-30% when moving from printed material to online reading (Anderson 2003; Kurniawan & Zaphiris, 2001; Muter & Maurutto, 1991). In addition, research will also need to investigate the specific forms or methods of reading instruction that can be most beneficial to our students, who now encounter technology-rich learning environments, as well determine the differences in reading behaviors and strategy use in computer-enhanced environments between second language and foreign language readers to better inform instruction. Finally, computer-based testing needs to go beyond computer-adaptive testing so that tests can actually assess and diagnose a person's language and skill development, certainly highly needed tools given the proliferation of distance education programs and an increased need for assessments that grant credentialing or certification (Chalhoub-Deville, 2001).

Conclusion

Research shows that computer-assisted instruction and computer programs to teach reading can become powerful instructional tools that increase students' engagement in reading, enhance reading comprehension, and improve reading skills. Such tools can also assist the teacher in developing a truly individualized reading program that can better meet the varied needs of students found in most classrooms. By using such a tool, teachers can vary the pace of instruction, review and reinforce learning, teach and address specific skills, provide immediate feedback and improve motivation. Given the importance of proficiency in processing multimedia and Internet information in the context of education and in the workplace, issues of technology integration across the curriculum, technology access for all students, combined with instruction on using technology must be addressed by administrators and teachers. We have only begun to look at the possibilities of how computers can enhance the development of reading comprehension skills. As newer applications and innovations are introduced, learners will be provided with even more effective learning tools allowing them to succeed as learners today and in the future.

Summary

Research in the area of computer-assisted instruction and reading has been carried out to assess the effectiveness of various kinds of computer uses, programs, and interventions on reading comprehension and reading speed. For the most part, provided that programs are pedagogically well-designed and there is consistent use on part of the learner, reading comprehension, skill development, and strategy use has shown to improve. Several other studies have examined multimedia reading software on reading comprehension and vocabulary acquisition and have found that glossing and multimedia annotations have generally led to an improvement in vocabulary acquisition, a deeper level of comprehension and retention. Recent research in this area has been concerned with tracking the behavior of students as they work on tasks to assist in more pedagogically effective programs. Other current studies have begun to examine online reading behaviors and strategy use of second language learners and how this may be similar to or different from those exhibited when reading traditional print materials. Finally, as discussed in this chapter, in addition to stand-alone software programs, more sophisticated web-based materials and activities are being created for both teacher and student use.

Discussion Questions and Activities

1. In small groups, examine and evaluate a commercially prepared reading software program. Comment on its appropriateness of content, organization and pedagogical approach to teaching reading given its goals, purposes, and intended audience.

2. Select an Internet site that presents reading practice activities or interactive exercises. Make a short presentation to your class about this site.

3. Select a recent article dealing with reading and technology. Write a short summary of the article.

4. What are some of the advantages of computer-assisted reading instruction over traditional forms of instruction?

5. In this age of information technology, many believe that we must equip our students with the necessary skills to deal with online materials and texts. What kinds of skills and strategies do we need to teach students to be more effective readers and learners in online environments? Share your responses with your peers.

6. What experiences have you had with computers and reading? What is your opinion concerning the use of computers in an ESL or second language reading class?

Chapter 4
Factors Influencing L2
Reading Development,
Performance, and Comprehension

This chapter addresses some of the factors that influence reading in an L2/FL. More specifically factors to be examined are the cognitive development at the time of L2 study, language proficiency in the L1, metacognitive knowledge of L1 structure, grammar, and syntax, the degree of difference between the L1 and L2 in terms of writing systems, language proficiency in an L2/FL and strategy use, and prior knowledge. While the research in this domain encompasses a great deal of literature, which cannot possibly be covered in its entirety here, it is hoped that this discussion will nonetheless provide readers with an overview in this area. Readers will note that much of this discussion is tied to the research presented in Chapter 2. Readers are advised to consult that chapter for a more detailed analysis of these factors within the context of research studies. The intention of this chapter is to specifically highlight some of the main factors influencing the reading comprehension process and the pedagogical implications as related to these factors.

Factors Influencing Reading

Reading, whether in a first or second language context, involves the reader, the text, and the interaction between the reader and text. Although reading in the L1 shares numerous important basic elements with reading in a second or foreign language, the processes also differ greatly. Because the reading process is essentially "unobservable," teachers need to make significant efforts in the classroom to understand their students' reading behaviors and be able to help students understand those behaviors as well. It is, therefore, important that teachers know as much as possible about the linguistic and educational backgrounds of their readers since many of the factors that influence reading in an L2/FL context relate to these areas. The main factors to be addressed in this chapter include cognitive development at the time of L2 study, language proficiency in the L1, metacognitive knowledge of L1 structure, grammar, and syntax, the degree of difference between the L1 and L2 in terms of writing systems, language proficiency in an L2/FL and strategy use, and prior knowledge.

Cognitive Development

Current theoretical and empirical work provides somewhat contradictory answers to when reading instruction in the L2 should begin. Many researchers believe, however, that L2 reading instruction should be delayed until initial literacy has been achieved in the L1 (Cummins, 1979; McLaughlin, 1984), however, reading teachers have little control over when students begin to study the second language. Similarly, the cognitive, mental, or developmental levels at the time of the L2/FL study also vary. As Aebersold and Field (1997) point out, the learning strategies of a young child are in fact quite different than those of an adult. Their L1 reading levels, background knowledge, reading strategies acquired in the L1, and most aspects of the reading process will have been influenced by this difference. Segalowitz (1986), for example, hypothesizes that L1 and L2 reading use different underlying cognitive processes. Grabe (1991) also notes that students begin reading in an L2 with a different knowledge base than they had when starting to read in their L1. For example, L1 readers already have a sufficient vocabulary base and know thousands of words before they actually start to read. They also have some grammatical knowledge of their own language. L2 readers, on the other hand, do not share these advantages. It must also be noted that older L2 learners do have a great deal of world knowledge. Such knowledge is sometimes called content knowledge or background knowledge, or the reader's schema and is defined as "organized knowledge of the world that provides much of the basis for comprehending, learning, and remembering ideas in stories and texts" (Anderson, 1984, p. 243). At the same time, older L2 learners also have more highly developed cognitive and metacognitive abilities, which younger L1 students do not possess (Aebersold & Field, 1997). In terms of cognitive development then, all factors that influence L2/FL reading have to be considered in relation to when the L2 learner began reading.

Language Proficiency in the L1

It appears that the level of reading proficiency that the reader has in the L1 also appears to be a factor in the development of L2/FL reading skills. Although the research is not entirely conclusive in this area, it seems to be the case that the skilled L1 reader has the potential for using L1 skills to enhance L2/FL reading. In other words, L1 readers can transfer effective reading skills from the native to the target language.

Clarke (1998) attempted to determine if proficient first language readers transfer their reading skills to the second language. On the basis of cloze tasks and oral reading, Clarke found that although there is some transfer of skills, since successful readers perform better than poor ones in both their native language and target language, limited language proficiency seems to exert a powerful effect on the behaviors utilized by the readers. According to Clarke, limited control of the language "short circuits" the good reader's system causing him/her to revert to poor reading strategies when confronted with a difficult or confusing task in the second language. Royer and Carlo (1991) conclude that there is transfer of reading skills from the L1 to an L2 and that teaching reading skills in the native language may in fact facilitate the transfer. In other words, the more the reader has learned to be an adaptable, questioning, comprehension-monitoring reader in the L1, the more likely that these behaviors will be exhibited in the L2/FL. The unskilled reader, or preliterate L2/FL language learner, will not have such skills, but can improve skills in their native language through reading skills and strategy instruction.

Cummins (1985) states that the development of skills in the L1 can transfer positively to the L2. He offers two possible explanations in this domain. First, the transfer threshold explanation states that "To the extent that instruction in Lx is effective in promoting proficiency in Lx, transfer of this proficiency to Ly will occur provided there is sufficient exposure to Ly (through the school or environment) and adequate motivation to learn Ly" (p. 143). So while surface aspects of languages may be quite different, according to Cummins (1985), there seems to be an underlying cognitive academic proficiency that is common across languages. This common underlying proficiency makes possible the transfer of cognitive academic or literacy related skills across languages. Transfer of academic skills and strategies occurs then between languages. There are times, however, when such transfer fails to occur. Second, Cummins (1985) suggests that this transfer is related to the level of proficiency attained by bilingual or second language learners. There may be a level of proficiency that students must attain in both languages. While the studies to date in this area involved readers who were proficient in their L1, there is little information about the extent of that proficiency.

Transfer is certainly a critical issue and further careful study of factors influencing transfer in the area of reading is warranted. Studying the question of when and under what conditions such transfer occurs would be profitable. Such factors as the necessary level of competence in the first and second language, the level of literacy concepts upon entering school, and the similarity between the first and target languages, may all strongly influence the degree to which the transfer of skills and strategies occurs. Certainly understanding the nature of this transfer can lead to a sound theoretical and empirical base.

Metacognitive Knowledge

Metacognitive knowledge refers to the learner's ability to discuss, describe, give rules for, and comment on L1 language use (Anderson, 2002). Metacognitive knowledge would differ by age; for example, a young child may have an unconscious awareness of the grammar, syntax, and pronunciation of their language but may not be able to explicitly talk about the language itself, and hence limited metacognitive knowledge. When teaching a second language a teacher may not be able to use complex grammatical explanations about the language with such students, but with older students who possess this knowledge, it may in fact enhance the L2/FL learning process (Devine, 1993). Those students who have a strong background in the metacognitive knowledge of their L1 may be able to apply this knowledge to their L2 reading process. Several studies, as discussed in Chapter 2, have shown that there is in fact a strong relationship between metacognitive awareness and reading comprehension (Anderson, 2002; Barnett, 1988; Carrell, 1989; Devine, 1987; Sheorey & Mokhtari, 2001).

Degree of Difference between the L1 and L2

The differences between the writing systems and rhetorical structures of the native language and the target language may be another factor that influences reading. Orthographic systems vary widely and while some languages may contain many numbers of symbols, other languages contain a limited number. For example, Chinese calligraphy is a writing system with numerous symbols and one that has strong aesthetic elements thereby differing from English. Arabic also has a unique writing system in that it is written and read from right to left. These kinds of differences in writing systems can pose difficulties for second language readers. Research has shown that fluent reading in a second language was associated with efficient decoding strategies and knowledge of the orthographic patterns and redundancies of the target language. Chapter 2 provides an overview of the studies in the area of orthographic knowledge and reading and Koda (1997) provides an extensive overview of the studies carried out in this area.

Language Proficiency in the L2 and Strategy Use

Second language proficiency is another strong factor in L2 reading. Numerous studies have looked at proficiency in the L2 and it has been found that proficiency is related to strategy use, which in turn affects how successful a reader is. Some studies have investigated the reading strategies used by successful and unsuccessful language learners and have found that successful readers use a wider range of strategies and use strategies more frequently than less successful readers (Anderson, 1991; Block, 1986; Hosenfeld, 1977; Knight, Padron & Waxman, 1985). Various other studies in the area of reading strategies have found that younger and less proficient students use fewer strategies and use them less effectively in their reading comprehension (Garner, 1987; Waxman & Padron, 1987). Strategy-training studies have shown the beneficial effects of training indicating the importance of direct instruction in strategy use and application in a variety of contexts and with a range of text types. Chapter 2 provides a more detailed discussion of the above studies.

Prior Knowledge

Schemas, or schema as they are sometimes known, have been described as "cognitive constructs which allow for the organization of information in long-term memory" (Widdowson, 1983). Cook (1989) states, "the mind, stimulated by key words or phrases in the text or by the context, activates a knowledge schema" (Cook, 1989, p. 69). Widdowson and Cook both emphasize the cognitive characteristics of schema which allow us to relate incoming information to already known information. This covers the knowledge of the world, from everyday knowledge to very specialized knowledge, knowledge of language structures, and knowledge of texts and forms they take in terms of genre, and organization. In addition to allowing us to organize information and knowledge economically, schemas also allow us to predict the continuation of both spoken and written discourse. The first part of a text activates a schema, that is, calls up a schema, which is either confirmed or disconfirmed by what follows. Rummelhart (1977) provides a nice example of the above process. He provides a brief fragment of a story which reads: *Mary heard the ice cream man coming down the street. She remembered her birthday money and rushed into the house...*These two sentences would be enough information for a reader to determine why Mary ran back into the house. To most readers it would seem obvious that she wanted to take the money and buy an ice cream. This interpretation, unless contradicted by information that follows the sentence, is plausible. Concepts which help the reader interpret the text are called cognitive schemata, a term first used by Bartlett in 1932 (Nunan, 1995). In the above example, the reader's background knowledge and linguistic cues in the text are organized into interrelated patterns which are used to reconstruct meaning. The linguistic cues activate the reader's schematic knowledge.

As previously discussed, the literature in reading research and methodology commonly refers to three types of schemata, the knowledge of which are necessary if readers are to make sense of text; these are content, formal, and linguistic schema. Content schema, which refers to a reader's background or world knowledge, provides readers with a foundation, a basis for comparison (Carrell & Eisterhold, 1983; Carrell, Pharis, & Liberto, 1989). Formal schema, often known as textual schema, refers to the organizational forms and rhetorical structures of written texts. It can include knowledge of different text types and genres, and also includes the understanding that different types of texts use text organization, language structures, vocabulary, grammar, level of formality/register differently. Schooling and culture play the largest role in providing one with a knowledge base of formal schemata. While formal schemata cover discourse level items, linguistic or language schemata include the decoding features needed to recognize words and how they fit together in a sentence. First language readers, may through repeated examples be able to generalize a pattern or guess the meaning of a word, which may not have initially been part of their linguistic schema. The building of linguistic schema in a second language can proceed in the much the same way.

Schema clearly plays a crucial role in text comprehension, both in the L1 and L2 context. For example, whether reading in a first or second language, one can assume that both native and non-native readers will understand more of a text when they are familiar with content, formal, and linguistic schema. An L2 reader, however, who does not possess such knowledge can experience schema interference or lack of comprehension, ideas which were examined further in Chapters 1 and 2 in light of the discussions pertinent to relevant research in this area. If we consider the above example again, a second or foreign language reader who does not understand who or what the ice cream man refers to, or what he does, would not be able to connect the two ideas, nor understand why Mary rushed into the house. While this is a very simple example, clearly lack of schematic knowledge, specifically content, formal (textual organization) and linguistic (language) knowledge, can inhibit comprehension of even what appears to be straightforward in meaning.

Cultural Citations

One area related to the discussion of prior knowledge, specifically content knowledge, is cultural citations. While L2 readers might be familiar with a particular topic and have sufficient vocabulary to understand a text, the reader may encounter words which are not in a dictionary and which assume experience with the culture, or at least knowledge of the context in which reference is being made. The following sentences, most of which will be understood by an adult American, are some examples of cultural citations.

- *The velvet décor of Heinz Hall is the color of ketchup.*
- *Regarding the earthquake, Seattle is shaken, not stirred.*
- *He described "Crouching Dragon, Hidden Tiger" as Bruce Lee meets Jane Austin.*
- *When he came by tonight he gave me a few bucks, about what it'd cost for a burger and fries at Mickey D's.*
- *Qatar is located on the Persian Gulf about 100 miles from Saudi Arabia and is about the size of the State of Connecticut.*
- *Her skin was as tender as DiMaggio's glove.*

(Reprinted from Language and Culture Bulletin, Vol 4, No.6)

Clearly references to events or people occurring before the reader's life experience and those occurring outside of the reader's culture may pose problems for readers. The ability to comprehend literary allusions and culturally-based metaphors will also depend on the reader's educational background. Finally, readers' personal interests and their environmental context are other variables affecting comprehension of various cultural citations.

Pedagogical Implications as Related to Factors Influencing Reading

While it was not possible to consider all of the factors that influence L2/FL reading or the scope of research that has been carried out in this area, it is hoped that this chapter provided some insight into some of those key factors. Given what we know about the reading process and the factors that affect reading comprehension, teachers can take several steps to engage students in activities that will minimize the effects of such factors, allowing them to develop and acquire those skills necessary for comprehension.

It is clear that orthographic knowledge has an important role to play in reading acquisition. Because differences between the L1 and L2 can affect the rate of reading and recognition of characters, teachers need to help learners develop fast and accurate decoding skills. Students need to be provided with instruction that develops knowledge of the sound-symbol relationships and enough practice to develop automatic decoding skills. For younger, less proficient readers, a program that integrates phonics instruction into meaning-based curricula is most effective.

Learners should have opportunities to develop their language skills. Any reading program should allow for activities that integrate reading and writing. Learners should also be encouraged to share their discussions and writings about texts and teachers should design activities which also encourage the practice and development of the four language skill areas, reading, writing, speaking, and listening. For example, students can participate in debates about an issue in a text or a story, the stories can be acted out, learners can role-play the main characters in a text, or learners can participate in literature circles. Many of these activities serve to foster language skills but also lead to a deeper understanding of issues and ideas within texts. Several chapters in this text consider these kinds of activities in more detail. Explicit strategy instruction should also be a part of the reading course. Chapter 5 illustrates how this can be accomplished in the classroom. Doing so makes students more aware of strategies that can be used to facilitate text comprehension and the ways in which strategies can be effectively applied.

Research on the effects of prior-knowledge on L2 reading comprehension reveals the importance of sensitivity to the prior-knowledge demands of texts. Teachers should, therefore, inquire about students' prior knowledge in terms of content-matter, cultural knowledge, and knowledge of texts. Such information would assist teachers in the selection of reading materials and the areas that of instruction that require greater attention. Teachers should provide materials to build background knowledge and vocabulary. In addition to building students' vocabulary, strategies for dealing with unfamiliar words in texts should be taught. Chapter 7 considers such strategies in more detail and also describes activities to build vocabulary. Students should also be introduced to a range of text types to build students' knowledge about text structure knowledge. Direct instruction on the differences and similarities between text types would provide a greater understanding of text purposes and organization, and in turn facilitate comprehension. Teachers should also use authentic texts of appropriate difficulty level as it enhances knowledge of language and syntactic patterns found in the L2. Specific activities to build schemata such as pre-reading activities and use of advance and graphic organizers are further discussed in the following chapter.

Figure 1 illustrates some of the factors influencing comprehension discussed above and suggestions to improve comprehension skills. It must be pointed out, however, that regardless of the factors, the suggestions below should be part of any balanced reading program. The emphasis a teacher places on such activities will depend on the reading task and purpose, student's level of reading and language proficiency, and their needs.

Factors Affecting Reading Comprehension	Suggested Areas of Instructional Focus
Cognitive Development and Language Proficiency in the L1	• Focus on language acquisition and vocabulary. • Read aloud to students and use books with visual aids. • Provide visual support for reading activities. • Develop phonemic awareness, which is how to break apart and manipulate the sounds in words. • Assist students in decoding-applying their knowledge of letter-sound relationships to sound out words that are new to them. • Build prior knowledge in all areas-content, formal, and linguistic schemata.
Metacognitive Knowledge	• Teach metacognitive strategies and provide opportunities for students to apply them. • Teach strategies for constructing meaning from text, and for problem solving when meaning breaks down. • Provide explicit instruction in what the task is, what the objectives are, and how to assess progress or completion. • Help students link newly acquired knowledge to previously learned information. • Read and think out loud while solving a problem. • Explain the process of deciding how to attack a problem, issue, or task. • Guide students as they work on tasks, suggesting various strategies for solving or completing a task. • Use metacognitive prompts such as asking students what is relevant, identifying what strategies are useful for the task, and identifying the goal of the exercise.
Degree of Difference Between the L1 and L2-Orthography	• Develop an understanding of how print works, for example, in English reading goes from left to right. • Focus on phonics and decoding activities (for beginning levels of proficiency), working as much as possible in context. • Expand sight vocabulary-the number of words that can be identified automatically.

	• Develop a high level of accuracy in word recognition. • Maintain a rate of reading brisk enough to facilitate comprehension. • Use phrasing and expression so that oral reading sounds like speech. • Transform deliberate strategies for word recognition and comprehension into automatic skills.
Language Proficiency in the L2 and Strategy Use	• Provide opportunities to use and apply different strategies in different contexts. • Embed skills and strategy practice within meaningful activities. • Use both direct instruction and independent practice to further and foster reading. • Promote basic skills as well as higher-order reasoning tasks and critical thinking skills. • Incorporate tasks and activities that encourage and promote critical thinking. • Provide students with opportunities that immerse them in real reading for real purposes. • Provide students frequent opportunities to read. • Focus on language acquisition, expand vocabulary and syntactic knowledge-(how English works-grammar and sentence structure).
Prior Knowledge	• Assist students in expanding their vocabulary and syntactic knowledge. • Provide students with a wealth of materials differing in topic and genre to build background knowledge and schemata.
Cultural Citations	• Provide students with a variety of experiences and reading materials on a given topic. • Provide books, TV programs, videos, and movies that expand cultural knowledge. • Explain that cultural citations are often not found in the dictionary and can be explained by someone more proficient in the cultural and linguistic nuances of the language.

Figure 1 Factors Influencing Comprehension and Suggested Areas of Focus

It must also be pointed out that despite the differences between L1 and L2 reading, the two processes are similar in some ways, and students' perceptions of their reading difficulties are also similar in many ways across languages. Readers, especially L2/FL readers, can better understand some of those similarities if teachers take the time to question students about their reading and reading behaviors, as students themselves, can offer tremendous insights into both their L1 and L2 learning experiences.

Finally, one last observation is important. It has been common to emphasize word identification strategies at the primary level at the expense of comprehension strategies, and at the higher grades, to emphasize the teaching of content area subjects with less emphasis on the reading process and strategies to facilitate understanding of those texts and their features. However, by understanding the factors that influence reading performance, teachers can provide a more balanced instructional program, providing the necessary resources and adjusting instructional strategies so that students at all levels can improve their reading skills.

Summary

Teachers of second language/foreign language readers must understand that there are many factors that influence their students' reading processes and hence, comprehension of texts. While additional research continues to be carried out in this area to better understand the effects of these factors, teachers who are aware of these factors can recognize them at work in the classroom and how they affect their students' performance, so they in turn can better assist their students. A student's cognitive development at the time of second language study can affect how well a student reads, how easily he or she can grasp concepts, and how effectively he or she applies strategies. Much research has shown that students who have higher L2 proficiency levels are more likely to transfer reading and writing skills from their first language to the second. Students who are more likely to be able to describe their own strategy and skill use, or those who are more metacognitively aware are also likely to be stronger readers. Research has also shown that the greater the differences between the native language and the target language in writing systems and rhetorical structures, the more difficult it is to acquire the second language and to become a proficient reader in the target language. Those students who are also struggling with the target language will tend to have more difficulties in the areas of reading and writing unless a certain threshold of language development has been attained in the target language. Finally, students' knowledge about concepts, texts, language, and the reading process itself will affect their reading comprehension so teachers must take the necessary steps to build background knowledge in all of these areas.

Discussion Questions and Activities

1. Interview a reading teacher to determine from their point of view the kinds of difficulties their readers have.

2. How would you define reading comprehension? Share your responses with your peers.

3. Interview a second-language student about their reading skills. Ask them to describe what a "good" reader is and what a "good" reader does while reading. Have them orally read a short story or passage they are currently studying in their class and then ask them to re-tell the story. Record your observations.

4. Based on your previous learning or teaching experiences, do you think that there are cultural differences in the organization and presentation of ideas in texts? Why?

5. If you have studied a second language, what memories do you have of learning to read in that language? What did you consider most difficult about reading in a second language? Why? In retrospect, what might have helped? With a small group of classmates, share your experiences.

6. From your own experience, write a short personal essay describing a time when your content or linguistic schemata failed you. It may be a joke you did not understand until…or a time you did not understand a situation until….etc. Also think of examples in your own reading in which inappropriate or inadequate prior knowledge interfered with text comprehension.

Chapter 5
Process, Practice, and Pedagogy

This chapter specifically takes the reading instructor through the unconscious and conscious processes that readers often use and the ways teachers can make students more aware of their processes and reading strategies. This chapter begins by providing a basic outline of reading strategies. The chapter also covers reading activities, skills, and strategies that can be employed during the pre-reading stage, the during-reading stage, and the post-reading stage. These sections describe methods for knowing and improving reading comprehension and strategies as well as specific activities and tasks that a teacher can implement in the reading class.

What is Reading?

In a general sense, reading is what happens when people look at a text and assign meaning to the written symbols in that text. The text and the reader are both necessary for the reading process to begin. It is, however, the interaction between the text and the reader that constitutes actual reading. Reading is an interactive process in which readers interact with the text in order to make meaning. This process involves the use of comprehension or reading strategies. Readers bring to each text, areas of knowledge (content, formal, and linguistic schema), plus reading strategies that are crucial in shaping what happens in the reading process. While the text remains the same, the information the reader brings to the text fluctuates as comprehension grows. Content schema refers to systems of factual knowledge, values, and cultural conventions. It provides readers with a foundation or a basis of comparison. For example, a reader may be very familiar with how a marriage is performed in his or her own culture but may not be aware of these cultural conventions in another culture or context. Formal schema, which is also referred to as textual schema, has to do with organizational forms and rhetorical structures of texts and genres (mystery novels, recipes, advertisements, autobiography, plays, letters, short stories, journal articles, newspaper articles, etc.). Schooling and cultural experiences provide a knowledge base of formal schemata. Linguistic schema, sometimes known as language schema, refers to sentence structure, grammatical inflections, vocabulary, cohesive structures. For example, if one has studied a particular grammar rule in their first language, they might be able to make use of that information to decipher the meaning of a word, phrase, or sentence. In essence, to read effectively, readers must make use of reading strategies and various types of schemata. The following section outlines those various kinds of reading strategies. It is important that students become familiar with the terminology related to such strategies and that they learn how to effectively implement such strategies before, during, and after the reading process.

General Reading Strategies

Research has shown that all students can benefit from instruction in learning strategies. Chamot and O'Malley's (1994) work with second language learners reinforces the idea that students who learn to consciously monitor their own learning, and who have a storehouse of strategies to use when learning becomes difficult, fare better than students who do not have such strategies. The same notion holds true for reading strategies. Reading strategies indicate how readers conceive of a task, how they make sense of what they read, and what they do when they don't understand. Such strategies are used by the reader to enhance reading comprehension and overcome comprehension failure. Therefore, teaching readers how to use strategies should be a prime consideration in the reading classroom to assist students in becoming more effective and efficient readers (Anderson, 2003; Chamot, Barnhardt, El-Dinary & Robbins, 1999; Janzen, 2001; Weaver & Cohen, 1997a, 1997b). When teaching a reading strategy, teachers should identify the strategy, explain why it is useful, demonstrate its use, give students practice in applying the strategy, and show them how to evaluate its effectiveness and what to do if it does not work. Chapter 2 discussed the extensive research in the area of reading strategies and second and foreign language learning, which clearly shows the relationship between reading strategy use and knowledge, and reading proficiency. Based on previous work on learning strategies (O'Malley & Chamot, 1990; Oxford & Crookall, 1989), Singhal (2001) has compiled the following list of specific reading behaviors or reading strategies successful readers use when reading. While this list is not exhaustive, it addresses the general domain of reading strategies used by effective readers.

Reading Strategy	Description of Reading Strategy
COMPREHENSION STRATEGIES (Cognitive, Memory, and Metacognitive Strategies)	
Paraphrasing/Summarizing	The reader rephrases content using different words but retains the same sense.
Anticipating/Predicting	The reader predicts what content will occur in succeeding portions of the text.
Previewing Text	The reader previews the text to see how it is organized and related to what they know.
Employing Context Clues	The reader uses clues in the text in order to make predictions or increase understanding. The reader uses lexical or syntactic context to determine word meaning.
Repeating Words	The reader repeats unknown words.
Analyzing	The reader analyzes word structure, grammatical structures, expressions, text format, or author's argument and strategies to determine the meanings of these words/sentences/expressions and text overall.
Word Division	The reader divides the words into parts to make it comprehensible.
Using Illustrations	The reader uses illustrations/graphs, etc. in order to facilitate understanding of the text.
Using Titles	The reader uses titles/headings to facilitate understanding of the text.
Using Textbook Aids	The reader uses textbook aids such as glossaries, appendices, and indexes to aid comprehension.
Rereading	The reader rereads parts of a text several times in order to facilitate comprehension.
Reading for Information	The reader can identify topic sentences, thesis statements, stated and implied main ideas, major and supporting details.
Using Prior Knowledge	The reader uses prior knowledge such as context, textual, and linguistic schema to make sense of text.
Guessing/Hypothesizing	The reader guesses the general meaning of a word by using context clues.
Associating	The reader creates an association between new material and what is already known.
Word Grouping	The reader places the new words in a group with other similar known words to determine meaning.
Word Associating	The reader associates a word with a known word in order to determine meaning.
First Language Associating-Cognates	The reader remembers a new word by identifying it with a word in their first language.
Monitoring	The reader self-monitors their own understanding of text/pacing/pronunciation of words.
Correcting Errors	The reader tries to correct their language/reading errors.
Word Recognition	The reader is able to recognize unknown words by repeating them.
Recognizing Text Organization and Rhetorical Modes	The reader recognizes the rhetorical pattern of the text.
Recognizing Genre	The reader recognizes the type of text/genre.
Recognizing Connectors	The reader recognizes connectors as they are used by the writer to continue ideas/themes.

Recognizing Textual Features	The reader recognizes specific textual features such as literary devices and/or rhetorical strategies.
Distinguishing Information	The reader recognizes what is important and not important and can skip those words or information.
AFFECTIVE AND SOCIAL STRATEGIES	
Self-Encouragement	The reader makes encouraging statements to his/herself and pays attention to factors that may interfere with performance or comprehension.
Clarifying	The reader asks for clarification when something is not understood.
Verifying	The reader asks for verification that something has been understood or said correctly.
Seeking Feedback	The reader asks others for feedback about his or her reading, responses, etc.
INTERPRETATION AND EVALUATION STRATEGIES	
Reacting to Text	The reader can react to a text and express opinions about the text and textual characteristics or features.
Judging Evidence	The reader can evaluate logical evidence or arguments in a text.
Evaluate Writing Techniques	The reader can evaluate the effectiveness of a writer's techniques which include style, purpose, point of view, slanted writing, etc.
Distinguishing Fact and Opinion	The reader can distinguish between fact and opinion and can understand how this contributes to a text.
Interpreting Text	The reader draws a conclusion about the text in terms of theme, author's message or interpretation of text.

Figure 1 Reading Strategies Used by Successful Readers

It is imperative that teachers take the time to help their students become familiar with such terminology as it enables them to better understand the reading process and the skills facilitating text comprehension and critical thinking. Writing teachers, for example, spend a great deal of time teaching their students the terminology related to the writing process and strategies resulting in effective writing, and the same should be true for reading. Eventually, it is hoped that such skills are applied automatically without much conscious thought. While the above strategies are not used together, or in any particular order, but rather are dependent on the reading task at hand, some strategies can be useful before, during, and after reading. The following part of this chapter describes *Pre-reading*, *During Reading*, and *Post-Reading* activities and the specific kinds of strategies that can be most helpful to students at each stage.

Pre-Reading

Pre-reading activities involve establishing expectations so that readers can better comprehend more of the text and how the information will be organized. Teachers can accomplish this by making students more aware of why they are reading a text selection. Students can also be provided with a framework for making sense of information which might include previewing titles, sub-titles, sub-headings, illustrations, graphs and tables, text organization and style. In addition to focusing attention on text features, teachers can assist students in becoming more aware of pre-reading techniques such as reading introductions and identifying key issues, reading the concluding paragraphs, skimming the text to get the gist, reading the first sentence of each paragraph, and scanning the text for specific information. The following section considers some of these approaches in more detail.

Establishing a Purpose

Students often are unable to state why they are reading a text or what they are supposed to do with the information later. Without a clearly stated purpose, they are likely to read the information and quickly forget. Teachers can prepare students for reading efficiently by clearly stating why they want their students to read a text and what they will do with the information later. While this takes only a few moments, doing so allows students to understand the point of the reading and enables them to better remember information they have read. In any case, regardless of the assignment or reading task, students must be clear about the expectations and must be provided with the adequate background knowledge needed to access the information in a text.

Activating and Building Background Knowledge

It is important that readers have an introduction to the topic of a text before they begin to read. Doing so can help students recall any information that they already know about the topic, namely content schema, either from personal experience or other reading. This knowledge will help students make sense of the information they encounter in the text as they read. Some kind of introduction to the topic can also arouse their interest, thereby enhancing the motivation to read. An introduction might also bring to attention the cultural factors, or vocabulary relevant to that topic. There are several activities that can help students activate prior knowledge. Students can brainstorm, that is engage in free recall activities that encourage them to list everything they know about the topic. They can participate in role plays which often work best if the teacher provides some short scenarios and assigns characters; they can go on field trips, or teachers can provide more structured activities including short reading and writing assignments related to the topic. Such activities can build a foundation allowing students to better understand the text. Students should also be made aware that they can use self-questioning techniques to activate their prior knowledge. (See Figure 3 for a list of questions). Teaching students to consider these kinds of questions can be useful as it provides students with a strategy to use in any academic context.

Using Subheadings, Headings, and Visuals

Another strategy that can be used before actual reading of the text is to preview text. Readers can use a number of features of the text to help them predict what the text will be about and to gain a general sense of its content. Such features include the title, the author, subtitles and subheadings, and photographs, graphs, charts, and other visuals. Teachers must emphasize that such features often provide important clues which can aid readers in predicting content and in determining the framework and organizational structure of a text.

Structured Overviews

Structured overviews are visual displays of information that provide readers with a basic outline of a text. Structured overviews can take the form of graphic organizers, flowcharts, maps, or formal outlines. Structured overviews emphasize important information and represent the interrelationship of ideas within a text, assisting students with comprehension and memory of key concepts. Teachers can also use structured overviews, specifically outlines, to represent the rhetorical organization of the text which will allow students to better understand the organization of ideas.

Explicit Instruction in Text Structure

Teaching text structure can lead to improved comprehension and more effective storage, retrieval, and retention of concepts. Text structure refers to the organization or sequencing of ideas. Text structure such as compare and contrast, problem-solution, cause and effect, argumentative, narrative, etc. differ in their patterns of organization and in the types of cohesive ties and signal words that are used. Making students more aware of text structure allows students to remember information they have read, but also provides a conceptual framework for organizing the information presented. Teachers can use a variety of visual/spatial charts to teach text organization. For example, teachers can use form templates which are blank or which are partly filled in so that students can make predictions about the ideas in a text. Venn diagrams can be used for compare/contrast essays, while maps or structured overviews can be used for more complex structures. Some research also suggests that different cultures structure texts in different ways (Connor & Kaplan, 1987; Hinds, 1983; Peregoy & Boyle, 2001) and therefore explicit instruction in text structure may benefit students who are less aware of common text structures found in English.

Anticipation Guides

Anticipation guides can help students to predict what will happen in a text (Holmes & Roser, 1987; Peregoy & Boyle, 2001). Teachers can use anticipation guides before so students can engage in predictions, but they can also be revisited after reading to confirm predictions. The following chart illustrates a prediction guide for a reading about food safety.

(Before reading) Your opinion	(After Reading) Text Information	Statement or Question
		1. All street vendors undergo food safety training.
		2. Food poisoning can cause death.
		3. Any kind of food can be sold on the street.

Figure 2 Anticipation Guide for *Threat of Sickness Lurks in Street Vendors' Smorgasbord*

Pre-reading Techniques

Finally, students need to learn the techniques that can create expectations about text content. Reading the introduction and conclusion, as well as the first sentence of the body paragraphs can provide an overview or gist of the text. Students can also skim the text and visuals to obtain information before reading or scan parts of the text for specific information. In sum, pre-reading strategies help students establish a purpose and build background knowledge, in turn allowing them to better comprehend text and retain information. Students can ask themselves the following questions, and with teacher assistance can engage in the following strategy-building activities.

Pre-reading questions	Pre-reading strategy-building activities
• What subject is this passage going to be about? • What do I already know about this subject? • Have I read any other articles or watched any TV shows related to this topic? • Have I learned about this topic in any other class? • What have I experienced in this area? • What opinions, thoughts, or beliefs do I have about this subject? • Do I know anything about the author's credentials and background? • Based on my quick read, how would I classify this piece in terms of genre? What features characterize a text of that genre? • What is the main idea of the text? • What is the overall structure of the text? • What is the focus and perspective of the piece?	• Teachers can discuss the content with students first. • Teachers can read the selection aloud to students before they read it themselves, helping them with difficult concepts and words. • Teachers can review text-specific vocabulary. • Teachers can help students become more aware of text structure. • Students can watch a filmstrip or movie on the text, or related concepts/topic. • Students can brainstorm and share what they know about a topic. • Students can predict what will happen by examining the illustrations that accompany the text or by using anticipation guides. • Students can begin by surveying the text-that is reading the introduction, and the first sentence in each paragraph, including the conclusion. The main goal here is to develop a general idea of structure. • Students should skim the text by doing a quick read in order to get the gist of the text. • Finally, students can scan parts of the text to locate specific information.

Figure 3 Pre-reading questions and strategy-building activities

During Reading

Many pre-reading strategies described above can be used while students are engaged with a text. However, one of the important areas that teachers must help students develop is the ability to evaluate and monitor their reading process. To become better readers, students need to be aware of how they are reading and what they can do to enhance text comprehension. Research in L2 reading has demonstrated that when readers consciously control and monitor their reading by paying close attention to text, think about the elements in text, and identify the various interactions that take place during the reading process, comprehension is improved. This is referred to as metacognitive awareness – that is, understanding the processes of reading, knowing, or how readers know and perceive. In order for such strategies to be acquired, teachers must introduce and explain reading strategies and then model them through whole-class readings and collaborative activities. Teachers can read a text out loud with students and can stop at various points to ask questions that not only enable students to learn the types of monitoring-comprehension questions they should be asking, but also how and when such strategies can be applied while reading a text. The objective of working in this manner and using a directed-reading or guided reading approach is to make students more conscious of such strategies so that use of such strategies eventually becomes automatic. Teachers who are much more aware of the L2 reading process and these kinds of strategies will be more effective in the reading classroom. The following set of questions was used by the author in a reading of a text entitled *Sociolinguistic Rules*. The teacher read the text out loud as the students followed. The students were given a series of questions which were addressed during the reading of the text. The questions allow students to monitor their reading process, but also enable them to practice a range of reading skills and strategies while making sense of the text.

Close Reading of *Sociolinguistic Rules*

Before reading the text itself, I will ask you some questions.
1. What do you think this text will be about?
2. How do you know? – Can you give me some examples of sociolinguistic rules? What about in your own culture?
Let us now read the text together. We will read the entire text once through. Then we will re-read. **I will stop at various points so we can discuss the answers to the following questions.**
Students read the entire text. Teacher asks:
3. Tell me what this text is about? Provide a summary.
4. The writer of the text offers a specific example of an incident between an American host and a student. What is that all about?
5. Can you give me another example that is similar to this to make the author's point?
Teacher and students read the text together. Teacher asks:
6. What is the writer saying in paragraph 3? 4? 5? Paraphrase these sections, identifying main idea in each paragraph).
7. What does "linguistic competence" mean?
8. Define the following terms. (Do not use a dictionary): In addition, tell me how you determined the meanings of the words. Be very specific about this. -unintentionally (paragraph 1) -reinforced -sufficient -shortcoming -sociolinguists (paragraph 2) -hypothetical -breakdown

9. In paragraph 3, it states "These rules are acquired and applied...." What is "these rules" referring to?

10. In paragraph 5, what is "this question" referring to?

11. What does "empirical data" mean in paragraph 4? Read the first sentence. What kind of information do you expect to read in this paragraph? How do you know?

12. Who is Christopher? What does 1982 mean? How do you know? (paragraph 4-this was a question about recognizing a citation)

13. What comparisons can you make between South Asians and Americans? (Apte, 1994). Where will you look to find this information related to Apte, 1994? How will you find this information quickly?

14. What is meant by "socially inappropriate behavior?" How do you know?

15. Define the following terms. (Do not use a dictionary): In addition, tell me how you determined the meanings of the words. Be very specific about this. -intercultural (paragraph 6) -attribute -universal -modify -conform -conventions

16. Where might you find such a text?

17. What kind of text is this? (story, poem, etc?) What are the references at the bottom of the page? In other words, why are these references needed and what do they tell us?

18. Have you ever been in a situation where you feel there was a misunderstanding between you and a native speaker of English? Did the misunderstanding occur because of linguistic or sociolinguistic problems?

19. Write a brief outline of this text.

20. Does this text have a recognizable structure? What is it? In other words, can you classify this text of being a specific type in terms of rhetorical structure?

Figure 4 During-Reading-Strategy-Building Procedure (DRSBP) for *Sociolinguistic Rules* Singhal (2002).

In the above strategy building procedure, the teacher has activated the students' prior knowledge by asking some very simple questions and by asking them to make predictions. She shows them how to make predictions based on the title and headings. As she reads with them, her questions allow them to practice a range of skills including paraphrasing, main idea recognition, understanding of purpose and use of cohesive ties, use of context for determining word meanings, identification of text specific features, and connection to personal experience. She also provides them with opportunities to monitor their comprehension by asking how they determined the answer to a specific question. In essence, such a procedure combines aspects of pre-reading activities and questioning-while-reading procedures (DRSBP) to assist students' comprehension.

In addition to using the procedures described above, teachers should teach their students to self-monitor and to ask questions while they read. There are numerous strategies students can employ to enhance text comprehension. The following chart lists during-reading questions and strategy-building activities that students and teachers may find helpful.

During-reading questions	During-reading strategy-building activities
• Did I identify the main idea of this paragraph? • Did I identify the supporting details of this paragraph? • Did I make use of the context clues on the page such as illustrations and charts? • Do I understand this paragraph and do the ideas connect to the previous paragraph? • Given the information in this section, what do I think the following section or paragraph will be about? • Did I guess at meanings of words I was unsure about? • Did I confirm my predictions? • Did I identify transitional sentences and phrases? • Does the author present ideas in a logical manner? • Do the ideas of the text fit with the stated focus of the text? • Did I ask questions as I read through the text? • Did I distinguish between fact and opinion? • Did I recognize the author's tone or attitude towards the subject? • Did I pay attention to the author's use of language to set tone and register? • Did I paraphrase or summarize sections as I read through the text? • Was I able to separate relevant information from less relevant information? • Did I re-read sections I did not understand? • Did I make associations wherever possible to help with comprehension of the text?	• Students can identify main ideas and supporting details. • Students can guess word meanings. • Students can make associations with prior knowledge. • Students can make and confirm predictions. • Students can analyze and evaluate the order of ideas and arguments presented. • Students can re-read to facilitate comprehension. • Students can use features of the text or genre-specific features to facilitate comprehension of the text. • Students can use their knowledge to facilitate recognition of textual features ie. literary features which will enhance comprehension. • Students will keep author's purpose in mind as they read and evaluate how additional information in the text supports author's purpose. • Students can recognize the influence of the author's personal beliefs. • Students can establish the assumptions underlying the text. • Students can use both bottom-up (word/phrase level) strategies and top-down (global) strategies to make sense of text.

Figure 5 During-reading questions and strategy-building activities

Post-Reading

Just as pre-reading and during-reading strategies must be taught, post-reading activities require instruction as well. It is rare that upon completion of a reading, students will engage in evaluative discussion of text, often because L2 readers are uncertain of what they have read, because they may lack sufficient language skills, or because they are apprehensive to share what they have understood. Therefore, teachers need to teach post-reading strategies and employ post-reading activities in the class to build a repertoire of reading skills, but also to check for comprehension. Chapter 8 considers assessment of reading in more detail and the kinds of tasks that can be used to assess comprehension. There are, however, different strategies that students can use to review, discuss, and evaluate information in a text. For example, students can write a summary of the text, orally re-tell the story or text, record thoughts and important points in a journal or learning log, evaluate arguments in the text, or write essays on the topic. The following list of questions and strategy-building activities can help to develop post-reading skills.

Post-reading questions	Post-reading strategy-building activities
• Was I able to understand the text and was I able to recall specific information as well as concepts described? • Can I use the knowledge from this text and apply it elsewhere? • Was I able to fully comprehend the organization of ideas? • Did I understand the relationships between ideas? • Did I synthesize parts of the text in order to see a structure or pattern of ideas? • Am I able to evaluate the text? • Can I effectively judge the content and the arguments made give the author's purpose?	• Students can write a summary of the text. • Students can orally re-tell the story. • Student can write to the author of the text, responding to a particular point or issue. • Students can analyze parts of the text to determine which sections are most important to the purpose of the text. • Students can make inferences and support those inferences by returning to the text. • Students can distinguish main ideas from details. • Students can write an outline of the text. • Students can draw a graphic organizer of the text. • Students can evaluate the logos-that is whether the text presents information in an organized, logical manner and whether

	relevant information is missing.
	• Students can evaluate whether the text presents opposing perspectives.
	• Students can evaluate the language of the text and how this affects readers.
	• Students can determine whether the text offers support for arguments, ie. facts, statistics, and whether the author cites reputable sources and authorities.
	• Students can evaluate ethos – that is whether the author is credible as determined by experience, education, knowledge of the topic, affiliations, and author bias.

Figure 6 Post-reading questions and strategy-building activities

One further point of clarification when implementing post-reading activities to assess comprehension is that teachers must keep in mind that their students can only demonstrate comprehension if they are familiar with the reading task. For example, students may read a text and be asked to summarize it, but without clarification or an understanding of what a summary entails, demonstration of comprehension becomes difficult. Teachers, therefore, have to explicitly teach students the purpose of graphic organizers, summaries, and outlines. They have to teach students to recognize pathos (emotional appeals a writer makes to readers by inspiring empathy or sympathy, and through the writer's awareness of the audience's cultural and emotional background such as race, age, sex, habits, educational level, ethnicity, values, and beliefs), logos (the evidence a writer provides in a text such as examples, facts, statistics, expert testimony or opinions; organizational pattern of the argument; relevance of the evidence; and relationship of this argument to similar ones), and ethos (the writer's credibility such as familiarity with the subject; reasonableness and good judgment; respect for others' values and integrity; and confidence shown by using his or her own voice, understanding reader needs, and treating the reader as an equal). In addition, readers need to recognize textual features and other writing strategies within text before teachers can use such tasks as assessment tools or as evidence of text comprehension. Post-reading activities are important at any level of reading and assist readers in acquiring the academic skills essential in any subject area.

Post-Reading Strategies for Organizing and Remembering Information

Post-reading activities may also include the reformulation and re-presentation of ideas in the text through graphic organizers, mapping activities, and concept analysis activities. Such activities allow readers to re-organize information in a more visual manner, resulting in increased comprehension and retention of information. Graphic organizers allow for ideas in text to be represented visually. For example, a venn diagram, represented by two interlocking circles, serves to illustrate similarities and differences between two concepts, characters, events, etc. Mapping, as a visual and spatial strategy, can be used to assist students with organizing and remembering information. A map can represent information using headings and subheadings as presented in a text, or it may synthesize the information according to the reader's understanding of the text (Peregoy & Boyle, 2001) Concept analysis charts, sometimes referred to as semantic feature analysis charts, a graphic method of listing and analyzing essential traits or features that define examples of a category or concept can also be used to reinforce important concepts and terms after reading. Such charts allow students to illustrate the relationships between concepts and can be used to distinguish one concept from another. In addition, such activities reinforce vocabulary, and the similarities and differences between lexical items and semantic categories. The following are some examples of graphic organizers and concept analysis charts which can be used by students, or even generated by students, after reading to organize information visually. Teachers can provide blank templates or once students have been familiarized with graphic organizers, they can generate their own. While these illustrate only a few examples, teachers can find numerous other printables in reading texts or on the Internet, or can even use automatic generators available on the Internet to create their own graphic organizers for classroom use. Graphic Organizers are available at <http://www.eduplace.com/graphicorganizer/index.html> and <http://www.teach-nology.com/web_tools/graphic_org/>.

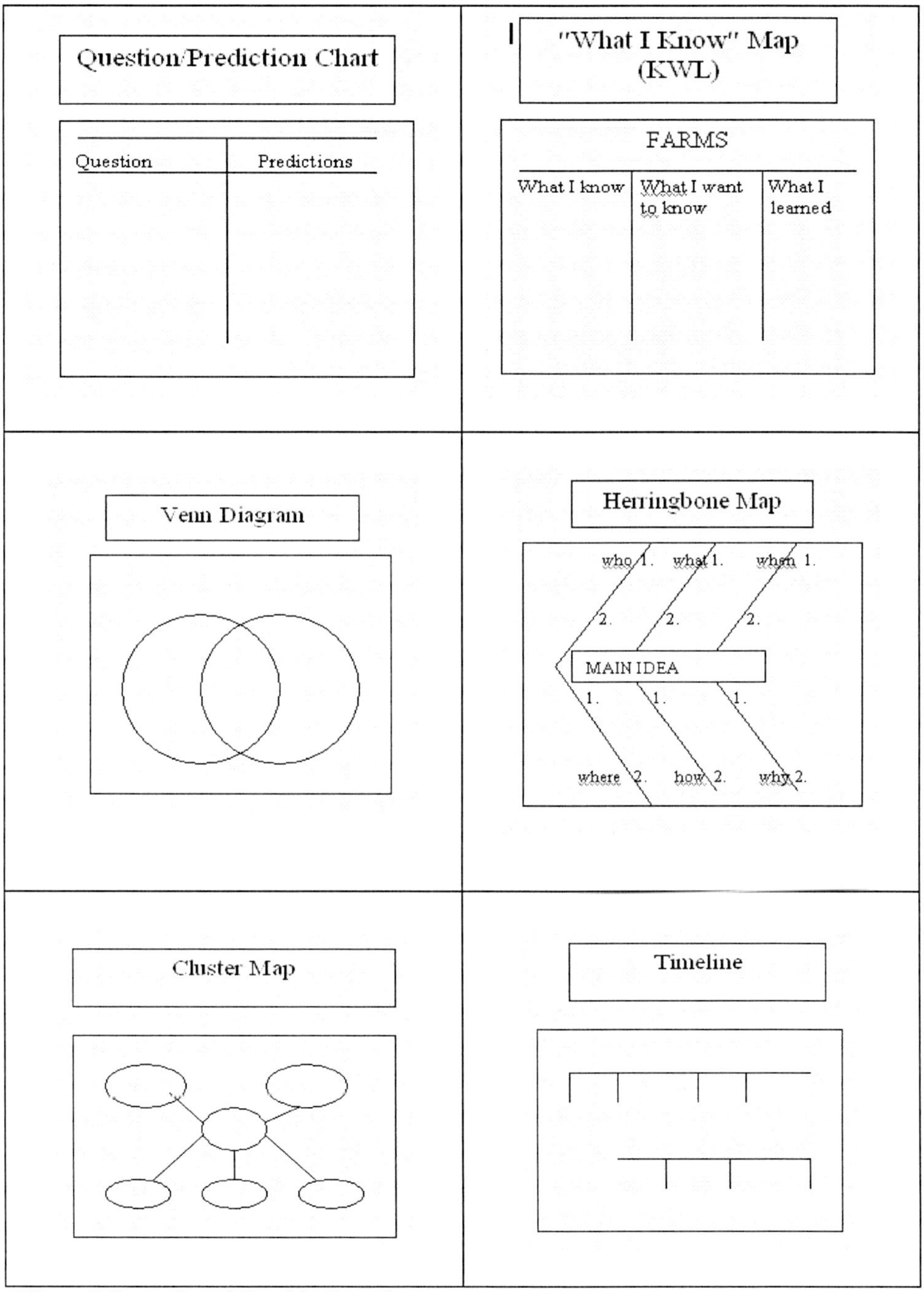

Figure 7 Examples of Graphic Organizers

Post-Reading Summary Writing

     Teachers should also directly teach the process of retelling or summary writing in order to provide practice in the extraction of main ideas and supporting details, the identification of relevant information, and the attainment of academic language. Figure 8 provides an overview of how summary writing can be taught. It can also serve as a handout on summary writing.

How to Summarize an Article

Your summary should convey an accurate understanding of the controlling idea, main idea, or thesis of the source. It should also demonstrate your accurate understanding of the major points the author uses in developing the controlling idea, main idea, or thesis. Read the passage carefully. Determine its structure. Identify the author's purpose in writing. (This will help you to distinguish between more important and less important information).

1. Read the article once and put it aside. If you had to describe what the article is about in one sentence, what would you say? This is the main idea of the whole article. In other words, it is the thesis-a one-sentence summary of the entire passage.

2. Reread the article and underline the key terms and ideas, and main ideas.

3. It may help to create a summary chart where you list the main idea or key idea/terms for each paragraph. Focus on the central idea of the passage. Sometimes a paragraph will list many details, but think about what the passage is "mainly" about. Think about what the author's main point is. Sometimes it will be directly stated and sometimes you will have to infer it from the information provided.

Paragraph 1	food safety is important
Paragraph 2	cooking foods at proper temperatures
Paragraph 3	important to store foods at proper temperatures
Paragraph 4	food safety rules are very lax

4. Once you have a summary chart for all the paragraphs, write the first draft of your summary by (1) combining the thesis with your list of one-sentence summaries or (2) combining the thesis with one-sentence summaries plus significant details from the passage. In either case, eliminate repetition and less important information. Disregard minor details, or generalize them. Use as few words as possible to convey the main ideas.

5. Use proper summary language and style. For example, use verbs to retell the author's ideas.
The author claims, argues, suggests, focuses on, expresses, analyzes, explains, describes, declares, justifies, defines, attributes, etc. The first sentence of your summary should include the author, title of article, and the main idea. For example, "The article "Food Safety Among Street Vendors" by John Marshall describes the importance of food safety and the steps people can take to prevent food-related illnesses."

Occasionally remind the reader that you are retelling someone else's ideas. John Marshall states that ….Marshall emphasizes that people should ……He also points out that…..

6. Check your summary against the original passage and make whatever adjustments are necessary for accuracy and completeness.

7. Revise your summary, inserting transitional words and phrases where necessary to ensure coherence, and check for any errors.

8. Here is an example of a summary.

> The article "Private Detectives and Investigators" by Michael Ryall describes the duties, working conditions, and qualifications and training of detectives and investigators. Ryall begins by describing the various duties of detectives and investigators. He *states* that private detectives and investigators help both businesses and the public with many different kinds of issues and problems. They engage in a variety of tasks including gathering evidence and carrying out investigations. In addition to these tasks, they perform surveillance and search for records and other useful information by interviewing people, by collecting evidence, or by verifying facts. Private detectives and investigators who are employed by stores are responsible for controlling the theft of products. They are responsible for protecting store merchandise and for arresting anyone who steals. Ryall also discusses the working conditions of private detectives and investigators. Sometimes detectives and investigators work from their offices but at other times they are expected to do work in places ranging from seedy bars to more luxurious and pleasant environments. They may have to work long hours especially when performing surveillance. Finally, Ryall concludes the article by informing readers about the necessary qualifications needed to become a detective or private investigator. Normally a high school diploma and strong communication skills are enough to become a private investigator; however, sometimes detectives may have to undergo specific training through specialized courses.

Figure 8 Handout on How to Summarize an Article

Reading and Less Proficient Readers

It must be recognized that when we teach reading, our underlying assumptions are that reading must be for meaning, and that we learn to read by reading. Readers need repeated opportunities to practice, and they need a guide to get into, through, and beyond a text. Teachers should therefore encourage the use of reading strategies at all levels, and extensive reading by finding selections that will help promote competency in the strategies students have learned. The following list of suggestions may help teachers in assisting beginner level and less proficient readers.

Guidelines for Working with Beginner Level/Less Proficient Readers
• Read to students and teach basic vocabulary and sight words.
• Use picture books to practice such skills as sequencing, predicting, and inferencing.
• Use cartoon strips and blank out words so students can write their own stories/texts.
• Build background knowledge prior to lessons.
• Use familiar patterned books for modeling and reading.
• Encourage student to use verbal strategies when they read/guided reading.
• Introduce content at a simpler level.
• Expand vocabulary (topic-specific/content-specific).
• Teach strategies for getting information from reference and non-fiction texts.
• Provide practice in using strategies – skimming/scanning, paraphrasing, summarizing, anticipating, using context clues, main idea extraction, etc.
• Use graphic organizers-text reconstruction/comprehension.
• Encourage variety in length and difficulty of texts.
• Use books on tape.
• Have a discussion about students' outside class reading.
• Have students keep journals that record what they have read.
• Allocate time to talk with each student about his or her current reading and reading interests.
• Encourage students to read works by the same author, or works of the same genre or same topic as this often coincides with their interest.
• Retell the story through another medium such as drama, poetry, or song.
• Include discussions of text to see if students' ideas and attitudes, and interpretations have changed as a result of reading the text.
• Provide a supportive environment by being flexible and allowing students to self-select materials that are developmentally appropriate.
• Include texts that reflect the students' cultures and experiences.
• Provide enough time to read, respond, and discuss texts.
• Recognize that errors are a natural part of the reading process.

Figure 9 Guidelines for Working with Beginning or Less Proficient Readers

Effective teachers of reading recognize that each reader is unique and brings a unique set of experiences to the reading experience itself. Readers may differ in how they use their background knowledge due to individual differences, and their knowledge about texts. While information in a text remains the same, the information the reader brings to that text fluctuates as they begin to employ an elaborate set of reading strategies, enabling them in turn to enhance their comprehension of the text. Teachers must plan carefully and ensure that strategy-building activities encourage use of and engage all levels of cognition and higher-order thinking skills in order to build meaningful reading comprehension skills that will carry over to all reading tasks and subject areas. Chapter 8 addresses the importance of designing tasks that promote higher-order and critical thinking skills in more detail. Strategy-building activities can be used to assess students' strengths and weaknesses, or to build comprehension skills. The key, however, to effective reading instruction is to provide balanced, flexible, and carefully planned reading activities that are developmentally appropriate for all readers in the classroom.

Summary

Teaching readers how to use strategies should be a prime consideration in the reading classroom to assist students in becoming more effective and efficient readers. Teachers should have readers engage in pre-reading, during-reading, and post-reading activities to assist them in developing their reading skills and refining their strategy use. Pre-reading activities involve establishing expectations so that readers can better comprehend more of the text and how the information will be organized. During-reading activities involve making students more aware of how they are reading and what they can do to enhance text comprehension. Post-reading strategies need to be taught and employed in the class to build a repertoire of reading skills and to check for comprehension. Research in L2 reading has demonstrated that when readers consciously control and monitor their reading by paying close attention to, thinking about the elements in text, and identifying the various interactions that take place during the reading process, comprehension is improved. In order for such strategies to be acquired, teachers must introduce and explain reading strategies and then model them through whole-class readings and collaborative activities.

Discussion Questions and Activities

1. Select a reading passage suitable for intermediate-level students and modify it so that it is comprehensible to beginner-level students. Explain your rationale for the modifications made.

2. Design a short reading lesson to teach identification of main ideas and supporting details.

3. Select an article from a newspaper or magazine and design three pre-reading activities related to it.

4. Examine and evaluate a commercially prepared reading textbook. Comment on its appropriateness of content, organization, and pedagogical approach to teaching reading given its goals, purposes, and intended audience.

5. Design a lesson plan form/template that would be useful to you when teaching reading.

6. Make two sequential lesson plans for the class for which you would use the textbook you chose in question 4. Use the lesson plan form you created in question 5. The lesson plan should address how you will use the pre-reading, during-reading, and post-reading model to teach the lesson. Share your form and lessons with your peers.

7. Discuss the following question as a class or in small groups: Can reading be taught in the classroom through a range of tasks and activities? Why or why not? Give specific examples and provide evidence.

Chapter 6
Using Literature in the L2 Reading Course

Reading textbooks for the second language or foreign language reading classes, especially higher-level classes frequently contain literary texts such as short stories, poems, and excerpts from longer works of fiction. This chapter discusses the issues, benefits, and adjustments that may arise when incorporating literature in the reading or writing class. More specifically, this discussion on the approach to using literature in the ESL classroom touches on four main considerations: (1) the reasons for and advantages of using literary texts to teach language, (2) some features of literary texts, (3) criteria for selecting literature, and (4) specific examples of assignments and activities incorporating literature in the classroom.

Reasons for and Advantages of Using Literary Texts

The question of whether literature should be part of an ESL curriculum is often met with apprehension. While increasingly more programs focus on meeting the specific academic and occupational needs of these students, any emphasis on literature in the second language classroom is seen as unnecessary. Those who argue against the use of literature in the L2 classroom state that the main goals of a language curriculum are to teach students language. The complexities inherent in literary works simply do not allow for the teaching of grammar and language in a system way or in a way that facilitates language development. Others argue that the inclusion of literature does little to support the academic goals or the skills needed to succeed in a range of academic subjects. Still others argue that because there are so specific examination requirements and very little time to cover the curriculum, use of literary texts is redundant. Finally, because literature can be linguistically and conceptually complex, it is too difficult for most second language students. Despite these objections many teachers incorporate literature into the L2 curriculum for a variety of reasons. Many of these reasons in fact, contrary to what some may think, relate to the development of linguistic knowledge and language skills and usage.

Literature can serve many functions in the classroom but if literature is to be used in the second language class, it is to be used as a language teaching resource rather than as an object of literary study (Carter & Long, 1991; Kline 2002). Literary works can be used so that students become more interested in reading literature and reading itself. For some students literature may provide the affective and attitudinal factors which will motivate them to read. Collie and Slater (1987) point out that very often the process of learning itself is "essentially analytic, piecemeal, and, at the level of the personality, fairy superficial" (p. 5). The engagement with a literary text over a longer period of time can in fact draw the student into the text to the point where the reader is more interested in finding out how events unfold, or for instance, what might happen to some or all of the characters in the work. Students can begin to engage with the text and use of literature can develop the students' pleasure in reading thereby broadening their experiences with texts, in turn leading to both personal and intellectual growth.

Literature can also allow students to become more familiar with various aspects of a culture (Agathocleous & Dean, 2003; Carter & Long, 1991; Collie & Slater, 1987). Many language learners learn a language knowing that they may never have the opportunity to visit or live in the area where that language is spoken. For such learners, literary texts provide an indirect route to an understanding about the culture and way of life of people. The literary text can offer the reader a full and vivid context in which characters from many social backgrounds can be depicted. The language learner can begin to understand the norms, rules, codes, and structure of a given society and better understand what life was like in another country or place or in another time (Collie & Slater, 1987). An added advantage of using literature for this purpose is that literature, which presents a particular register or dialect that is embedded within a particular cultural and social context, thereby enables students to develop an awareness of language use as well. Literature becomes a window to a culture helping students to understand and appreciate other cultures and people in the world.

Literature can also lead to language enrichment. Literature provides a rich context in which lexical and syntactical items are made more memorable. Literature can expose students to a variety in language in terms of sentence structure, function of sentences, and ways of connecting ideas. A longer work such as a novel or long play will develop student ability to make inferences, predictions, and deduce meaning from context, important academic skills needed across the curriculum (Carter & Long, 1991; Collie & Slater, 1987; Draper, 1993). While the language of literary works is not typical of daily language or textbook language, the elaborate or compressed quality of much literary work can lead to a density of meaning not possible in non-literary works. The richness, variety, and use of figurative language itself can allow students to understand a concept, idea, or situation in a new light, allowing them to experience and understand it from an entirely new perspective. The inclusion of literary works allows students to understand both the various ways writers use language and literary features to convey a message and the more subtle conventions of various genres of fiction. Such genres may include poems, more specifically love poems, sonnets, epic poems, comic verse) dramas and plays, or fiction which might include short stories, mysteries, romance novels, science fiction, horror, and historical novels to name a few. These genres have different purposes, and as readers we have different expectations of such genres; therefore identification of a genre work and comprehension of it features will help the student focus on the understanding of the work under study. Use of literature, therefore, enables the expansion of content, linguistic, and textual schemata, all of which are necessary for the improvement of language skills and for developing and promoting the students' higher-order and critical analysis thinking skills.

Features of Literary Texts

Because academic or informative texts are different than literary texts, teachers need to be aware of these specific differences in order to draw students' attention to the specific features that characterize these texts (Parkinson & Thomas, 2001). Academic or informative texts usually contain a main idea with supporting points. Supporting points are often comprised of evidence that may take the form of facts, statistics, or previous work or research. The credentials of a writer are also important in determining the credibility of a piece. Such a text is usually labeled as a particular rhetorical structure such as arguments, descriptions, or cause and effect pieces for example. They might include visual information such as graphs, charts, and tables. Literary texts, on the other hand, include different elements such as plot, setting, character development, theme, figures of speech, and descriptive vocabulary for instance. Because of these elements, or the lack of understanding of these elements, second language students will often be frustrated when faced with literary works. It is, therefore, crucial that teachers spend time explaining and illustrating what these features are, how they function within a text, and how a writer makes use of such features to convey a message to readers. For example, in order to better understand a short story or novel, it can be extremely useful to familiarize students with the terminology used to describe the parts of a story or novel. A teacher might begin by using a story like *Cinderella,* which is familiar to most learners. As students retell the story out loud, the teacher can outline and label the parts of a story on a plot diagram on the board. The following guide can be provided as a reference.

Guide to Short Story and Novel Elements

PLOT

Plot is the sequence of incidents or events that comprise a story. Most plots have a number of common features:

Protagonist: The central character in the conflict

Antagonist: The force(s) or people against the protagonist

Conflict: The story begins with some problem or conflict.

There are four types of conflict:

character versus nature

a character versus other characters

a character versus a social or economic situation

a character versus him/herself

Exposition: Introduces the characters, the setting, and the situation

Initial incident: the first happening that sets the main characters in action

Rising action: The series of happenings in the story that build suspense

Climax: the point of highest interest or excitement in the story that will determine how everything turns out

Falling action: The events after the climax

Denouement/Resolution: The resolution of the conflict, for better or worse, or by being accepted or seen in a different way. Sometimes there is a happy ending and sometimes a sad one, depending on the author's view of reality and the point he/she is trying to make.

CHARACTER

1.Characterization: The author can describe a character in a number of ways:

tell the reader directly

by the character's actions

by the character's words

by what the character says about himself

by what other characters do or say

2. Character Types

Round character: A round character has many traits, and it could take a full essay to fully analyze and describe the character.

Flat character: We don't learn much about a flat character, so he/she can be summed up in a sentence or two.

POINT OF VIEW

This refers to the perspective of the narrator.

Omniscient: The narrator can see into the minds of all characters; written in third person

Limited Omniscient. The narrator can see into the mind of one or more characters (but not all of them); written in third person

First Person: The narrator is a character in the story; written in first person

Objective: The narration is like a camera and records only what it sees; written in third person

THEME

This is the controlling purpose or central idea of the story. The theme of a story dramatizes an idea and it is usually expressed as a statement. Usually stories have two purposes: to entertain or to dramatize a statement about life or the human experience. Sometimes a theme can be a lesson or moral of a story. Remember, that some stories are simply meant to entertain and therefore not all stories have a theme.

Figure 1 Guide to Short Story and Novel Elements (Mount Royal College-Languages Institute - Reading Practice Exercise)

Once students become familiar with the parts of the short story or novel they can begin to analyze other stories through this structural lens. The lesson below allows students to better understand the part of the story, *A High Dive*. The story is about a circus manager who is worried that he will be unable to keep his circus business alive because attendance is dropping. In order to attract more crowds, he decides to find someone who can perform a dangerous act. After reading the story, students are provided with a list of questions specifically focusing on short story elements.

Read the story *A High Dive* and answer the following questions:

Comprehension Questions and Short Story Elements
1. Why was the circus manager concerned?
2. What happened when the manager tried to bring in the Wall of Death?
3. What did the mysterious man claim he could do?
4. Why did the man refuse the job?
5. What did the manager think of the mysterious man?
6. Outline the plot. Identify the climax of the story, and the other events. Label these elements.
7. Who is the protagonist of the story?
8. What are the conflicts? What types of conflicts are they?
9. What point of view does the story use?
10. Use one adjective to describe the young man. What method(s) does the author use to develop that character?

Figure 2 Comprehension Questions from A High Dive (Mount Royal College-Languages Institute - Reading Practice Exercise).

Comprehension of poetry can also be problematic for second language students. Students often claim that they avoid reading poetry because they dislike it, they do not understand it, and in some cases, even fear it. For the most part, this is because they have a very traditional idea of what poetry is. Another reason students avoid reading poetry is because they have not developed the strategies that can help make sense of poetry. The following strategies can be used by teachers to help their students better understand poetry, and perhaps even develop an appreciation for poetry.

Initial Reading - Students should first read the poem. Teachers should encourage readers to read actively and to get involved with the piece by writing in the margins. Difficult words, lines and passages should be underlined and the poem should be read several times both silently and out loud.

Examining the Subject of the Poem - The students should consider the title of the poem and examine what it might reveal about the poem's subject, tone, and genre. The title must be revisited throughout reading and analysis of the poem. Students must continually ask themselves the question: "What is this poem about?"-and then return to this question throughout their analysis.

Examining Elements Relevant to the Poem - Students must also consider some basic elements such as characters, setting, point of view, and author's attitude toward the subject of the poem. They need to consider the basic situation and what is going on in the piece. Questions such as: Who is talking and to whom? Under what circumstances? Is it a dialogue, a monologue, or a letter? What is the narrative structure of the poem? Are there flashbacks? Is a story being told? Where? About what? can be extremely helpful in the interpretation of the poem. They also need to consider the structure of the poem. Consider the narrative structure of the poem. For example, questions such as: Does perspective shift? Do the above parts relate to each other? How are they appropriate for this poem? How are the ideas in the poem ordered? Is there a progression of some sort? From past to present? From one place or setting to another? Is there a clear beginning, middle and end? Is there a climax of any sort? What are the form and genre of this poem? How does the poet use the form? Writers will often use specific forms to create meaning and therefore students need to understand that form and meaning can have an important relationship.

Paraphrasing the Poem - Students may also find it helpful to paraphrase the poem in order to unravel any complex sentence structures. Questions to ask can include the following: Is the poem built on a comparison or analogy? If so, how is the comparison appropriate? How are the two things alike? How different? Does the poem appeal to a reader's intellect? Emotions? Reason? How does the poem affect you as a reader?

Analyzing the Context - Teachers must emphasize that works are not created in a vacuum but rather within the framework of a specific context. This context might include the writer's feelings, beliefs, past experiences, and physical environment as well as broader contexts such as biographical socio-cultural, political, psychological, and historical contexts for example. Contexts affect the writer and what they create. They might make references to other historical figures or events Students need to consider these contexts carefully in order to discover inherent meanings.

Examining the Form of the Poem - Students can examine how the poem is constructed and the specific units of organization (quatrains, paragraphs, couplets, etc.) They can examine the metric pattern of the poem and rhyme and whether they relate to the poem's meaning. They might consider if there is any alliteration, assonance, or onomatopoeia and how these relate to the poem's meaning. Teachers would have to provide and explain the uses and meanings of such literary devices.

Examining Word Choice of the Poem - Teachers must also spend some time showing students how writers use language. Effective readers are sensitive to the implications of word choice. Even if they are slightly unsure about the meaning of a word, they should be encouraged to consult a dictionary, which will reveal the various possible meanings and parts of speech. Students should also consider various possible meanings of a word and be alert to subtle differences between words. Words will also help to create mood and tone and are also used to appeal to a reader's sense of emotion. Students must consider whether the language used is abstract or concrete and whether this is appropriate to the poem's subject as authors will often use words that are related in theme or will use similar words to emphasize their message. Writers will also use figurative language and therefore teachers must spend the time discussing the terminology and such literary devices. Students must consider if there are any consistent patterns of words. While reading, students can also try to identify as many literary devices as possible and consider how these devices were used to help get the writer's message across. The guide below provides basic definitions of the more common literary devices but teachers may wish to provide more comprehensive glossaries of literary terms.

Figurative Language and Literary Devices

Here are some examples of Figurative Language. This is language that uses figures of speech, such as hyperbole, simile, metaphor, personification, and symbolism or other forms of imagery. It is used to gain impact, freshness of expression, or pictorial effect.

Metaphor - A figure of speech in which a word or phrase literally denoting one kind of object or idea is used in place of another to suggest a likeness or analogy between them: a comparison. Sometimes an entire piece/poem can be a metaphor.

Simile - A comparison of two things using the words "like" or "as".

Personification - Attribution of personal/human qualities to something inanimate.

Imagery - Mental images or the products of imagination.

Symbolism - The art or practice of using symbols, especially by investing things with a symbolic meaning or by expressing the invisible or intangible by means of visible or sensuous representation: the use of conventional or traditional signs in the representation of divine beings and spirits.

Paradox - A self-contradictory statement that at first seems true. An argument that apparently derives self-contradictory conclusions by valid deduction from acceptable premises, or a tenet contrary to received opinion.

Diction - Verbal description, choice of words, especially with regard to correctness, clearness or effectiveness or vocal expression. Sometimes you will notice that words used in a poem fall into categories, i.e.) death, black, mundane, cold, terror, trapped, cracked, etc. or glassy, prismatic, mirror, shine, shell, enamel, gloss, etc.

Irony - The use of words to express something other than and especially the opposite of literal meaning. Incongruity between the actual result of a sequence of events and the normal or expected result.

Tone - Style or manner or expression in speaking or writing. Note that an author can create tone through diction (use of words) or even use (or lack of) punctuation, sentence length, etc.

Mood - A conscious state of mind or predominant emotion; feeling; a distinctive atmosphere or context, aura.

Setting - The time and place of the action of a literary, dramatic, or cinematic work. The setting can be real, imaginary, historical, or any combination of these. It can be stated or suggested.

Character Portrayal - The way in which characters are represented or depicted in a literary work. How does the character behave? What does this behavior indicate? What does the character look like? What do other characters say and think about this character?

Narrative Structure - The form or shape a narrative takes. Form or shape can be altered by words on a page/spacing or by use of time and place, i.e. story follows a chronology, story is told as a series of flashbacks, a letter, a dream told in first person, etc.

Flashback - A flashback is an interruption in a story to show an event that happened before that particular point in a story/poem. Because the entire action moves to a new place and time, the reader may be caught unaware, thus becoming confused. Look for this technique in your reading.

Foreshadowing - Occurs when a writer uses hints to suggest events that will happen later in a story.

Figure 3 Figurative Language and Literary Devices

Teachers can use similar guides to teach the various elements of literary texts; however, while initial learning might necessitate the separating of these elements, it must be emphasized that these elements are not separate from the reading task and that writers use several of them simultaneously. It is also important to note that students bring their own cultural knowledge of such texts to the class and initial discussion of various literary genres should address those culturally shaped expectations.

The lesson described below uses a piece by Donne, *Death be not Proud.* Students read the poem and following explanations and discussion of the analysis of poetry, literary devices, and figurative language are given an opportunity to work through the poem to uncover its meaning, purpose, and the elements used by the author to create meaning and accomplish his purpose. Teachers may use similar activities with poems of varying complexity depending on the age and language abilities of their students.

Read the following poem by John Donne. As you read, think about what the poem means? Why have you come to that conclusion? What message is Donne trying to convey? What was his purpose in writing this piece? What literary devices does Donne use to get his message across? (metaphors, personification, similes, narrative structure, point of view, symbolism, imagery, diction, pathos, tone, etc.)

Death be not proud, though some have called thee
Mighty and dreadful, for, thou are not soe,
For, those, whom thou think'st, thou dost overthrow,
Die not, poore Death, nor yet canst thou kill mee;
From rest and sleepe, which but thy pictures bee,
Much pleasure, then from thee, much more must flow,
And soonest our best men with thee doe goe,
Rest of their bones, and soules deliverie.
Thou art slave to Fate, Chance, kings, and desperate men,
And dost with Poyson, Warre, and Sicknesse dwell,
And poppie, or charmes can make us sleepe as well,
And better then thy stroake; why swell'st thou then?
One short sleepe past, wee wake eternally,
And death shall be no more, death thou shalt die.

1. Who is the author addressing? How do you know?
2. Why are some word spellings different?
3. Where and when was John Donne born?
4. Why are some words capitalized?
5. Based on what we have studied, which literary devices are being used? Give examples from the poem?
6. Why do you think Donne uses these literary devices?
7. What do you know about poppies?

8. What do you think the word "charme" means? Can you relate it to any word?
9. What does the last line of the poem mean? What happens to Death?
(Singhal, 2002)

Figure 4 Comprehension Questions to Analyze a Poem-Death Be Not Proud

The above two lessons illustrate how students can become more familiar and perhaps more comfortable with the literary pieces they are exposed to in a classroom once they learn the terminology and language associated with each genre. Many concepts and elements inherent in literary works can become even more transparent as they work through the process of text comprehension.

Criteria for Selecting Literature

Choosing materials that can be effectively integrated in the ESL class can be a somewhat complex task because students in such classes do not *study* literature per se, but rather reading and writing skills are developed by planning lessons around literature. The goals and objectives of the course must be met through inclusion of literature in the course. Having said that, there are; however, four main criteria that can assist in the selection process: (1) the level of language in the literary texts, (2) the cultural and social content of the works, (3) the relevance of the works to the lives of the students, and (4) the quality of the literary texts (Aebersold & Field, 1997; Carter and Long, 1991; Tomlinson & McGraw, 1997).

Level of Language -To meet the diverse needs of the students, the teacher must consider the complexity of the texts and the experiences of the students. Beginning readers need predictable, repetitive texts to capture their imaginations and provide the richness and rhythm of language. The teacher will also have to make a decision about using modified or authentic texts. The choice to use either type will mean weighing the advantages of a controlled level of grammar and vocabulary against the richness of authentic texts. Therefore the language proficiency of the students may determine the appropriate type of text to be used.

Cultural and Social Content - Literature that is culturally authentic or rich in cultural context can help students in developing an appreciation for and an understanding of persons from a variety of cultures and social settings. However, teachers must also keep in mind that cultural content can be too implicit in some texts, causing second language learners increased anxiety and frustration due to the complexities and lack of comprehension. The selection of multicultural literature also necessitates various considerations. The following questions may aid teachers in selecting appropriate literary texts:

- Is there a balance of high-quality, unadapted fiction and nonfiction?
- Have I included a range of literature and resources at a variety of reading levels?
- Are they appropriate and appealing to my students?
- Will the literature motivate my students to engage in further reading and writing?
- Are the literature texts and resources multicultural?
- Are they written by authors of diverse backgrounds?
- Do these multicultural works represent a variety of perspectives?
- Do the multicultural works accurately reflect a broad range of cultural, linguistic, and historical perspectives?

Relevance of Works to Students' Lives – When selecting literary texts, there should be some degree of match between the students' interests, needs, backgrounds, lives, and the literature they are reading in class. This can lead to increased motivation and an increased desire to read. Teachers must probe for and listen to their students as they discuss what appeals to them. A teacher who is aware of student preferences will be better able to make appropriate and effective choices.

Quality of Literary Texts – Although the assessment of the quality of literary texts is somewhat subjective, literature should be able to stand the test of time and value if it represents good writing, hold students interest and fosters imagination and carries the reader to the end. These general guidelines can be used to determine overall quality of literary texts including multicultural literature.

- The language used is rich and varied and is appropriate for age group, and student proficiency and developmental level
- The works contain up-to-date terminology, and authentic use of dialect.
- The language and content stimulates critical thinking skills.
- The works provide depictions of realistic and multidimensional characters.
- The works adhere to high standards of creativity and/or scholarship.
- The literary works authentically portray thoughts and emotions.

- Cultural information is presented in a manner consistent with the storyline.
- The content is free of stereotypes.
- The literary works contain a humanistic element appealing to readers.
- The works offer situations creating genuine interest and enthusiasm in the reader.

Incorporating Literature in the Classroom

Once the selection of literary texts has been accomplished, the issue of how to deal with such texts in the classroom must be carefully considered. Having said that, it is important to recognize that literature is used so we can learn something about the world and so we can learn something about language. Seeing literature solely as a language learning or teaching tool undermines the purposes and benefits of using literature in the class (Agathocleous & Dean, 2003). Rosenblatt's distinction between efferent and aesthetic reading illustrates the above point more clearly. Approaching the text efferently means that the reader uses the text to gain information. Aesthetic reading is more concerned with the experience itself. This kind of reading relates to the enjoyment attained when the reader interacts with the literary work. The following discussion provides examples of how literature can be used in the language classroom. These examples focus on both the efferent and aesthetic purposes of reading, how the two interact, and illustrate how literature can be used to further both language and intellectual development.

The following exercise was intended for students to do a close reading of the text *We Do Abortions Here* written by Sally Tisdale, a nurse and author. By answering the following questions, students would further their understanding of how the writer appeals to an audience's sense of emotion and the kinds of writing strategies used to do so. Students realize that texts involve a transaction between the reader and the writer and the writer's background, coupled with writing strategies, create powerful texts. A discussion of the rhetorical triangle prior to analysis and close-reading of the texts would facilitate students' understanding of the piece. Teachers should discuss the relationship between the reader, writer, text, and the three appeals: ethos, pathos, and logos. While it is not necessary to use these terms, students will come to better understand the three appeals and how they correspond to three elements of the rhetorical situation, sometimes represented as the "communication triangle." To evaluate the effectiveness of a text, readers have to answer questions about the resources available to writers in a given situation. How does the author claim authority (ethos)? How are readers' experiences or feelings represented to them (pathos)? How is the topic defined and reasoned (logos)?

We Do Abortions Here by Sally Tisdale

1. In the essay, who is the writer and what does the writer do for a living? Where does she work?
2. Which magazine published this essay?
3. What do you know about this magazine? Based on this, what kind of an audience is Tisdale addressing?
4. What are four adjectives that come to mind when reading this essay? (What did you feel/your reaction?)
5. Which part(s) of the essay had the greatest effect or impact on you? Why?
6. What kind of an audience is the writer addressing? (Who is the writer addressing?)
7. In your mind, what is the purpose of this essay?
8. Does the writer help to resolve the abortion issue? Why or why not?
9. What are the writer's feelings about abortion? How do you know?
10. Where in the story does the writer reveal her own position on the issue? (Quotation)
11. Does the writer experience any sort of dilemma? If so, what is the dilemma?
12. When we discussed the rhetorical triangle, we talked about appealing to an audience and the ways in which that can be done. Pathos is often described as emotional appeal. Does the writer use pathos? How? Also, explain how ethos is established, if at all.
13. Does the writer offer a definition of abortion?
14. On page 705, (para 21) what does Tisdale mean when she says, "Abortion is a matter of choice, privacy, control. Its uncertainty lies in specific cases: retarded women and girls too young to give consent for surgery, women who are ill or hostile or psychotic. Such common dilemmas are met with both compassion and impatience: .."
15. On page 709, (para 39) the author writes, "Abortion requires of me an entirely new set of assumptions. It requires a willingness to live with conflict, fearlessness, and grief." Interpret and explain the above.
16. Identify two examples of rhetorical/writing strategies the author uses throughout this essay Go one step further and explain how these strategies tie into the context (or the purpose of the essay). *In other words, I want to know what was used, but also, why and how it was used.*

(Singhal, 2002)

Figure 5 Close-Reading to Analyze Writing Strategies in *We Do Abortions* Here by Sally Tisdale

The above activity also makes students as readers more aware of the writing strategies employed by writers. Again this type of activity emphasizes the connection between reading and writing and it is important that students see the reading process and writing process as inseparable. For example, the following chart adapted from *A Student's Guide to First Year Composition* by Wurr, Eroz and Singh-Concoran (2000) can be provided as a guideline to learners working with higher-level texts. It explains the various kinds of writing strategies and techniques used by writers to appeal to and connect with readers. Teachers can use something similar in their courses to explain writing strategies to their students.

What is a "Writing Strategy" and How Do I Know One When I See One?

Personal Experience is one strategy that writers use to appeal to readers. Because the author may describe his or her experiences in such a vivid way, it is easier for readers to believe the situation and see the issues from the author's perspective. Sharing personal experiences is also an excellent way for the author to "deflect potential rebuttals." It is much more difficult to question someone when only they have gone through that particular situation so this works well as a strategy.

Style is another writing strategy that can be quite effective. For example sentence length can indicate tone. Short sentences can not only seem abrupt, but can seem terse. A longer sentence might sound more gentle or even create a more dramatic effect. The style of writing can create a certain rhythm and in turn then create a certain mood. For example, some writers are very descriptive; others use literary devices in their writing. Whatever the case, different writing styles have different effects on readers as well as different rhetorical effects.

Diction, or otherwise known as word choice, is really important in writing. The way an author says something will impact both effect and meaning. Think about how someone who uses big words makes you feel. Sometimes readers will view the author as an authority while other times the author may appear pretentious. Other times the author might be viewed as highly educated and therefore believable. Word choice can also indicate the author's affiliations and beliefs. At times more than one language may also be used to make a connection to the reader.

Nods to the Opposition refers to acknowledging the other point of view. For example, if the writer is making an argument but despite that, will acknowledge that other or opposing positions are also valid to some degree, readers might have more respect for the author. Sometimes, however, authors will use this strategy only to show how weak other arguments or positions are.

Point/Counterpoint is used by writers when they "set up an argument as a debate." This strategy helps the reader see where opposing sides agree and disagree.

Questioning the Motivation of the Opposition is an interesting strategy because it creates doubts in the reader's mind. If someone makes an accusation or even slightly questions the other groups' beliefs or actions, this undermines the credibility of those groups or individuals. We have seen this time and time again the political arena.

Stereotyping the Opposition means that the writer presents a distorted view of opponents. This can be done by making fun of them or by misrepresenting them. There are numerous groups in society or those who hold various beliefs who have been stereotyped like pro-life or environmental groups.

Targeting the Concerns of the Audience occurs when the author writes about events or situations the readers can most relate to. Sometimes the author will use a specific language style or diction, or even describe events with such emotion so as to connect with the reader. If the reader can relate to what the writer is saying, the reader is more likely to take action or believe the writer.

Knowledgeability refers to the knowledge of the author. The author may demonstrate his knowledge of a subject by quoting others. This shows the reader that the author is well-read and has done the research. Sometimes the author will speak of his or her own experiences. For example, if the author is a doctor, and is writing an article on the effects of smoking, this carries a lot of weight. References to authority have to be perceived as real by the reader otherwise the reader may see it as a poor attempt to change the reader's mind or position on a subject.

(Adapted From Wurr, A., Eroz, B., and Singh-Corcoran, N. (2000). *A student's guide to first year composition.* Boston: MA, Pearson Custom Publishing).

Figure 6 Guide to Recognizing Writing Strategies and Techniques

As students are presented with opportunities to practice and analyze how authors are presenting their arguments, eventually, they will acquire a repertoire of techniques to use as they evaluate others' work and as they develop as writers, leading them to become more careful and critical readers.

The following activity enables students to come to a better understanding of a character in a text. In this exercise, students use a series of questions intended as guidelines to help them write a journal entry. The example used the story *The Yellow Wallpaper* by Charlotte Perkins

Gilman. By considering responses to the questions listed below (answered in a journal entry), students come to appreciate the issues surrounding the character and the various issues inherent in the story itself. By allowing students to step into the shoes of a character, they are often able to see issues they may otherwise not pick up through a simple reading of the story. In the story *The Yellow Wallpaper*, the unnamed first-person narrator descends from neurasthenia into insanity during the course of her enforced rest (imprisonment) in a bedroom with yellow wallpaper. At first she speaks with a perky and optimistic voice, dwelling on the view from her room and the interesting associations she finds in the wallpaper's pattern. She has little or no emotional support. Her husband thinks that there is no reason for her to be suffering; it's just a case of "nerves." As time goes on, she comes under the hallucinatory power of the figure in the wallpaper. Eventually the narrator decompensates to the point of crawling around the room on hands and knees, and stripping the paper, first with her hands, then with her teeth. Her husband faints when he comes in and sees her doing this.

Journal Entry-*The Yellow Wallpaper*

Part I

Imagine that you are a character in *The Yellow Wallpaper*. Write a 2-3 page interior monologue about yourself to provide answers to the questions below. Do not answer these questions in the order given or mechanically, one by one. Instead, fashion your answers in a diary-like entry that captures the personality of the character you have chosen. First, look at the questions carefully and decide what to start with - begin with something that would appeal to your character, something about which s/he would have a lot to say. I do not expect you to answer each and every question, but you want to try and answer most of them in some way or another.

The purpose of this assignment is to bring together your impressions of this character, to increase your understanding of this character, and to begin to identify and explore the themes and concerns Gilman conveys through this character.

1. What do you care about passionately? What are the most important forces, beliefs, desires in your life?
2. Who do you love the most or feel closest to? Why this person?
3. When in your life were you the happiest (or unhappy). Describe what happened.
4. What have you done in your life that you are the proudest of? Why?
5. What have you done in your life that you most regret? Why? What have the consequences been?
6. Whom do you fear, hate, or resent? Why?
7. What quality in yourself most disturbs or bothers you? Why?
8. What quality in yourself most pleases you? Why?
9. How do others see you? What quality in you most disturbs or bothers them?
10. What experience in your life do you relive over and over again in your mind? Why is this experience so important to you?
11. How do you feel about the future, either yours in particular or the future in general?
12. If you could be granted one wish, any wish at all, what would it be?

Part II

In a separate section, write about the themes or concerns that Gilman conveys through this particular character. (Your themes may vary a great deal in terms of issue/topic-which is perfectly fine). What kinds of things does this character force us to think about or pay attention to? What problems does Gilman examine by using this character? What questions does she pose through this character?
(Singhal, 2002)

Figure 7 Journal Activity for *The Yellow Wallpaper*

In addition to understanding the story itself, closer analysis of the language in the text helps students to understand how form of the language conveys meaning and how something is said also provides insight into a character's feelings and thoughts. They can begin to understand the significance of one waiter's shorter sentences and the other waiter's longer phrases. They also begin to understand that literary works, including their own, are not created in a vacuum, but rather often stem from some experience the writer may have had. This allows students to make connections to text as well. They in some ways see how his life fits into the text, and how his experiences enabled him to write this piece. The questions below also ask students to use clues in the story to determine time, place, setting, and the context in which this story takes place. They also consider writer strategies such as language form and style, use of Spanish, tone and character development used to convey the message/theme of the story.

Understanding Reader Response: A Closer Look at *A Clean Well-Lighted Place*
by Ernest Hemingway

Spend 10 minutes providing biographical information on Hemingway (available from the Internet or the Library).
1. Provide each student with a copy of "A Clean Well-Lighted Place."
2. Read the story as a class. Stop at various points to ask questions:
a. From what you have read so far, what time period might this be? How do you know?
b. Where do you think this is taking place? How do you know?
c. What do the following words mean? (Spanish words in the text)
d. What has happened up to this point in time?
e. Who are the main characters? How are they similar/different?
f. How does this section of the text differ from the second part (pace, sentence structure), etc., Old waiter, young waiter, old man – each a different writing style, etc., pace, outlook on life as reflected in the text structure.
g. How does this related to content? Do you see a relationship between form and meaning here?
3. Ask students to write a short journal response to the story. Then discuss their responses. Some students may have made connections to the text in terms of personal experience. Perhaps the situation or character reminds them of something or someone. Others may have made connections to the story in terms of their reading/writing experiences.
(Singhal, 2002)

Figure 8 Reader Response Activity for *A Clean Well-Lighted Place*

This activity encourages students to anticipate the storyline based on clues the writer has given them in the story. Some paragraphs of the story have been printed below to illustrate this prediction activity.

A High Dive

The circus manager was worried. Attendances had been falling off and such people as did come-children they were, mostly-sat about listlessly, munching sweets, or sucking ices, sometimes talking to each other without so much as glancing at the show.... What did people want? Something that was, in his opinion sillier and more pointless than the old jokes; not a bull's-eye on the target of humor, but an outer or even a near miss-something that brought in the element futility and that could be laughed at as well as with; an unintentional joke against the joker.

The clowns were quick enough with their patter but it just didn't go down; there was too much sense in their nonsense for an up-to-date audience, too much sense in their nonsense for an up-to-date audience too much articulateness. They would do better to talk gibberish perhaps. Now they must change their style, and find out what really did make people laugh, if people could be made to; but he, the manager, was over fifty and never good himself at making jokes, even the old-fashioned kind. What was this word that everyone was using-"sophisticated"? The audiences were too sophisticated, even the children were. They seemed to have seen and heard all this before, even when they were too young to have seen and heard it.

"What shall we do?" he asked his wife. They were standing under the Big Top, which had just been put up, and wondering how many of the empty seats would still be empty when they gave their first performance.

"I don't see what we can do about the comic side," she said. "It may come right by itself. Fashions change, all sorts of old things have returned to favor, like old-time dances. But there's something we could do."

"What's that?"

"Put on an act that's dangerous, really dangerous. Audiences are never bored by that. I know you don't like it, and no more do I, but when we had the Wall of Death-"

Her husband's big chest muscles twitched under his thin shirt.

Prediction:
What is the conflict that begins the story? What possible solution does one of the characters offer? How can you tell that the other one doesn't like it? What do you think the "Wall of Death" is? Will the man and woman probably agree or disagree as they talk about it?

(story continues, etc.)

Figure 9 Predicting Practice Activity for *A High Dive (* Mount Royal College-Languages Institute)

Numerous activities which encourage students to think critically and analyze the structure of the text and the inherent message can also be designed around literature. These activities can also ask students to analyze language and use of detail. Some typical textbook questions relating to literature might be as follows:

Questions for Critical Thinking

1. What do you think is the writer's thesis? Consider the title and the first sentence. Is this a case of a thesis where the attitude about the topic is unstated but the writer can assume that readers would understand from the very beginning what a mother's attitude would be?
2. In this essay, how many stories are told?
3. Narration involves a story usually with a sequence of events. This essay uses elements of narration to develop the main point. What is the sequence of events that the author has chosen for this essay?
4. In order to achieve coherence, writers need to use transitions of time in narrative pieces. Review the essay and underline all the transitional expressions you can find.
5. What does the final quote mean? How does it relate to the overall theme of the story?

6. Comment on the author's use of language and use of detail. How do both of these elements affect her writing and the point she is making?
7. What kind of literary devices are used in the text?

Figure 10 Critical Thinking Exercise for a Short Story

The exercise below is another reading comprehension activity based on a short story. By answering the following questions, students learn to use and become aware of a range of reading strategies that can be used to create meaning as they read. Teachers may even use this as a think aloud to determine the kinds of strategies students are using. How do they use context? How to they determine the meanings of unknown words? Are they able to comprehend the literary devices such as personification and metaphor? The story can also be used to point out such features and the way in which the author uses them to achieve his message.

The World We Lost by Farley Mowat

Before reading the text itself, ask the students question 1.

1. What do you think this text will be about? How do you know?
Allow students to read the story.
1. What do you think the "thunderous roar" is referring to?
2. Tell me what this text is about. Provide a summary.
3. From whose point of view is the story told?
4. Why did the author need to see inside the wolf den? How do you know?
5. Why was it difficult for the author to get into the den?
6. What did the author see upon entering the den?
7. Who is Angeline? Who is George? How do you know?
8. What or who is the Norseman? How do you know?
9. What is the Norseman compared to? How did you determine that?
10. What are the four green lights the author refers to?
11. Define the following terms (do not use a dictionary). In addition, tell me how you determined the meanings of the words. Be very specific about this.
-diameter, burrow (paragraph 1), -moss, esker (paragraph 2)
-shed, tunic (paragraph 3), -squirmed, claustrophobia, admit (paragraph 4)
-murk (paragraph 6), gopher (paragraph 8)
-save (paragraph 10), -bravado (paragraph 11)
-rage, brute (paragraph 13), -somber, engendered (paragraph 14)
-appalled, refuge (paragraph 15)
-alien (paragraph 16)

1. In paragraph 15, why does the author say he was shamed? What does he mean?
2. What is the author's overall message he wants to get across to readers?
3. What is George's howl compared to?
4. Explain what the last paragraph of the story means?
5. Where might you find such a text?
6. What kind of text is this?
7. Did this text remind you of any event, person, or specific experience? Explain?
8. Write a brief outline of this text. Does this text have a recognizable structure? What is it? In other words, can you classify this text of being a specific type in terms of structure?
9. Is this fiction or non-fiction? How do you know?
(Singhal, 2002)

Figure 11 During-Reading Strategy-Building Procedure (DRSBP) for *The World We Lost*

Following the above activity, the students were asked if they could make a connection to the story and one student stated the following:

When I was in the army I we got an assignment to take over a base camp for 30 days. The base was located near our border with Jordan. Our mission was to operate from this camp by doing patrols along the border in order to prevent any dangerous individuals from entering Israel or any drug trafficking. The Israeli fence is an electronic sensory fence and any touch will send signals to the basecamp in a specific area and will alert armed patrol cars to the location. Lots of wildlife animals live in this area, and in most cases, pigs cause the fence to go off. Sometimes we get permission to "eliminate" the problem. One day while on patrol, as the commander, I answered a "code red" for the fourth time that day. Until that time we only spotted the wild pig. I got off the armed car and yelled, "He is mine!" I ran 100 feet aimed my M-16 at the pig who was about 300 yards away. It took four quick shots to stop the pig from running. I felt very bad about taking the pig's life for such a stupid reason - for just touching the fence.

Literature can be used to inspire students to write their own works, and as seen in the above example, can also encourage them to tell their own stories. This student was able to connect to the text and further his understanding by drawing a parallel between his experience and that of the writer's. It also enabled him to understand the overall theme of the piece.

This activity encourages students to think about how literary works are created and the underlying meanings behind the story and characters.

Textual Contexts

Biographical: How would knowing about the author and his/her life further your understanding of the novel and issues presented within it? Where did the author grow up? What do you know about his/her education, family, religious background, relationships, other works, etc.

Gender: Think about how women/men are represented or portrayed in the story and also consider gender relationships/roles in the story.

Historical/Social: What historical events occurred during that time period? Are these in any way relevant to the reading/interpretation of the story? Consider the values of the time, the social customs, marriage laws, the notion of class and social status, economic conditions of that time/place, etc. You might use some of the problems or ideas you find in *The Yellow Wallpaper* or *Sonny' Blues* to comment on some contemporary political or social problem. How might such factors help you to better understand the story, the actions of the characters, and the events that took place?

Psychological: For example, you may apply some sort of psychological framework here. In *The Yellow Wallpaper* you might examine the idea of the conscious versus the subconscious, or you might examine how this story was written to describe psychological processes, or you may examine they way in which such patients/people were seen by society at that time (social).
(Singhal, 2001)

Figure 12 Framework for Understanding a Text in Context

The exercise below gets students to think about another literary device-point of view. Students can rewrite this piece in first person, first from the composer's perspective and then from the artist's perspective. Encourage students to read their works out loud. Such an activity helps students to understand that literature is about the human experience. They also understand how point of view re-creates or distorts a written text and the interpretation, or even how their own beliefs and influence their interpretations and perspectives.

A Story About the Body by Robert Hass (portion of text below from Human Wishes)

"The young composer, working that summer at an artist's colony, had watched her for a week. She was Japanese, a painter, almost sixty, and he thought he was in love with her. He loved her work, and her work was like the way she moved her body, used her hands, looked at him directly when she made amused and considered answers to his questions. One night, walking back from a concert, they came to her door and she turned to him and said, "I think you would like to have me. I would like that too, but I must tell you that I have had a double mastectomy," and when he didn't understand, "I've lost both my breasts." The radiance that he had carried around in his belly and chest cavity-like music-withered very quickly, and he made himself look at her when he said, "I'm sorry. I don't think I could." He walked back to his own cabin through the pines, and in the morning he found a small blue bowl on the porch outside his door. It looked to be full of rose petals. But he found when he picked it up that the rose petals were on top, the rest of the bowl-she must have swept them from the corners of her studio, was full of dead bees."

Figure 13 Exercise to Understand Point of View

ClassZone.com publishes numerous activities including those under the title *The Language of Literature Teacher Center.* This website can be found at: <http://www.classzone.com/disc_languagearts.cfm>. Numerous literature pieces are online with various types of questions. These include an overview of the story, an instructional focus area which assists teachers in designing class tasks, class discussion activities with comprehension questions, think-pair-share activities, role playing activities, and real world connection activities. Overall, the literature activities on the site provide excellent examples of the range of activities given any piece of literature.

Numerous similar activities can be found at: <http://www.eastoftheweb.com/short-stories/teacher.html>. This site, East of the Web, includes a variety of genres including fiction, non-fiction, science-fiction, short stories, humor, horror, and hyperfiction. The link above also includes lesson plans and reading activities and materials for the stories provided online for teachers to use with their students. Other literature resources can be found at: <http://www.readingmatrix.com/archivedir/Literature_and_Poetry/>.

The above lessons and examples describe some of the ways in which literature can be incorporated in the language classroom. Teachers are continually using their expertise, experience, and imagination to create a range of tasks and activities centered on the literary text that go beyond simple comprehension question-answers which provide little room for student responses or their personal involvement. While it is simply not possible to describe all of these literature-related tasks and activities in a single book, let alone a chapter, the following chart does provide an additional list of possible ideas, activities, and techniques teachers may find useful when using literature in the language class. Several others provide even more concrete ideas of how literature can be incorporated in the language classroom (Agathocleous & Dean, 2003; Carter & Long, 1991; Collie & Slater, 1987; Duff & Maley, 1990; Gower & Pearson, 1987). Others provide instructors with strategies and advice for incorporating elements of computer technology into the literature classroom (Agathocleous & Dean, 2003; Kline, 2002).

Literature-Related Ideas and Activities

- Ask students to make predictions about the book, story, and its mood by examining the title, cover, and illustrations.

- Have students create the first scene of the book based on their predictions. They can share their scenes with their classmates.

- Use pictures of characters or people who may be similar to characters in the book in terms of occupation, etc and ask guided questions to make students more aware about the issue(s) in question.

- Write a note or letter to a character in the story.

- Take on the role of a character and write a diary entry in first person.

- The teacher selects key words from the first part of the text. Students can work in groups to brainstorm possible narrative links between the words.

- Have students listen to a recorded discussion about the book and have them comment on what they agree and disagree with.

- Have students create a biographical montage on the author of the book and present it to the class.

- Take a section of the story and delete every seventh word and use as a cloze-exercise.

- Devise comprehension questions based on significant passages.

- Have students write endings to the various chapters before reading them. Students can discuss and compare their responses.

- Students can choose a character and come up with a product that they would endorse. Each student has to explain why he/she felt the product ties in with the character.

- Have students work in groups to discuss possible continuations. They improvise them and act them out.

- Each students takes on the role of a character. The teacher gives them a scenario and the students role play the situation based on how they believe the character would respond.

- Have students write paragraphs that come immediately before the first section of the work they have just encountered.

- Choose a section of the text and have students work as editors to make suggestions and changes. They have to explain the rationale for their changes.

- Have students write a summary of a portion of the text or whole text. Summaries can be compared.

- Students are given a jumbled list of a certain number of events that occur in the passage, which students have read and they are asked to place them in the correct sequence.

- Have students identify the moral of the story. Give students a list of morals and have them choose and explain their selection(s).

- Select a portion of the text in which there is no speech. Ask students to write a dialogue involving characters, allowing them to explore their view of a character or fictional situation.

- Use matching exercises such as words from the story or poem to a definition.

- Create a multiple-choice question sheet to check for comprehension.

- Create true-false quizzes to check for comprehension.

- Create worksheets with incomplete sentences based on content and situations in the story. Students must fill the blanks. Answers may differ leading to class discussion.

- Create a poster containing only visuals (magazine cut-outs, drawing, charts), which depict a chosen theme in the story. The teacher may choose to have a formal Poster Session such as at a conference where students discuss and explain their poster.

- Teacher can have students answer a question sheet or grid related to a character in the work. The same questions can be given again at a later point in the story so that students can draw on their expanded knowledge of the character. Question sheets and grids can be compared.

- Students can write a synopsis for the back cover of the book or a critique of the book.

- Students can write a newspaper article or magazine article about a particular scene.

- Students can write an epitaph on a character, which in many ways helps them to better understand the character.

- Students can participate in mini-read alouds to develop their awareness of intonation, rhythm, stress, and other aspects of oral language.

- Students can give oral summaries and these can even be recorded and compared by the class.

- Teachers can prepare statements relating to the literary work that students are asked to agree or disagree with. This can promote class discussion and students will have to explain why they made such choices.

- Students can be given a series of issues related to the literary work and the teacher can set up debate teams to debate these controversial issues.

- Students can work in groups to analyze one particular aspect of the literary work. These might include imagery, paradox, foreshadowing, repetition, recurring themes, use of particular objects, etc. The material gathered can even be used to support the writing of an essay.

- Students can work together to videotape and create a film trailer for the literary work.

- The teacher can have students listen to a critical commentary on the book and then note-take and respond to the commentary.

- A section of the work can be re-written for a different or very specific audience.

- Teachers can have students choose an issue and write a Text-in-Context essay in which they examine that issue and support their claim by using support from the literary text itself and secondary research sources.

- Teachers can have students write a Literary Analysis Essay in which they explain the purpose of the text and analyze the literary elements used by the writer to accomplish that purpose.

- Students can write a Reader-Response essay in which students describe how the book helped them to better understand a personal issue and how their perspective on that issue has been impacted.

Figure 14 Literature-Related Ideas and Activities

Without a doubt literature does have a place in the second language classroom. For many students literature can motivate them to read in the language. Literature illustrates how language is used and the contexts in which it is used. It builds on students' existing knowledge and furthers their content, linguistic, and textual schemata. Literature encourages cultural understanding, language development, and personal growth, all reasons for using literary works in the classroom. Teachers' success in using literature, of course, greatly depends on the selection of texts and way in which they are incorporated. In essence, one of the most effective ways of teaching second language students is through the reading and writing of literature. Literature can be extremely inspiring, can prompt students to write their own stories, and can encourage them to take risks as readers and writers, ultimately promoting their interest in reading itself.

Summary

The inclusion of literature in the second/foreign language reading class can be extremely beneficial to L2 readers. Literature can engage students' interest thereby motivating them to read more. It allows students to become familiar with different places and different people, beliefs and cultures. Because literary texts often include authentic language and dialects, exposure to such texts further enables learners to develop an awareness of language use as well and leads to language enrichment. Therefore, use of literature in the L2 classroom expands content, linguistic, and textual schemata. When selecting literary texts, teachers should choose texts of appropriate difficulty level, those that are rich in cultural and social content, and those that are relevant to their students' lives. Learners need frequent opportunities to read so sharing and collecting good literature with them will aid this process and create readers who will take control of their own learning. Finally, literature-based activities should emphasize both efferent reading, the ability to understand a text and obtain information from it, as well as aesthetic reading, the ability to interact with the text and the textual elements, and to appreciate the text as a literary piece. In sum, through literature, learners can extend their experiences and knowledge, compare ethnical concepts and values, and discover the beauty and grandeur of language.

Discussion Questions and Activities

1. Select a literary piece such as a short story or poem and create a lesson plan for a group of beginner-level learners.

2. Observe a class with students working in literature response groups. What are the advantages of literature response groups? Are there any disadvantages? Would you do anything differently from the classroom you observed?

3. Develop a Reader's Theater script for a group of adult language learners.

4. Observe several classrooms in which teachers feel that literature is central to learning. Describe some of the literature-based activities students participated in. Describe the views of the teacher towards literature study? What role does the teacher play? What are the students' attitudes toward literature? Do they read in their free time?

5. Read "A Clean-Well Lighted Place" by Ernest Hemingway. Write 8-10 comprehension questions and 8-10 questions focusing on the language or literary elements.

6. Select a novel appropriate for intermediate-level learners. After becoming familiar with the text, describe 10 different activities related to the novel you could have your students participate in throughout the semester. These activities would be designed to both enhance their understanding of the text, and build their language and critical thinking skills.

Chapter 7
Vocabulary Issues and Reading

Vocabulary knowledge is a central component to understanding texts. Therefore, teachers need to find ways to help their students develop their vocabulary knowledge and their skills to deal with unknown words. This chapter begins by providing an overview of the various approaches to vocabulary instruction. It then illustrates problems unique to the second language learner. Finally, the chapter discusses the ways in which vocabulary can be successfully taught by considering effective vocabulary learning strategies and methods of teaching vocabulary.

Introduction

Vocabulary is extremely important for extracting meaning from text. Second language or foreign language learners most commonly claim that vocabulary is one of their main weaknesses and that they need to learn vocabulary so that they can understand the texts they are reading. While comprehension of language structures such as syntax helps learners understand the relationships between sentences and ideas, it does not provide direct access to the meaning of the sentence. Although teachers do spend time teaching vocabulary, time constraints and coverage of large numbers of vocabulary items is often not possible. Typically learners' receptive vocabulary, that is words they recognize but don't use, is larger than their productive vocabulary, words they use when they speak and write. While not every word learners are exposed to needs to become a part of their productive vocabulary, learners to need to expand their vocabulary knowledge base to better understand both academic and literary texts. Although vocabulary teaching is often viewed as being straightforward in that learners simply need sufficient exposure to words, it is a much more complex task than many learners themselves realize. As Nation (1990) points out, learning a word means recognizing form (recognizing the word in print and distinguishing the grammatical forms of the word), position (understanding the grammar patterns and structures in which a word can occur), function (knowing the situations and contexts in which the word would most likely occur), and meaning (knowing the various meanings, nuances and subtleties of a word as well as its synonyms). Teachers are continuously faced with the task of deciding which words students need to know, and the most appropriate, effective, and useful ways of teaching those words to their students. While this chapter focuses on vocabulary instruction, readers may wish to consult Read (2000) for a comprehensive review of research related to vocabulary assessment and a range of procedures for assessing the vocabulary knowledge of second language learners.

Approaches to Second Language Vocabulary Acquisition

This section describes the main approaches to L2 vocabulary instruction. It is beyond the scope of this chapter to discuss the numerous vocabulary studies related to each approach or vocabulary acquisition research; however, this section does address the rationales proposed by advocates of these approaches. For an extensive discussion of the studies supporting these approaches readers are encouraged to consult the works cited and for a fuller discussion of L2 vocabulary research issues and studies, readers may wish to consult (Coady & Huckin 1997; Coxhead, 2000; Coxhead & Nation, 2001; Nation 2001; Schmitt, 2000). While several main approaches are presented here, it is important to keep in mind that a variety of approaches are often used in the classroom depending on a number of factors including student proficiency level, task or activity, and the purpose of the activity.

Context Studies

One position taken is that students will learn all the vocabulary they need from context alone by simply reading extensively, as long as there is comprehension. Krashen (1989) for example, argues that vocabulary is acquired by reading. He states that students should read large quantities of reading materials that interest them. His main argument is that comprehensible input is what leads to language learning and therefore large amounts of comprehensible input in terms of reading materials will lead to vocabulary acquisition. Research by Nagy and Herman (1984) and Nagy, Herman and Anderson (1985) shows that children do learn large numbers of words by means of incidental learning from written context, but if a child were to encounter 10,000 unknown words in a given period, he or she might learn 1000-1500 of them. It seems logical then that readers should be taught to use clues in the text to help decipher new words and a blend of direct-definition instruction, and vocabulary learning through context clues can be more effective than one method alone.

Strategy Instruction Studies

The proponents of this view also support the context view of vocabulary acquisition but also emphasize the teaching of specific learning strategies so that students can effectively learn from context. It must be noted that most of these studies have focused on advanced L2 learners who have significant competence in the target language already. Specific vocabulary instruction strategies might include using the key word method (learning new words by learning a keyword "word clue" for each vocabulary word); associating (making associations to other L1 or L2 words or concepts); incidental learning (learning through reading or listening to others read); repeated exposure (using new vocabulary across the curriculum); pre-teaching vocabulary (explicitly teaching word meanings, parts, and usage before reading); restructuring reading materials (substituting an easier synonym for a harder word, summarizing or paraphrasing, or dramatizing a text); and the context method (using clues in the text to help decipher new words). In essence, researchers emphasize that because of the great variation across learners, the teaching of vocabulary learning strategies is essential. Studies by Ahmed (1989) found that successful learners used more vocabulary learning strategies and more frequently than less successful learners, and Oxford and Crookall (1990) concluded that different vocabulary learning strategies may be appropriate to different students. Other studies have found that direct instruction in a range of strategies including keyword approaches, and metacognitive awareness has led to greater vocabulary acquisition (Altman, 1997; Hulstijn, 1997; Nation, 2001; Oxford & Scarcella, 1994; Parry, 1997). The main position of proponents of this view is that the development of extensive vocabulary knowledge requires some direct instruction and strategy training, as well as extensive reading.

Explicit Vocabulary Instruction

Research in this area has for the most part focused on elementary learners of English and has shown that explicit teaching of certain types of vocabulary using a range of techniques can lead to acquisition. Because the focus has been on the younger learner, there is a greater emphasis on the vocabulary skills needed by students at an earlier stage in their acquisition of the language. Nation (1990, 2001) for example, argues that the 2000 most frequent words need to be learned as quickly as possible. Context-specific vocabulary must also be addressed. For example, students using language for academic purposes should be exposed to and should learn academic vocabulary. The University Word List (UWL) first published in 1984 (Xue & Nation) is a list of vocabulary items common in academic texts. It is composed of 808 words, divided into 11 levels. This list is designed to be a list of specialized vocabulary for students who know about 2000 generally common words and plan to study in an English-language college or university. This list has now, however, been replaced by a new word list. Most recently many reading programs have included a component focusing on teaching words from the *Academic Word List* compiled by Averil Coxhead at Victoria University of Wellington in New Zealand (Coxhead, 1998; 2002). The list was developed from a corpus of approximately 3,500,000 running words of written academic text by examining the range, frequency and uniformity of occurrence of words outside the first 2,000 words of English (West, 1953). This corpus contains four disciplines, which include arts, commerce, law, and science, and each discipline is made up of seven subject areas. The AWL highlights the words which learners will meet in a wide range of academic texts and also provides a useful basis for further research into the nature of academic vocabulary. The division of this word list into smaller sublists helps in the sequencing of teaching and materials, so that a systematic approach to vocabulary learning can be taken. In general, the format would be as follows: Learners would read academic texts and listen to academic lectures and discussions. Where possible, the written and spoken texts would not be too difficult for learners, with no more than about 5% of the running words in the texts being new words for the learners. Learners would also have opportunities to speak in academic discussions and write academic texts using academic vocabulary. Finally, learners would directly study words from the list using word cards and engaging in intensive study of short academic texts (Coxhead & Nation, 2001). In sum, those who include a focused study on vocabulary in such a way would clearly say that a second lexicon can be identified and the effects of knowing them predicted. Furthermore, the goal for L2 readers would be to arrive at a point where 95% of the words are known in an average text which is the point at which independent reading and further acquisition can take place. Other studies have shown that explicit instruction coupled with contextualized reading can lead to greater gains in vocabulary acquisition (Nation, 2001; Paribakht & Wesche, 1997; Zimmerman, 1994).

Classroom Activities

Advocates of this view believe that vocabulary words are best learned through traditional classroom activities, which are often found in practical handbooks for teachers. These books do not advocate any particular methodological approach but offer a variety of activities that teachers can choose from. Beginner level activities, for example, might include communicative activities, picture-matching, and games. Intermediate level activities might include task work, simplified readings, and many other vocabulary activities, many of which are described below in Figure 5. Advanced students might benefit from dictionary work, vocabulary learning strategies, and comprehension work on reading passages. In short, the basic view here is that teachers can use a number of different kinds of activities, several of which are discussed in a latter portion of this chapter, and integrate them into the classroom situation when the need arises.

Lexical Problems in Vocabulary Acquisition

The comprehension of text is affected by textually relevant background knowledge and the application of general reading strategies such as predicting the context of the text, guessing unknown words in context, making inferences, recognizing text structure, and so forth. Yet research in both first and second language students has shown that reading comprehension is strongly related to vocabulary knowledge (Coady & Huckin, 1997; Laufer, 1997; Nation, 2001). These studies indicate that an improvement in reading comprehension can be attributed to an increase in vocabulary knowledge and that increased proficiency in high frequency vocabulary also leads to an increase in reading proficiency. Research has also demonstrated that while many L2 readers make use of various reading strategies such as syntactic knowledge and background knowledge, most readers in interpreting texts, tend to regard words as main landmarks of meaning. Background knowledge is relied on to a lesser extent and syntax is almost disregarded. These studies mainly indicated that lexical problems in large part hinder successful comprehension.

Laufer (1997) points out that there are three main lexical problems that may affect reading comprehension which include the problem of insufficient vocabulary, misinterpretations of deceptively transparent words, and the inability to guess unknown words correctly. L2 readers often have difficulty applying reading strategies to texts that they do not understand. For example, if a reader had to determine the main and supporting ideas of a text, it would be difficult to do so unless he or she had a fairly good understanding of the text. On the other hand, identification of text structure might be a simpler task, provided the text had a number of discourse and text markers. For example, a text with such words as "argument," "supports," "evidence," might suggest to the reader that the text is an argumentative one in which the writer makes an argument and then supports it with evidence. However, this strategy itself is of little use if the reader is still unaware of overall meaning and what the specific claims and evidence are. It is, therefore, essential that L2 readers reach a threshold vocabulary. While there is some disagreement over how many words one must know in order to be able to use higher level processing strategies effectively, results of several studies suggest that vocabulary should not be below the minimum of 3,000 word families or 5,000 lexical items.

The second problem affecting reading comprehension is deceptive transparency of words. Words that look familiar will be interpreted to mean what the learner thinks they mean. There are five main types of deceptively transparent words. The following chart, a summary of Laufer's (1997) findings, explains and provides an example of each type.

	Explanation	Example
Words with a deceptive morphological structure	Words that look as if they were composed of meaningful morphemes. The learner assumes that the meaning of a word equaled the sum of meanings of its components.	*Outline* is misinterpreted as *out of line*
Idioms	The learner assumes that the meaning of the whole was the sum of the meaning of its parts.	*In the same boat* or *add fuel to the fire*
False Friends	The learner assumes that if the form of the word in the L2 resembled the form in the L1, the meaning does as well.	*Tramp* interpreted as *lift* because in Hebrew it is *tremp.*
Words with multiple meanings	Learner assumers that the familiar meaning of a word is the only meaning.	*Abstract* means *not concrete* (in all cases) but it can also mean a *summary*
Synforms	The learners misinterpret synforms (pairs/groups of words that are similar in form (sound or morphologically similar).	(cute/acute), (conceal, cancel) (economic/economical), (reduce/deduce).

Figure 1 Types of Deceptively Transparent Words

Given the kinds of errors related to deceptive transparency, it is imperative that readers have a better awareness of deceptively transparent words. Doing so will result in a larger number of correctly interpreted words which in turn will enhance text comprehension.

The third major lexical problem that affects reading comprehension is related to the inability to guess words correctly. This occurs when the reader is trying to guess unknown words, those that are unfamiliar to them. Guessing may be possible to some extent but there are a number of factors that interfere with guessing attempts of the reader. The following chart, which summarizes Laufer's (1997) findings, explains each type.

	Explanation
Nonexistent contextual clues	Clues may not always be available in the text and therefore readers cannot simply "discover" them.
Unusable contextual clues	The learner may not be able to use all the clues in the text because the clues might not be understandable to the reader.
Misleading and partial clues	The reader might assume that because something looks right in a context, it is right but this may not be the case. Readers may be deceived by the notion that there is no need to understand the precise meaning of words when the reader may be satisfied with what makes sense in the context, whether is it right or wrong.
Suppressed Clues	If the reader's schemata, expectations, and concepts are different than the author's, readers may disregard information or may impose their own interpretation on the text, suppressing clues that are relevant and suggest a different meaning. The reader's background knowledge may be so strong that it overrides lexical and syntactic clues to meaning.

Figure 2 Factors interfering with identification of word meanings

Given the above discussion, without a doubt, effective reading requires vocabulary knowledge. This is not to say that reading comprehension and vocabulary are one in the same, or that reading quality is determined by vocabulary alone. But while reading strategies are employed by readers to make sense of text, they are of little use if the words of the texts themselves are incomprehensible to the reader.

Methods and Strategies in Vocabulary Teaching
Pre-Reading Vocabulary

Once teachers have selected the text to be used, they need to decide which vocabulary words to teach before students begin to read. This decision is based on what students already know, what they need to know to comprehend the text, and what they will need to know in the future.

Teachers may find it useful to begin by teaching students topic-specific or content-specific vocabulary. For instance, if students will be reading an article on the Internet, it would be useful to present words that might appear frequently in such a text. For example, these words might include *website, URL, hypertext, password, WWW, search engine, browser, cyberspace, chatroom*, and so forth. Working with such vocabulary prior to the reading will enable students to have a general understanding of these words and recognize them when they encounter them in the text.

To present vocabulary before reading, teachers can use exercises presented in textbooks or can create their own activities and exercises. As stated, students can benefit from previewing topic-specific or content-specific vocabulary. By doing so, teachers create the concept or meaning of the word before students are exposed to it in the text. It is crucial therefore that vocabulary is introduced in the context of the topic of the reading text rather than simply a list of vocabulary words that are separate from the topic. This framework of the context enables students to both comprehend and remember words, which in turn facilitates their learning of the word. As Silberstein (1994) points out, the ability to determine the meaning of vocabulary items from context is one of the most important aspects of successful reading. Activities of this type provide practice in inferring meaning from context, which is an important reading skill, and the additional contexts introduced by the teacher provide semantic links that aid readers in remembering items. While vocabulary from context activities are often practiced using reading passages or full discourse context, teachers can create sentence-level activities that ensure students will gain a general sense of the term. Sentence-level items can be taken directly from the text to be read, and teachers can create additional new sentences rich in context. Silberstein (1994), as shown below, also points out that it is important to make students aware of the types of contexts that provide meaning of an unfamiliar word. Figure 3 provides some examples.

Examples: This neighborhood is so *affluent* that most residents have swimming pools and luxury cars.
My friend loves collecting *antiques* and has a garage full of old items such as old radios, clocks, and sixteenth century dolls.

Synonyms: She seems to have an *innate* talent for learning languages. Being able to speak so many languages at such a young age requires an *inborn* gift.
Your instructions were quite *explicit*. Without such *clear* directions we never would have found the place.

Antonyms: His mother was *lenient* when he lied about doing his chores, but when she found out he lied about missing school, she was *harsh* in her punishment.
Utah's population is fairly *homogeneous*, but in Long Beach there are people from all over the world so the population is quite *diverse*.

Description: My mother received a *topiary* as a gift. It is a plant trimmed into a fanciful, round shape.
I love *strudel*; it's a pastry made of very thin sheets of dough baked in long rolls that are filled with fruit, nuts, cheese, or vegetables.

General Sense of the Sentence or Passage: The police *quelled* the demonstration before it got out of control.
Grasp your mother's hand tightly when you move through the crowded streets so you don't lose each other.

Figure 3 Types of Context to Determine Word Meaning

During Reading Vocabulary

Teachers should emphasize that vocabulary takes time to acquire and that the primary way to expand vocabulary is to read more. The more students read, the more the process will occur naturally. However, as students read, there are specific strategies that should become second nature to them. These include phonics, context, word structure analysis, and dictionary use. Many students have been taught to use phonics or to "sound the word out" in order to determine an unknown word. While phonics often has no connection to actual word meaning, this can still be a good idea in college reading because occasionally hearing the word will trigger something familiar to the student. The next two strategies, context and word structure, both discussed in more detail below, are other strategies students can use to determine meaning. And finally, if that does not work, students should consult a dictionary (Nation, 1990).

Using Context

The use of context as a strategy is vitally important while students are reading. Guessing the meaning of a word from the other words around it, the context, is perhaps the most useful vocabulary skill that readers can have. The ability to use the words and information around an unknown word in order to guess or infer what that word means in a general sense will serve students well in almost every reading situation. Students should begin by examining the unknown word and determining the part of speech. Looking at the relationship between the clause or sentence containing the unknown word and other sentences or paragraphs can sometimes be very helpful in deciphering word meaning. Sometimes this relationship will be signaled by a conjunction like *but, because, if* or *when*, or by an adverb like *however*, or *as a result*. Once a guess has been made, substitution of that word within the sentence can usually determine if it is an effective choice. Students can also verify that their guess was the same part of speech.

Given the above, it is also important that students learn to determine whether or not the meaning of the unknown word is vital both for the purpose for reading the text and for their comprehension of the material in the text. Readers should know that if they can get the overall gist of the text and understand it, they can probably skip over words they are unfamiliar with, provided they are not key words. Various strategies can be modeled so that students learn to distinguish key and non-key words. Teachers in fact can model such strategies while reading. For example, when reading out loud, and when faced with an unfamiliar word, the whole sentence should be read and then the students should be asked whether they understand the overall meaning of the sentence. If not, it is important to determine the meaning of some key words in that sentence. Another strategy is to examine the grammatical function of the word. If it is a function word such as an adverb or adjective, rather than a content word such as a noun or verb, the reader may be able to do without the meaning of the word (Aebersold & Field, 1997).

Word Structure Analysis

At the same time students are examining the context of the sentence, they should also look at the different parts of the unfamiliar word to see if there is a word part that they recognize. For example, they may be familiar with what "pre" or "re" mean especially before words like *preschool* or *regain*. When faced with less familiar words such as *presumption* or *reexamine*, students might recognize that these words are comprised of "pre" and "assumption" and "re" and "examine" respectively. Therefore, use of context in addition to word structure analysis can enable readers to determine word meanings in a given text. Teachers can also spend some time teaching students Latin and Greek stems and affixes that can provide clues to meaning. Charts and tables that students can fill in can be useful exercises because they encourage students to find groups of words containing those stems and affixes which can facilitate the acquisition of words as words can be learned as groupings. It is often the case that words containing these elements are best practiced in their original contexts and teachers simply need to draw students' attention to the fact that use of both content and word structure analysis can help them identify the meanings of unknown words.

Dictionary Usage

The dictionary plays an important role for college readers; however, most students tend to go to one extreme or the other when using the dictionary. Many students, in an effort to be careful and conscientious, will stop and look up every unfamiliar word they encounter. While for many students this may seem like a good idea, in practice it simply does not work for several reasons. First, it breaks the flow of reading, and it is difficult for the reader to remember what has been read previously. Second, it takes a tremendous amount of time, especially for college students who will encounter new terminology on a regular basis. Finally, this method requires students to have a dictionary with them at all times. Often as a result of encountering the problems just mentioned, students will simply stop consulting the dictionary altogether. Students should learn that the dictionary is a valuable resource after they have already tried to determine the meaning of an unfamiliar word through context and word structure analysis. For instance, there are times when a student might use both of these strategies, and the meaning is still unclear. Other times students may notice several unfamiliar words within the same sentence. Under these circumstances, students should refer to a dictionary for assistance.

Teachers must also spend some time teaching students how to effectively understand the information presented in a dictionary and how to best use their dictionaries. Dictionaries often present a great deal of information but because students are not clear about what this means, they often overlook some very helpful details. Students can benefit from being aware of the following information:

Guide to Using the Dictionary

Guide Words: These are the two words found at the top of each page. They tell the reader the first word entry on the page and the last word entry on the page. These words can help a reader to locate a word more quickly than by scanning down each page looking for the word they want.

The Entry Word: This is the boldface word to the left of the definition. Entry words are listed in alphabetical order and are usually divided into syllables.

Superscript Numbers: Occasionally there are words that have identical spellings but distinctly different meanings and origins. Each of these may be listed separately with a small raised number following.

Pronunciation: The pronunciation of a word is usually in parentheses after the entry word. A key to using the pronunciation symbols usually appears at the bottom of each page as well as in the front of the dictionary.

Part-of-Speech Labels: Most dictionaries give an abbreviation indicating the part of speech of the entry word. These abbreviations are simply the first letter(s) of the part of speech. For example, "adj." would be used for an adjective.

Definitions: Many words in a dictionary have shades of meaning or slight variations of the basic definition. These are listed separately after the entry word in most dictionaries. These definitions are usually preceded by a number and, in some instances, may be subdivided and set off by letters in order to show a related sense of the word.

Etymologies: Following the definition(s) of a word is the etymology or word origin, which is usually in brackets. This tells the reader where the word originated. The etymology will also tell readers how the original word was spelled and its meaning in that language. Often there is a direct connection between a current definition and the history of the word.

Synonyms: Word entries might be followed by word synonyms, a list of words with similar meanings. Synonyms can be especially useful to students when writing.

Adapted from *Strategies for Interactive Reading* (Zinn & Poole, 1996)

Figure 4 Student Guide to Using and Understanding the Dictionary

The above information can assist students in using their dictionaries more effectively. There are, however, various other kinds of problems readers may encounter when using a dictionary. Students may have trouble when a form of the word is contained in the definition. For instance, if a student were looking up the meaning of *accusation* and within its definition found the word *accuse*, it would then be necessary to take that extra step by looking up *accuse*. The same is true if the definition contains an unfamiliar word or two. This is one reason it is especially important that teachers assist students in selecting the best dictionary for them – preferably those that also contain example sentences. Students most frequently complain that they have trouble deciding among the several definitions listed for multiple-meaning words. Once again, teachers must encourage students to revisit the context of the sentence in order to select the most appropriate meaning for a word.

Post-Reading Vocabulary

It is essential that students revisit vocabulary after the text has been read and discussed. Of course it may be necessary to do some vocabulary work prior to discussion of the text as comprehension and examination of the meaning of the text must come before examination of the language used to convey meaning, but that will depend on the difficulty level of the text itself. Teachers must therefore use their judgment in deciding how and when vocabulary learning will occur once text has been read. Revisiting vocabulary, however, can enhance student comprehension of the text and can promote vocabulary development. Textbooks often include vocabulary exercises both before and after readings often focusing on both recognition and production of words. Some texts include word lists at the back of books with definitions and students should be made aware of such resources. The following section on "Examples of Vocabulary Practice Activities" provides some examples of common types of textbook activities. While only one or two examples for each type are provided, teachers will have a sense of the range of possible vocabulary activities. As students become increasingly more proficient in the target language and more independent as learners, teachers can assist them in taking charge of their own vocabulary development. Teaching students a system whereby students can learn and develop their own vocabulary is vital for vocabulary improvement and for helping them become independent readers. Students can be encouraged to dialog with text as they read, noting the meanings of new words in the margins of the texts they are reading or on a separate sheet of paper. Students should be keeping vocabulary logs in which they write the word, write the pronunciation of the word, identify the part of speech of the word, record related family words, copy the dictionary example of the word, write the definition of the word, record any synonyms provided in the dictionary, and finally, write their own sentence using the word. This can be done in a traditional book format, for example in a spiral notebook, or students can carry index cards attached to a metal ring. Regardless of the form the vocabulary log takes, working with a word in such detail provides reinforcement and can lead to actual learning of the word. Students can also revisit words in the text and write paraphrases on the sentences in which those words are used, and can also substitute synonyms for those words. This kind of activity builds both paraphrasing skills and strengthens word association and use-of-context skills. In sum, no matter how much structure a teacher provides to help students learn vocabulary, ultimately students will have to take the responsibility of developing their own vocabulary. As teachers, we can however, provide them with vocabulary learning strategies they can use throughout their language learning experience.

Examples of Vocabulary Practice Activities

There are numerous types of vocabulary building exercises that teachers can use and create to facilitate vocabulary development. The following chart provides an overview of these kinds of activities.

Vocabulary Tips, Techniques, and Activities

Matching Synonyms

Tired ----- a. Upset
Angry-----b. Fatigued

Matching Opposites

Lethargic -------Energetic
Straightforward--------Vague

Matching Definitions

Band (verb) -------to enlist or draft someone into the army, to hire
Recruit ------- to come together as a group

Fill in the blank sentences
(cultured, antidote, cultured, anthropology)

1. The doctor prescribed an _____ for the poison.
2. I would like to take a course in _____ to learn about different cultures.
3. Sometimes writers or poets get their work published in an _____.
4. She is a very _____ woman who reads a lot and travels all over.

Fill in the blank (variation) – Choose all the possible answers.

He ate lunch at the _____.
cafeteria, dine, restaurant, deli, diner, salad bar, snack bar

Cloze Exercise

I went to the store to buy _____ bread. It was late and so the store was _____ by the time I got there.

Complete the Phrases

To achieve -------a. a skill
To master ------ b. a goal

Label the Diagram (provide a diagram with blanks-link to theme)

Mouse
Monitor
Mouse pad
Tower
Keyboard

Categories: Teacher gives the example; students give the category or vice versa.

Knife, gun, rifle – weapon

Furniture – table, chair, bed, sofa

Cross out the word that does not belong.

uncle / father / aunt / brother
robin/parrot/rat/canary
meadow / river / sea / lake

Complete the sentences (provide words or encourage use of context)

I felt so exhausted after_____.
It is ironic that _____.
I think he detonated _____.
An addition _____.

Analogies

easy : hard :: cold : _____ *(hot)*
skyscraper : city :: tree : _____ *(forest)*
warp : wood :: _____ : paint *(peel)*
shatter : glass :: _____ stone *(crumble)*

Which word is stronger?

Tired, Exhausted
Throw, hurl
Surprised, shocked

Arrange the words on a scale

hot - warm - luke - warm - cool - cold
despise - hate – dislike

Which word in each pair is *slang?*

___ a kid / ___ a child
___ disgusting / ___ gross
___ to fail / ___ to flunk

Which word has a more *positive connotation?*
***or* Which word would be more *polite* when talking about a person?**

___ thin / ___ skinny
___ fat / ___ overweight
___ frugal / ___ miserly

Choose the two answers that can complete each sentence.

He pondered . . .
(a) his future
(b) that he didn't know what to do. [*ungrammatical*]
(c) the meaning of life.

Guessing word meaning from context

His mother was *lenient* when he lied about doing his chores, but when she found out he lied about missing school, she was *harsh* in her punishment.
Utah's population is fairly *homogeneous*, but in Long Beach there are people from all over the world so the population is quite *diverse*.

Part of Speech Chart (place the following words in the appropriate category)
nice,   nicely,   literature,   literary
Adjective   Adverb   Noun   Verb

Act out/pantomime

Give students cards with instructions like the ones below. Have them perform the actions without speaking. The other students try to guess the word or expression the student is pantomiming.
Open the door *fearfully*.
Walk across the room *cautiously*.

Crossword Puzzles

Several software programs are available which allow you to make your own puzzles. Clues can be synonyms, opposites, fill-in-the-blank sentences, etc.

Enhancing Meaning

Have students, in small groups, expand the meaning/use of a word according to the following categories: general meaning; parts of speech; derivative forms; synonyms; antonyms; and categories.

Word Families

When introducing a new word, write it on the board, along with its part of speech. Ask students to provide other related words.

Prefixes and Suffixes

Form the students into pairs - one being the teacher, the other a student. Provide each "teacher" with a list of prefixes and sample words using each prefix; provide each "student" with a list of meanings. Have the "teacher" say the prefix 2-3 times with a sample word. The "student" guesses the meaning of the prefix from the list. The "teacher" corrects if the "student" does not guess properly after the third attempt.

Vocabulary Notebook or Log

Have students write down unfamiliar words from a reading. Encourage them to write the meaning, part of speech, the sentence itself, a newly created sentence, and a visual to help them remember the word.

Keyword Technique

Have the students learn to use a key word from their first language that is associated with the word to be learned in English.

Figure 5 Vocabulary Tips, Techniques, and Activities

Extensive Reading and Vocabulary Acquisition

L1 research in vocabulary acquisition has given rise to the incidental vocabulary learning hypothesis which proposes that most vocabulary is learned gradually through repeated exposure in varying contexts (Nagy & Herman, 1985). This view holds that on average ten to twelve exposures to the word are necessary over time in order to learn it well. Proponents of this view essentially argue that extensive reading can promote vocabulary growth more than explicit instruction in vocabulary alone. The same views are put forth for L2 learners. Several L2 studies have shown that vocabulary acquisition can improve through extensive reading. The question, however, is how language learners who do not know enough words in the first place to read well, acquire vocabulary. Laufer (1997) points out that a beginner would require knowledge of 3000-5000 word families to achieve even modest comprehension. Coady (1997) provides a preliminary answer to the paradox facing beginning readers. He suggests that the vocabulary acquired through the medium of reading by L2 language learners can be divided into at least three major developmental categories: "those whose forms and common meanings are recognized automatically irrespective of context (or sight vocabulary); those whose forms and meanings are to some degree familiar to the learner but are recognized only in context; and those whose meanings, and often forms, are unknown to the learner and whose meanings must therefore be inferred from the context, looked up in a dictionary, or left uncomprehended" (p. 232). Coady (1997) points out that sight vocabulary consists of medium- to high-frequency words that have been learned through repeated exposure and explicit instruction. Less frequent words will most likely be learned through incidental contact through extensive reading, but only after a critical level of automaticity has been achieved with the high-frequency vocabulary. The implication here is that teachers must assist readers in learning the 3,000 most frequent words so that they become part of their sight vocabulary.

One of the main issues of course is how to get learners to engage in extensive reading. Day and Bamford (2002) suggest that there are many factors, which are interrelated such as not understanding text, reading slowly, not reading much, and not enjoying reading, which can be either causes or effects of one another, constituting the vicious cycle L2 readers are often trapped in. Nuttall (1982) states that one must break the chain in order to move from the vicious circle to the virtuous circle in which one enjoys reading, reads faster, understands better, and reads more. As many proponents of extensive reading would argue, this is best accomplished through pedagogical efforts that emphasize reader interest, theme of text, match between reader's background knowledge and the text, and the linguistic and cultural authenticity of the text.

Regardless of the methods used, words are essential to language learning. The essential question is how one acquires them. Meaningful experiences and exposure to the target language will certainly lead to increased proficiency. Language acquisition in this case can occur over time through contextual use. If, however, students need to use language for academic tasks and have a limited amount of time in which to acquire these skills, then an instructional or strategy approach will be more beneficial. Moreover, the literature also suggests that systematic vocabulary instruction paired with reading can be a much more successful approach than approaches focusing on learning through context alone or vocabulary instruction alone.

Summary

Vocabulary instruction is an essential element of any reading class as it is vocabulary itself that provides direct access to the meaning of a word. There are numerous approaches to teaching vocabulary which range from emphasizing extensive reading to build word knowledge, strategy instruction which emphasizes the teaching of specific learning strategies so that students can learn from context and use word parts to determine word meanings, to explicit vocabulary instruction, which emphasizes the teaching of word lists, words groups, and academic vocabulary. Research in vocabulary acquisition studies has shown that lexical problems stem from inadequate background knowledge, insufficient vocabulary, misinterpretations of deceptively transparent words where a word may look similar to another word, but differs in meaning, and the inability to apply word identification strategies or the inability to guess unknown words correctly. Pre-reading strategies such as teaching topic-specific or content vocabulary prior to reading texts can help students to better understand concept or meanings before they are exposed to it in the readings. Phonics, context usage, word structure analysis, and dictionary use are the kinds of strategies students should be taught and have an opportunity to practice while reading. Meaningful activities that teach words connected to text topic and content, and activities that encourage the application of vocabulary learning strategies will lead to increased reading proficiency and more skillful readers.

Discussion Questions and Activities

1. Select a story that will be read to a group of students. Create a pre-reading exercise or activity and a post-reading exercise or activity that focuses on vocabulary.

2. Create a handout describing a technique that can be used with a group of students to note new vocabulary words. For example, one common technique is a vocabulary log which asks students to write down the word, part of speech, meaning and a sentence using that word. Make enough copies for your classmates so that you all have a selection of handouts to use and share.

3. Examine three or four L2/FL reading textbooks to determine what kind of vocabulary skills are emphasized before, during, and after reading. What kinds of instructional and learning strategies are emphasized through these activities?

4. Find a recently published article on vocabulary acquisition and second language learners. Write a summary of the article and share it with your peers.

5. Write a short lesson to explain the difference between the connotation and denotation of words.

6. Write a lesson which teaches students how to use context when determining the meaning of a word. You might want to use a short reading with your lesson.

Chapter 8
Reading Assessment

The teacher's role in the reading classroom is not only that of a facilitator but is also one of an assessor. Teachers encourage and facilitate learning but simultaneously evaluate what has been learned. In order to assess reading comprehension in a second or foreign language, it is necessary to understand what the reading assessment process entails. This chapter explores the various methods for assessing reading comprehension, which include journals, portfolios, reading logs, checklists, multiple-choice tests, recall protocols, cloze tests, vocabulary tests, comprehension questions, authentic and communicative tasks, and computer-based testing.

Introduction

Reading in a second language in many ways is similar to reading in the first language. However, L2 reading is often slower and less successful. There are several reasons for this. The slowness of L2 readers is often because their eye fixations are longer than native speakers (Adams, 1990; Rayner, 1975; McConkie, et.al, 1982). Many studies have shown that the difference between the eye movements of university-level ESL students and that of native readers was that the ESL students' eye fixations were almost three times as long. Second language readers are also faced with new and unknown vocabulary. In addition, the sentence structures may be too complex or very different from the syntax of their primary language. Learners can often misread sections of text because their expectations about the way grammar conveys meaning in the target language are conditioned by their experiences with grammar in their native language. Therefore, they may misinterpret structures that are not like those in their first language. Sentence complexity can be an impediment to grasping specific details, thereby affecting the learners' ability to adequately comprehend even the gist of the text. Thus, the lack of linguistic knowledge can cause difficulties for L2 learners. L2 readers may be less familiar with the rhetorical structures of different modes of texts or may be less familiar with the systems of factual knowledge values and cultural conventions. Hence, lack of textual and content schemata may be obstacles to comprehension. Given the array of factors that influence reading, it is absolutely necessary for teachers to find appropriate methods and a variety of ways to accurately assess their students to determine what they know and the areas that may need attention and practice. This chapter provides an overview of reading assessment and assessment tools. For a more detailed look at this subject, readers are advised to consult Alderson (2000) which reviews theory, research, and practice in the assessment of L2 and FL reading.

Assessing Reading Comprehension Ability

Over the years there has been a change in the way assessment of reading is viewed. The testing of reading is now more consistent with a strategic view of the reading process, rather than the idea that reading is a discrete skill (Alderson, 2000). Current theories of reading assert that the best assessment consists of having teachers observe and interact with students who are reading authentic texts for genuine purposes, and of having teachers see how their students constructed meaning.

Before considering the methods of assessment, it is important to understand the various types of reading assessed. Teachers must recognize that test items can be written so that they implicitly or explicitly call for different types of reading. For example, if a student is given a lengthy passage to read in a short amount of time, skimming the passage, that is inspecting it rapidly with occasional periods of close inspection, may be the only way to successfully handle the text. The students might also scan the text, that is read to locate specific information, or engage in a search reading wherein the reader is scanning without being sure about the form the information will take. Learners can also be given passages to read receptively or intensively, a form of careful reading aimed at discovering exactly what the author seeks to convey. Finally, students can read responsively with the written material acting as a prompt for them to reflect on some point or other and then possibly respond in writing. Testing formats in which questions are interspersed with running text may cater to such an approach. All of these types of reading can be assessed through various types of reading items and tasks. Learners should also be made aware of the different types of reading that are assessed on reading tests, and teachers or test constructers may even indicate to the reader the type of reading that is expected.

Types of Meaning and Knowledge Assessed

A reading test can tap various types of meaning and reader knowledge. When we are reading for the informational meaning of the text, our purpose is to determine what the basic concepts or messages are. In order to do this, readers must do enough analysis of the vocabulary to distinguish known and unknown words, concepts, and relationships between the ideas in the text. Nonnative speakers often have so much difficulty determining the literal or basic meanings of the idea units in a given text that determining the relationship between those ideas, the writer's attitude towards these ideas, or inferred meanings becomes secondary. Discourse meaning is another type of meaning that can be assessed. For example, an item may overtly or covertly require a reader to identify where and how something is being defined, described, classified, exemplified, or contrasted with something else. Such rhetorical functions are signaled by connectors or discourse markers. Less proficient readers may miss these markers--words or phrases like *however, thus, whereas,* and so on. Readers may also miss the transitional markers indicating time, sequence, etc. As Alderson (2000) emphasizes, given the different types of understanding, test constructors must consider the level of meaning they think their readers should have attained or ought to get out of a particular text when assessing how well or the degree to which they have understood the text in question.

Methods of Assessing Reading

Journals – A journal is a notebook or other semi-permanent container housing the writings of one student. Students in literature classes are frequently asked to keep journals in which they respond in writing to reading assignments. The journal can help students understand textbook material. Often, students make connections between what they read and their own lives, connections they sometimes do not make in more formal writing assignments. The journal also allows students to make connections between various selections they have read. They frequently pay attention to writers' styles because the journal encourages students to read more carefully.

It is important to note that teachers do not evaluate the journal for mechanics and usage. The entries, in essence, are rough drafts. However, teachers do respond to the content of the writing, pushing students to go beyond obvious or superficial comments and plot summary. Journals may be used as a basis for further student writing about topics found in the journals, topics which often deal with point of view, character analysis, or comparison and contrast. Students can also be asked to share entries with the class, and this frequently results in lively discussions because students have already done a great deal of thinking about the topic. The following is a list of beginning sentences that are useful in helping students start a reading journal:

- I like/dislike this idea because...
- This character reminds me of someone I know because...
- This character reminds me of myself because...
- This character is like [name of character] in [title of work] because...
- I think this setting is important because...
- This scene reminds me of a similar scene in...
- I like/dislike this writing because...
- This section is particularly effective because...
- The ideas here remind me of the ideas in [title of work] because...
- This incident reminds me of a similar situation in my own life. It happened when...

Figure 1 Journal Starters

Journals can be adapted in many ways and a number of authors provide effective examples of how journals can be used in the reading classroom (Green & Green, 1993). Student journals can be a highly effective way to keep learners involved in the processes of monitoring comprehension, making comprehension visible, applying knowledge, and gaining language proficiency.

Portfolios - Portfolios are systematic collections of student work over time. These collections help students and teachers assess student growth and development. It is essential that students develop a sense of ownership about their portfolios, so they can understand where they have made progress and where more work is needed. The content of portfolios will vary with the level of the student and will depend on the types of assignments they are given in class. The portfolio may include the student's journal, drafts of writing assignments for the class, homework exercises, tests, summaries of articles or other reading assignments, and statements of goals for reading. Reading logs and audiotape recordings can also be included. As portfolios are assembled, it is important that students keep them in a place where they have easy access to them. Students should be encouraged to browse through their portfolios and share them with classmates. Portfolio evaluation often occurs at three levels: the student, the student's peers, and the teacher. For each piece selected, students may be asked to describe briefly why they chose it, what they learned, and what their future goals are. Each portfolio entry needs to be assessed with reference to its specific goals. Since the goals and weighting of the various portfolio components has been predetermined, assessing the portfolio is not difficult. The following examples of assessment tools such as rating scales, checklists for the different skills, and self-assessment scales can be used and adapted according to a teacher's needs. Because students have invested a great deal of effort and time in their portfolio, it is recommended that the teacher provide feedback on the portfolio that is more than just a grade. One possibility might be to write a letter about the portfolio which details the strengths and weaknesses and generates a profile of a student's ability, which is then added to the portfolio. Teachers must also have short individual meetings with their students to discuss their progress and future goals.

Reading Portfolio Assessment Tools

Assessment tools related to portfolios include a wide range of such tools so teachers must develop and use those best suited to their needs. The following tables provide a small number of examples of the kinds of assessment tools inline with portfolio assessment (Singhal, 1999).

Self-Evaluation of Reading Strategy Use

Reading Strategies Check the box that best describes how you read.	Frequently	Occasionally	Rarely	Never
COGNITIVE STRATEGIES				
When I read part or whole of a story, I summarize or paraphrase those parts for a better understanding of the text.				
I use the title page and illustrations to help me understand the story.				
I use information in the story to help me determine the overall meaning of a text.				
If I don't understand the meaning of a word or expression, I spend time analyzing it for meaning.				
I reread the parts of a text several times if I don't understand.				
I preview the text to get a general idea of what it is about, how it is organized, and how it relates to what I already know.				
I use clues in the text to help me predict the outcome or future events of a story.				
I skim the reading passage first to get the main idea, and then I go back and read it more carefully.				
I find the meaning of a word by dividing the word into parts that I understand.				
I sound out words or repeat words that I do not know.				
COMPENSATION STRATEGIES				
If I don't know the meaning of a word I read, I guess the general meaning by using any clue I can find, for example, clues from the context or situation.				
If I don't know the right word for something or can't think of the correct expression, I find a different way				

to express the idea. For example, I use a synonym or describe the idea.				
I use reference materials such as glossaries or dictionaries to help me with the new language.				
MEMORY STRATEGIES				
I create associations between the new material and what I already know.				
I place the new word in a group with other words that are similar in some way.				
If I don't know the meaning of a word, I make an association with a word I already know rather than giving a nonsense word.				
I remember a new word by identifying it with a familiar word in my first language, which sounds like or resembles the new word.				
METACOGNITIVE STRATEGIES				
I am continually self-monitoring and evaluating myself while reading.				
I read without looking up every unfamiliar word.				
I try to notice and correct my language errors and find out reasons for them.				
I try to identify the purpose of the language activity.				
I direct my attention to the task.				
I read without omitting words or parts of words.				
I read without adding words or parts of words.				
I read without reversing order of letters in words or words in a sentence.				
I am able to recognize unknown words by repeating them.				
I am able to recognize what is important and not important and can skip those words.				
AFFECTIVE STRATEGIES				
I take risks wisely when I read.				
I make encouraging statements to myself so that I will continue to try hard and do my best.				
I pay attention to factors that may interfere with doing my best.				
I try to relax when using the new language.				
SOCIAL STRATEGIES				
I ask for clarification when I don't understand something.				
I ask people to verify that I have understood or said something correctly.				
I ask other people for feedback.				

Table 1 Reading Strategies Inventory Self-Assessment Chart

Portfolio Goals and Assessment Tools

Goal	Sample Classroom Activity	Portfolio Evidence	Assessment Tools
Understand articles discussed in class.	Read and summarize the texts.	Informal written retellings, main idea and summary chart, summaries of articles. Journal responses to articles.	Individual progress report, corrected summary items, self-assessment of summaries according to predetermined criteria-a checklist provided by teacher.
Understand simple short-stories.	Read stories. Identify the main events and characters. Plot diagrams.	Detailed plot diagrams. Journal response to particular aspect of story. Completed homework-comprehension questions.	Corrected test item-retelling of story and comprehension questions.
Appreciate Literature.	Reading of literature and poetry in class. Explanations of literary elements.	Reading logs and reading journal.	Self-assessment.
Critical analysis of arguments.	Close readings of argumentative texts. Explanations and practice with features of argumentative texts. Understanding writing strategies in argumentative texts.	Completed exercises including questions related to the text and the writer's strategies. Journal responses. Letters to the author.	Answer key to exercise questions.
Expansion of Vocabulary	Explaining vocabulary log and purpose of log. Studying affixes and roots. Defining words from an article in class and identifying part of speech. Identifying and defining words that are similar in form.	Ten new words a week in the Vocabulary Log which include the definition, part of speech, similar word forms, and example sentences using the words. Vocabulary quizzes.	Self-assessment of log and performance on quizzes, corrected test items, and completion of vocabulary log according to predetermined criteria.
Using simple resources and tools.	Work with a glossary, index, table of contents, dictionary. Search Engines	Alphabetizing words from a dictionary. Results of a search on the web as related to class topic.	Answer key to dictionary exercise. Appropriateness and usefulness of information obtained from the web. Information found, not found, partially found.

Table 2 Portfolio Goals and Assessment Tools

Assessment of ESL Student Reading Behaviors and Reading Level

READING BEHAVIORS AND STRATEGIES	Level 1 No or sometimes Emerging and Developing Reader	Level 2- On most occasions Expanding and Proficient Reader	Level 3- Always Highly Proficient and Independent Reader
COMPREHENSION-The reader demonstrates a thorough and insightful comprehension of the text.			
The reader makes insightful prediction about the text.			
The reader understands the purpose for his/her reading.			
The reader knows when he/she is having problems understanding the text and knows what strategies to use to improve comprehension.			
The reader can identify main ideas and supporting ideas.			
The reader can insightfully identify textual features and plot elements, and distinguish rhetorical modes and their features as well as locate details.			
The reader can thoroughly summarize the text using the most important information. The summary is focused and brief.			
CONTEXT - The reader demonstrates a thorough and insightful understanding of the context.			
The reader can identify the setting of the text and show how that setting affects the story.			
The reader demonstrates an insightful understanding of the contextual issues (political, historical, social, cultural, content area concepts).			
The reader understands the different points of views and perspectives (characters' points of view, subjects presented differently or within different paradigms).			
CONVENTIONS – The reader demonstrates a thorough and insightful understanding of text conventions.			

The reader can identify vocabulary, punctuation, and other grammatical conventions unique to the genre or rhetorical mode.			
The reader uses these features to read and understand the text.			
The reader can identify literary features and elements, and figurative language.			
The reader can identify the organizational conventions of the text and can use them to aid understanding.			
INTERPRETATION-The reader reads between the lines to make an insightful interpretation supported by thorough evidence from the text.			
The reader can insightfully identify problems, gaps, ambiguities in places where he/she must read between the lines and infer.			
The reader can insightfully locate details, clues, and evidence to aid in clarification.			
The reader can make insightful interpretations which are consistent with the clues and evidence in the text.			
EVALUATION – The reader makes an insightful judgment about the text and provides support for that judgment.			
The reader expresses insightful opinions about what he/she has read.			
The reader makes judgments that are thoroughly supported with details from the text.			
The reader challenges the text and the author when appropriate.			
The reader considers all sides of issue or argument in his/her judgment.			
The reader can respond to the aesthetic qualities of the text or literary piece and offer personal opinions.			

Table 3 Assessment Chart for ESL Student Reading Behaviors and Development Level

Reading Logs –Students can maintain a log of all their independent reading at school and at home. The log should include works completed and works started but not completed. In addition to the name of the book (article, etc.) and author, the log should include personal reactions to the selection. Periodic discussions of these logs will provide insight on how the student is developing as an independent reader and suggest ways in which the teacher can give added encouragement.

Checklists - Checklists can be completed by both readers and students. For example, a checklist can be used by a teacher to assess word and letter knowledge. The first step is to develop a list of the concepts to be tested. The student is then asked to demonstrate understanding of these concepts using a real book. The teacher uses the checklist to identify those concepts that have been mastered and those that need further work. Students can use checklists to review their own work. Teachers and students can prepare a list of specific skills that need to be worked on and students can then use this list to check their own work.

Multiple-Choice Questions - Multiple-choice tests are often favored as reading tests because their scoring is reliable and rapid. They are commonly used in standardized tests including language assessment tests like TOEFL. Reading books and tests will often have a set of multiple-choice questions following a reading passage. The choices in a multiple-choice question consist of a correct answer and a number of other responses called distractors. While multiple-choice tests are widely used, they are not without their shortcomings. Multiple-choice questions test only receptive knowledge and not productive skills. Guessing may have a considerable but unknowable effect on test scores, the format of the test is restrictive as it limits what can be tested, they are not effective teaching devices, and it is very difficult to construct successful multiple-choice questions.

Recall Protocols and Summaries - Reading protocols make the assumption that there is a direct relationship between what readers comprehend from a text and what they are able to recall. Therefore, those who recall to a greater degree and accuracy, comprehend to a greater degree. The basic procedure involves first selecting an unglossed text, approximately 200-300 words in length. Students should then be given opportunity to read the text as often as they like and when they finish, they are asked to put the text away and write down everything they remember. Many different methods are used to score protocols; however, a more expedient method involves obtaining the percentage of main ideas or main events inherent in the recall and the order of those ideas. For example, if the reader's recall protocol has a clear beginning, middle, and end and includes a sufficient number of main ideas and events to maintain the thread and gist of the text, that would indicate that the student comprehends the text. A rater might analyze a reader's retelling of a narrative using such questions as the following: To what extent was the reader able to: identify and describe the story characters, recall and describe the setting of the story, recall main ideas and events, retell the story events sequentially, relate the story to personal experiences and other selections. A rater could analyze a retelling of expository text by asking the extent to which the reader was able to: identify the central ideas, recall supporting details, and recall the organizational sequence of ideas. Teachers must also recognize that in order to obtain an accurate measure of assessment for each reader, and to maintain reliability, the instructions that the respondents are given regarding the completion of the task should be clear. For example, respondents should know whether they are to write a recall for a rater who is either fully familiar with the text or has never seen it before since this could affect the nature of the recall protocol. Respondents should also be told whether they are to produce the gist, or a complete recall with as many details as possible, and finally, whether they are to reproduce the surface structure of the text.

Recall protocols have been endorsed as an effective means of assessing L2 reading comprehension. Performance on such measures is consistent with performance on other language proficiency measures and scores from recall protocols are useful and interpretable because they provide both quantitative and qualitative information (Bernhardt, 1991; Singhal, 1999). Retellings also have further benefits as they show where a lack of grammar interferes with comprehension without focusing the reader's attention on linguistic elements, and they do not influence the reader's understanding of the text whereas other types of comprehension questions may form another "text" to be comprehended by the student.

Cloze Tests - The cloze test is another common type of assessment measure, more specifically a completion measure aimed at tapping reading skills interactively with learners using both bottom-up and top down global cues such as background knowledge to complete the task. The basic cloze test is a passage from which a word is deleted after every certain number of words according to the fixed-ratio procedure. In a cloze-test every fifth, sixth or seventh word might be deleted where in a fill-in-the-blank test, the teacher can determine which words the students are to recall. This type of test deletes words rationally on the basis of some linguistic criteria. The cloze test has been used as a measure of readability, global reading skills, grammar and writing. While such tests are easy to score and construct, it has been viewed as a micro-level completion test (a measure of word and sentence-level reading ability) rather than a macro-level of measure of skill at understanding connected discourse or the meaning of the text within a context. Teachers must also recognize that it is possible to do well on these tests without understanding the passage and without having an awareness of the context, and therefore it is unclear whether the reader understands the passage once completed.

Vocabulary Tests - Vocabulary assessment in an integral part of reading assessment, but it is not the same as testing reading comprehension. While textbooks often include vocabulary items, such exercises emphasize recall of word meaning rather than assessing what the whole text means. Students will often equate the learning and memorizing of vocabulary with reading improvement when in fact they may not understand how the words are used in context and the nuances of words. While vocabulary expansion is absolutely necessary and needs to be assessed, teachers must consider effective ways of testing vocabulary. Isolated matching exercises do little to improve student's word knowledge. While multiple-choice formats and matching exercises can be used to assess vocabulary recognition, the words on the exercises should relate to a reading passage and respondents should be asked to indicate what a word means within the context of a given passage. Tests that encourage the learning of the word, part of speech and appropriate usage given the context are more effective. For example, students might guess at the meanings of unknown words in a given passage. They should be encouraged to examine the context including the syntactic structure of the sentence. By determining the part of speech and attending to the contextual cues, work identification is facilitated. Students should be learning new words but should also be taught specific strategies to determine word meaning. Chapter 7 considers vocabulary related issues in more depth and provides examples of vocabulary tests and activities.

Questions and Short Answers - Another form of comprehension testing is the question and short answer. In this format, a set of questions usually follows a reading passage. The questions require students to write a few sentences or paragraphs in answer to a question about the reading. While some argue that such tests are biased in that they focus on a student's writing ability, the advantages of such tests far outweigh any drawbacks. Such tests demand production of language, reinforce writing skills, elicit responses to a range of reading strategies, and therefore test a range of critical and higher order thinking skills, and provide a more authentic task. The design of effective questions will require more time, and teachers must ensure that the structure and wording of the question does not lead students to provide a correct response without understanding the meaning of the text. Questions should test higher-order cognitive skills and should allow students to practice analysis, evaluation, and synthesis. *Bloom's Taxonomy of Cognitive Domains* has proven to be a useful framework for increasing cognitive responses through language. According to Bloom, there are six progressively complex domains of thinking which include *Knowledge, Comprehension, Application, Analysis, Synthesis, and Evaluation.*

Competence	Demonstrated Skills
Knowledge (recalling previously explicitly encountered information)	• observation and recall of information • knowledge of dates, events, places • knowledge of major ideas • mastery of subject matter • *Question Cues:* list, define, tell, describe, identify, show, label, collect, examine, tabulate, quote, name, who, when, where, etc.
Comprehension (recalling basic meaning and understanding what is read)	• understanding information • grasp meaning • translate knowledge into new context • interpret facts, compare, contrast • order, group, infer causes • predict consequences • *Question Cues:* summarize, describe, interpret, contrast, predict, associate, distinguish, estimate, differentiate, discuss, extend
Application (using learned material in new situations)	• use information • use methods, concepts, theories in new situations • solve problems using required skills or knowledge • *Questions Cues:* apply, demonstrate, calculate, complete, illustrate, show, solve, examine, modify, relate, change, classify, experiment, discover
Analysis (making connections among details)	• seeing patterns • organization of parts • recognition of hidden meanings • identification of components • *Question Cues:* analyze, separate, order, explain, connect, classify, arrange, divide, compare, select, explain, infer

Synthesis (combining elements into a new coherent whole)	<ul><li>use old ideas to create new ones</li><li>generalize from given facts</li><li>relate knowledge from several areas</li><li>predict, draw conclusions</li><li>*Question Cues:* combine, integrate, modify, rearrange, substitute, plan, create, design, invent, what if?, compose, formulate, prepare, generalize, rewrite</li></ul>
Evaluation (judging the adequacy of materials or ideas for a given purpose)	<ul><li>compare and discriminate between ideas</li><li>assess value of theories, presentations</li><li>make choices based on reasoned argument</li><li>verify value of evidence</li><li>recognize subjectivity</li><li>*Question Cues* assess, decide, rank, grade, test, measure, recommend, convince, select, judge, explain, discriminate, support, conclude, compare, summarize</li></ul>

Table 4 Bloom's Taxonomy of Cognitive Domains
Adapted from: *Bloom, B.S. (Ed.) (1956) Taxonomy of educational objectives: The classification of educational goals: Handbook I, cognitive domain.* New York, Toronto: Longmans, Green.

The above taxonomy provides a useful structure in which to categorize test questions. It also provides a helpful guide which teachers can use to design comprehension activities and questions which build both critical thinking and critical reading skills. Critical thinking is an on-going process all second language readers should engage in regardless of language proficiency level. Readers need to use information and knowledge in a variety of ways to allow them to seek alternatives, make inferences, pose questions, and solve problems. Activities that encourage such practice in critical thinking allow readers to develop their reading skills, enhancing their ability to understand increasingly complex texts.

Authentic and Communicative Tasks - More recently there have been great efforts in the area of language teaching and assessment to design truly authentic or communicative reading tests. This shift in large part is because test makers, teachers, and language educators have realized that when students can see the practical value in what they are learning and what they are being tested on, it leads to an increased motivation and an increased desire to learn and master the language. They also begin to see how their language abilities transfer to other subject areas and courses. As Canale (1984) points out, a good test is not only one that is valid, reliable, and practical in terms of administration and scoring, it must be regarded as fair, important and interesting by the students. Tests must also be able to provide clear, rich, and relevant feedback to the students. For example, a multiple-choice test following a reading passage, provides little feedback to a student other than a number, and has little to do with authentic language use. A more authentic task might be to examine the text for the author's main ideas. Such as task would more closely resemble work done in other courses and is testing a reader's ability to focus on the important ideas of a text rather than those that are less relevant to the meaning of the text. A number of different tasks can be designed to more accurately and authentically measure the reading proficiency of students. The following examples and reading tests/tasks were written by the author and used in an intermediate-level, academic ESL reading course.

Examples of Authentic Reading Tasks and Questions

1. This chapter dealt with immigration and migration. Write a one-page essay describing the reasons people move and the *advantages and disadvantages* of moving to a new place. In your essay, include at least *two examples* (situations or people) from at least two of the stories you have read that support what you are saying. You read, "The Great Migration" on page 134, "How to Eat a Guava" on page 139, and "The Circuit" on page 142.

2. In this chapter, we read stories involving anthropologists and ethnographers. Write an essay explaining who these people are and what they do. Use examples from the three readings to illustrate and support your descriptions of them. Your essay must have an introduction, body, and conclusion. Introduction - What is an anthropologist or an ethnographer? In general, what kind of work do they do? What kinds of information do they collect? What do they try to find out or learn? Where do they go to collect information? How do they collect it? What methods do they use? Body - In the body of your essay, you can be more specific. You can answer the above questions, but this time relate them to the articles. (Support what you have said in your introduction by telling us about the articles). In the articles, what were they trying to find out and how did they find this out? What methods did they use? You must provide specific examples from the articles. You must also paraphrase. Marks will be deducted if copying occurs. Conclusion-What do we learn from ethnographers? What is the benefit of their work?

3. Write a summary of the article *Childhood Obesity*. We have spent several classes discussing what a summary is. Your summary should present a clear and precise restatement of the article and should include the same content (information) as the article. It should include a topic sentence (your general statement) and information must be paraphrased. I expect very few, if any, spelling errors since you have the article in front of you, and you may also use a dictionary. You may also use a summary chart, but you cannot use a pre-written summary.

4. Read the article "America and Its Immigrants" by Lawrence Harrison. How does Harrison feel towards immigrants and their contributions to the country? What are some of his opinions or concerns related to our current immigration policy? Write a response to Harrison in the form of a letter in which you either support or refute his ideas. Include your personal experiences to make your point.

Figure 2 Examples of Authentic and Communicative Reading Test Questions and Tasks

Authentic tests offer several advantages to both teachers and students. Research into the use of authentic tests has shown that such tests provide a more realistic picture of a student's language abilities and reading proficiency. (Omaggio, 1986; Shohamy & Reves, 1985). Authentic reading tests and tasks allow students to actually use what is learned and there is a transfer from classroom teaching and learning to real-life application and performance. Students are also encouraged and called upon to use their skills to deal with authentic problems in language use rather than providing answers to problems often designed to test at the linguistic level only. Because testing more closely resembles learning, learners are much more involved in the assessment itself. Although these kinds of texts require more time to construct, authentic testing also allows teachers to more closely match course goals and course materials.

Computer-Based Testing

Technology is playing an increasingly more prominent role in the area of testing and more specifically reading assessment. Computer-based testing involves the computer as a tool for assessment instead of paper and pencil. Since answers to questions are input into a computer's memory, scoring systems are objective. Computer-based testing as evidenced in the literature, offers numerous advantages which include a reduction in testing time, immediate feedback and accurate evaluation, rapid access to test items, rapid editing of test times, and increased test security. Computer-based testing has also been shown to influence affective factors leading to decreased levels of frustration and boredom, and increased motivation. In addition, computer-testing can facilitate record-keeping and can also provide a wealth of information that can be managed easily and used for research purposes. Newer more advanced programming and authoring tools allow for a wider range of testing formats as well, including multiple-choice formats, fill-in the blank formats which might include deletion, insertion, and completion formats, matching formats, and drag-and-drop formats which usually involve matching and reorganization exercises. More recent authoring tools such as *Hot Potatoes* <http://www.halfbakedsoftware.com/> and *Script-0!* <http://www.readingmatrix.com/scripto/index.html> also make it possible to create tests that function online. Some of these authoring tools provide web forms that take teacher input and information and place it in a javascript. The resulting code is then written to a web server. Once the page has been created, it is no longer dependent upon the server where it was made and can be moved to any server. *Script-O!* also allows teachers to customize the output so that scores can be sent directly to the teacher via email and can be saved to a downloadable Excel file.

Computer-adaptive testing is a subtype of computer based testing. When an examinee is administered a test via the computer, the computer can update the estimate of the examinee's ability after each item and then that ability estimate can be used in the selection of subsequent items. With the right item bank and a high examinee ability variance, computer-adaptive testing can be much more efficient than a traditional paper-and-pencil test. In general, if the respondent answers a question correctly, one of greater difficulty if presented, and if the respondent answers an item incorrectly, then an easier item is presented. This pattern continues until enough information to assess the respondent's ability has been gathered (Cohen, 1994; Wainer, et.al., 2000). At present, most computer-adaptive tests are limited to multiple-choice formats, however, efforts are underway to produce assessment instruments both for computer-adaptive tests and computer-based assessment in general, that move beyond simply mechanizing existing product-oriented reading comprehension test item types to the inclusion of more process-oriented, interactive tasks. Chalhoub-Deville (1999) and Chalhoub-Deville and Deville, (1999) provide an in-depth discussion on reading comprehension and computer-adaptive reading tests by bringing together the work of experts in different fields relevant to the development of such tests. Developers are also now working on assessment tools that provide feedback but that also offer users ways to improve their performance and proficiency. One such project is the DIALANG system which provides diagnostic language tests in 14 different languages. The tests are for adult learners and include tests in reading, vocabulary, writing, grammar, and listening. Further information about this project can be found at <http://www.dialang.org/>.

The above section has presented and discussed a number of testing methods for assessing reading comprehension. It is important to note, however, that ideally, effective assessment should include more than one of these methods as no single test can accurately measure all that a student knows and is able to do. Therefore, to accurately and fairly assess each student's understanding, it is necessary to use multiple measures of assessment. In addition to assessment methods, teachers need to ensure that their assessment instruments are appropriate for the students, their level, and the task being measured. The following list provides some useful guidelines when writing and administering tests.

Guidelines for Writing and Administering Tests

The following guidelines may prove useful when creating reading tests and assessment tools.

1. *Consider the course objectives:* Teachers must be aware of the purpose of assessment and must be clear about what the goals of the course are and the kinds of reading tasks the students have been asked to do in the course, and will be able to do at the end of the course.

2. *Ensure the test is valid, reliable, and practical:* A test must test what it purports to test (valid), be dependable and consistent (reliable), and applicable to the situation (practical). A test is valid if it measures what it claims to be measuring. A test has content validity if it samples the content that it claims to test in some representative way. For example, if a reading test were meant to test reading vocabulary, then a test of reading would include tests of vocabulary. If a teacher has spent several classes focusing on main idea identification and features of a summary, an appropriate test might involve having students write a summary on a reading passage. Students would be required to identify the main ideas of the passage when putting it into summary form according to what was taught in class. The test itself would therefore match what is to be tested. Empirical validity is a measure of how effectively a test relates to some other known measure. One kind of empirical validity is predictive, or how well the test correlates with subsequent success or performance. A second type of empirical validity is concurrent, or how well the test correlates with another measure used at the same time. Teachers intuitively expect the better students to receive better scores and check for concurrent validity between the test and the student's daily performance. A test is reliable if it yields predictably similar results when it is taken again. While many factors can affect test performance, these kinds of variables usually do not introduce very large deviations in students' scores. A test may also be valid and reliable but may be too costly in terms of time and/or money. A highly usable test should be relatively easy to administer and score. Even when alternative methods of assessment such as portfolios are kept to document student progress, issues of practicality still emerge. The portfolio should be easy to maintain, accessible to students, and scored with rubrics.

3. *Be cautious of problematic test content such as bias:* Bias can take many forms and teachers must be aware of the different types. Linguistic bias can include geographic bias which happens when test items feature terms used in particular geographic areas that are not universally shared. Dialectical bias occurs when a student is tested using expressions that are known to certain dialect speakers that are not known to others. Cultural bias includes cultural content which may prove difficult for students without that cultural background. For example, American food items, American sports, or culture-specific stories may only be known to students familiar with that particular culture. Content bias may also be an important consideration as a reading test might be testing knowledge of other subject areas not known to students or may test several aspects of language proficiency rather than an area of reading meant to be tested by the teacher.

4. *Recognize potential difficulties in the testing situation:* The context in which a test is administered needs to be carefully examined to understand how culturally and linguistically diverse students might be affected. These factors include anxiety, lack of experience with testing materials, and time limitations. All students experience anxiety, but for many students anxiety can be compounded if the test is alien to the student's cultural background and experiences. Certain test formats such as multiple-choice or think aloud tasks may result in higher levels of anxiety as students may feel that these kinds of assessments inaccurately reflect their true reading proficiency. One way to reduce anxiety caused by these reasons is to allow students to take practice exams so they become familiar with various formats. Other accommodations such as simplified directions and permitting students to use dictionaries or word lists might be a consideration by the teacher. Time limitations is also an important consideration as some students may need more time than others because of time needed for mental translation and response formulation. Time extensions and untimed tests should therefore be considered. Cultural differences may also need to be addressed by the test administrator or teacher. Students from some cultural groups may not feel comfortable making eye contact with the test administrator. The student may be unfamiliar with the test format. Some students may be reluctant to guess on answers unless they are absolutely certain their responses are accurate and others may be embarrassed to volunteer a response or receive positive feedback about their performance (Cloud, Genesee, & Hamayan, 2000). In essence, administration procedures should also match classroom

instructional practices, and the assessment tasks should mirror learning processes with which students are familiar.

The assessment of reading comprehension can occur in several ways but the important point to remember is that assessment of reading will be more accurate and fairer if multiple measures of the same skills are used. Regardless of which assessment methods or instruments teachers may wish to choose, Swaffar, Arens, and Byrnes (1991) offer some basic principles to ensure that the methods being used work well for the students. It is important to choose texts that are familiar in content, interesting, unambiguous, and of appropriate length. It is also essential that teachers determine the reasoning behind students' conclusions and responses so that they obtain a more complete picture of what the student comprehends. The assessment tasks themselves should be designed so that students can demonstrate their knowledge including the content, textual, and linguistic schemata of the text. Finally, teachers should recognize and acknowledge that students will have individual interpretations of texts, and, therefore, this should be taken into account when evaluating responses.

Summary

There are several different methods of assessing reading. Before assessing readers; however, it is important for teachers to determine the purpose of the assessment and the specific types of knowledge to be assessed. Some methods of assessment such as journals, portfolios, reading logs, and checklists are ongoing and more student and learner-centered. More traditional methods of assessment include multiple-choice questions, recall protocols, cloze tests and completion exercises, vocabulary tests, open-ended short-answer questions, and authentic tasks. These kinds of tests are often used as achievement tests to determine student mastery of the material taught in class. When writing tests, teachers should ensure that course objectives are considered, that tests are valid, reliable and practical, that tests are free from cultural and linguistic bias, and that factors, which may interfere with performance, such as anxiety, lack of experience with testing materials, and time limitations have been carefully considered.

Discussion Questions and Activities

1. Read the story "Fish Cheeks" by Amy Tan. Design two questions for each of Bloom's Taxonomy Levels.

2. Standardized reading tests are often criticized for being biased. What are three possible sources of cultural bias which might affect these tests?

3. How can you determine if a low test score on a reading passage is because of lack of prior-knowledge, poor reading skills, or lack of preparation?

4. Select a short article and write 6 comprehension questions and 6 questions which cover a range of reading strategies and skills. Identify the specific strategy or skill addressed in each question.

5. Write a list of the pros and cons of each of the assessment methods described in this chapter. Share your responses with your peers.

6. Select a reading assessment instrument such as a standardized test, teacher-prepared test, or any other. Identify what is being measured and the appropriateness of the test questions to measure these skills. Compare your findings to someone who has chosen the same instrument.

Chapter 9
Planning and Designing the Reading Course

As teachers and administrators are well aware, the planning and design of a reading course involves many important decisions and a great amount of time. This chapter discusses the specific steps involved in this process. These steps include deciding what to teach in the reading course, the course goals and objectives, the structure or approach of the course, materials selection, and student and course evaluation. Throughout this chapter, examples from a specific ESL intermediate-level college reading course will be used to illustrate the various components that should be included in course design.

Conceptualizing the Reading Course

Before teachers begin to design a reading course, they must be able to conceptualize the purpose of the course. In other words, teachers have to formulate an overall description of the course which briefly explains what the course is about, and in general terms, what will be accomplished. A course description does not have to be complicated and can simply look like the following which is a course description for an ESL intermediate-level college reading course (*Effective Reading for ESL Students*).

Course Description
"Effective Reading for ESL Students" is designed to improve students' ability to comprehend written English, primarily academic prose and fiction, and focuses on using lexical and grammatical clues to derive sentence meaning; develop vocabulary; extract the main ideas; extrapolate information; draw conclusions; recognize basic written discourse conventions; interpret charts, timelines and tables; and interact with text through writing.

Table 1 Course Description for ESL Reading Course

Once the purpose has been established, teachers need to think about the course goals and objectives well in advance of any other aspect of course design. This is one of the most important tasks in the design of a reading course as the goals are used to guide teachers as they begin to plan the structure of the course and how students' performance will be assessed. Goals or course objectives can be stated in fairly general terms but they should reflect the expected outcomes, that is, the reading abilities that students should develop over the course and should indicate what students will achieve during the course. It is essential that before goals are written, teachers consider specifically what students must be able to do by the end of the course with the reading abilities. Students may need to meet specific standards or meet prerequisites for academic programs and courses. In essence, teachers should have a clear picture of where their students should and will be academically and therefore student needs play an important part in the formulation of course goals and objectives. The following statements are course objectives for the intermediate-level ESL reading course.

Expected Outcomes for Student-Course Objectives

1. Read with increased proficiency.
2. Comprehend selected non-adapted short stories written in standard American English.
3. Interpret and assess story lines and themes.
4. Distinguish and write about irony and figurative language.
5. Comprehend a corpus of non-technical and semi-technical vocabulary and compare and analyze similar terms for precise meaning and effectiveness within a piece of discourse.
6. Analyze single and multiple charts, tables, and timelines, solving problems, formulating conclusions and posing further questions in written and oral discussion.
7. Differentiate cohesive devices and their function across sentences and paragraphs.
8. Use flexibility in strategy application, depending on text complexity, purpose for reading, familiarity of topic, and learner strengths and weaknesses.
9. Examine author purpose in discourse text.
10. Compare narrative, descriptive, analytical, and argumentative rhetorical modes and combinations thereof.
11. Analyze and evaluate lexical choices.
12. Formulate conclusions; make assumptions, generalizations, and predictions.
13. Compare and contrast reader responsibility in American English discourse versus that of their own language/culture.
14. Select reading strategies appropriate to the task, situation, and personal learning style.

Table 2 Course Objectives for ESL Reading Course (Brazda & Singhal, 2002).

Once the goals or objectives have been identified, the teacher needs to select appropriate materials for the course. The materials will be used to fulfill the course goals. Most teachers will likely decide on one or two required texts and will also have a number of other texts on hand at the students' level of proficiency. Required texts, including nonfiction and fiction, must be chosen so that they include a range of readings in terms of genre and also provide the types of reading and reading skills and strategies teachers wish to cover in the course. The important point to remember, however, is that fiction and non-fiction texts have different textual features and readers need to be made aware of such features. A general distinction between nonfiction and fiction texts is that nonfiction texts present information and are generally the type of texts read throughout a reader's academic life. Fiction, however, can teach language and can also introduce readers to social, cultural, and political themes and issues. Both texts, as stated, are quite different and therefore require a teacher to use different methods when incorporating such texts in the course. Chapter 5 addresses various types of activities and approaches related to the teaching of nonfiction, and Chapter 6 discusses the selection and use of literary texts in more detail

The next phase of the course design, the course content itself, involves a great deal of planning and decision-making as teachers decide what is to be learned and the specific approaches through which course goals will be achieved. Approaches, as used here, refer to the theoretical underpinnings of language learning that guide or inform language practice and teaching. Teachers' approaches will vary depending on their beliefs about how reading and reading skills and best taught and learned. For example, Aebersold and Field (1997) point out that an extensive approach to teaching reading is based on the idea that when students read large quantities of text, their reading ability and reading comprehension will improve. In an extensive reading program or approach, students are given more choice in terms of what they want to read. They are often encouraged to read several texts about the same topic to build background knowledge. Reading in this type of approach is used to accomplish something else such as a written summary or report, group discussion, and so forth. The focus of the extensive reading program, therefore, is not on the detailed comprehension of the text itself or textual features which contribute to the meaning of the text, or even the building of reading skills or strategies through reading exercises, rather reading is a means to an end. On the other hand, an intensive reading approach is more commonly used and practiced in second and foreign language classrooms as texts are read carefully for comprehension. Students engage in reading exercises before, during, and after reading which allow them to practice a range or reading skills, and also which require them to focus on various aspects of the text. The content of a reading course is, therefore, in large part determined by the teachers' views on reading theory and pedagogy. The following provides an overview of the course content outlining the concepts and topics to be covered in this course. Instructors of this course employ an intensive approach to the teaching of reading.

Course Content

Part I. Grammar, linguistics, and strategy building for extended prose (12 hrs/2 wks)
 A. The structure of the English sentence as a key to meaning:
  1. Identifying the subject, verb, and complement in non-simple sentences; in periodic (subject postponed) sentences; and in sentences with verbal subjects
  2. Identifying noun modifiers: nouns, adjectives, prepositional phrases, adjective clauses, and reduced adjective clauses; and recognizing the punctuation of relative and reduced relative clauses as keys to their functions
  3. Identifying verb and sentence modifiers: adverbs, adverb clauses, reduced adverb clauses, prepositional phrases and their grammatical and semantic roles
  4. Formulating strategies to comprehend dense passages using basic element breakdown and modification information
 B. The verb form as a key to meaning
  1. Distinguishing tense vs. time aspect in finite verbs
  2. Recovering tense, time, and aspect information in non-finite verbs
  3. Formulating strategies to understand instructions and processes using tense, time, and aspectual information
 C. Voice as a marker of focus.
  1. Identifying lexico-grammatical structure in determining active, passive, and impersonal voice
  2. Making assumptions about the writer's reasons for choosing a particular voice.
  3. Formulating strategies to understand the focus of the sentence using voice information.
 D. The modal as a clue to a writer's attitude
  1. Distinguish between time and tense
  2. Interpreting the tense as past or non-past
  3. Determining modality: intrinsic freedom (having control over an event) vs. extrinsic freedom (not having control over an event)
  4. Disambiguating areas of semantic overlap
  5. Linking the modal to inference and speculation
  6. Formulating strategies to recognize, evaluate, and paraphrase a speaker/writer's attitude through an awareness of time, tense, and constraining factors of meaning
 E. Cohesive devices in English and their function across sentences and paragraphs

Part II: Vocabulary improvement (24 hrs/4wks)
 A. Prepositions
  1. Combinations with adjectives and verbs
  2. In phrasal verbs
 B. Strategies for understanding
  1. Using context clues
  2. Using thematic associations

3. Using lexicogrammatic markers
C. Mastering of selected words and idioms

Part III: Overall-comprehension-fostering strategies: semantic mapping/experience-text-relationship/(instructor's choice) (12 hrs/2wks)
 A. Research on using these reading strategies
 B. Intensive instruction in these strategies
 C. Selection and adoption by the student of at least one of these strategies
 D. Keeping a journal record of the experience and process with chronological, descriptive, and evaluative entries (optional but recommended)

Part IV: Academic readings (conceptual paragraphs and short chapters) (42hrs/7wks)
 A. Recognizing the author's purpose for writing
 B. Recognizing the main ideas and the major support details
 C. Extrapolating information--literal and inferred meanings
 D. Recognizing the writer's and reader's assumptions
 E. Drawing conclusions based on logic, lexical choices, assumptions, and weight of supporting evidence
 F. Interpreting charts, tables, and timelines
 G. Recognizing four basic rhetorical patterns, their markers and functions as an aid to making predictions (introduction)
 H. Interacting with the text in both written and oral discussion

Part V: The short story (18hrs/3wks)
 A. Analyzing and interpreting the text: (see Part IV A-E); making inferences; retelling the story
 B. Understanding literary concepts: identifying setting, plot, conflict, characterization, symbolism, and multi-level themes; interpreting figurative language; recognizing irony
 C. Identifying cultural influences: examining cultural values and behaviors that figure importantly in the text
 D. Interacting with the text in both written and oral discussion

Table 3 Course Content for ESL Reading Course (Brazda & Singhal, 2002).

Teachers also need to consider the amount of time to be spent on each aspect of the course, and this should be done while course content is being planned. This particular course is 18 weeks long, and the students meet twice a week for a total of six hours. The hours shown indicate the average number of hours that are spent on each topic. In this course, content is not necessarily covered in the order given, nor are components separated. Teachers may find it helpful to arrange the course content so that it is somewhat sequential in terms of skills. If skills are ordered progressively from easy to difficult, for example, such a logical progression will undoubtedly facilitate learning as students form the foundation for more complex skills and tasks.

While the above serves as an important and essential guide to teachers, it must be remembered that classes have a life of their own.

Unplanned events often occur in the classroom, and teachers need to take advantage of these moments and opportunities, which often lend themselves to great teaching and learning episodes. A student might ask a question which would require the introduction or explanation of a concept, or even practice of skills which was meant to be covered at a later time. Teachers need to be aware of these instances and be prepared to step away from a rigid, or pre-determined format or lesson to introduce or explain something new to their students.

Methods of Instruction

Methods of instruction must also be decided on when designing the reading course. Once again, the way in which content is approached in the classroom, and the activities through which students will enhance their reading skills will depend largely on teachers' views about how reading skills are best taught. The instructional methods and activities used in the classroom must be well thought out as they are used to meet the course objectives, and at the same time must expand students' opportunities to learn while maintaining their interest. The chapter on pedagogy discusses the specific kinds of activities that can be used to build reading skills before, during, and after reading. It is important, however, that teachers have a clear plan about the specific methods of instruction in their course. Teachers, therefore, need to identify and describe the typically used instructional methods as they relate to the learning objectives and content of the course. The following describes the instructional methods used in this course.

Methods of Instruction

Lecture
- Instructor lectures on features that facilitate comprehension of academic and literary texts (English rhetoric, rhetorical clues, organizational patterns, vocabulary building, and identification strategies, reading strategies, figurative language, literary concepts) and on techniques for further comprehending, analyzing, summarizing, organizing, and evaluating texts. Students demonstrate acquisition of basic principles in written and oral exercises/exams.
- Instructor explains note-taking symbols and effective note-taking methods.

Demonstration
- Instructor models how reading strategies can be used effectively in a variety of textual contexts.
- Instructor demonstrates critical reading strategies including summary analysis.

Discussion
- Students participate in discussions on issues and concepts in texts.

- Instructor guides students in discussions and exercises related to text content and text features.
- Instructor guides students in discussions on the effectiveness of rhetorical strategies used by the writer on a given text.

Technology
- Instructor utilizes online and software exercises for improvement of reading skills and strategies, and vocabulary expansion.
- Instructor incorporates wireless internet research for writing and discussion topics.

Video Presentation
- Instructor utilizes video content as listening practice. Videos on topics addressed in class build content knowledge.

Collaborative Learning
- Students participate in discussions on issues in texts.
- Students participate in group discussions on the effectiveness of rhetorical strategies used by the writer on a given text.
- Students engage in group and partner work in order to research and evaluate sources found on the Internet.

Table 4 Methods of Instruction for ESL Reading Course

Planning Course Assignments

Teachers must also spend some time thinking about the types of assignments that will assist students in achieving the learning objectives. The objectives, listed above for this for this particular course, are to improve and develop students' reading abilities, and reading comprehension skills and strategies. The assignments for this course include higher-level critical thinking skills and application of concepts so students have opportunities to apply and practice the skills that are taught.

Course Assignments
Essays • Students write essays and complete written homework assignments that challenge their ability to analyze, summarize, define, discuss, and examine texts and inherent issues and concepts. **Reading Assignments** • Students use critical thinking skills to demonstrate literal and general comprehension of assigned narrative, descriptive, analytical, and argumentative readings. • Students read an academic text covering several college-level topics in order to acquire skills in recognizing main ideas and supporting details, determining author purpose for writing, and formulating conclusions based on logic, lexical choices, assumptions, and weight of supporting evidence. • Students read ten short stories and identify the story line, formulating themes and discovering and evaluating for effectiveness elements of irony, foreshadowing, and figurative language. Students will examine cultural values and behaviors that figure importantly in the text. **Presentations** • Group presentation of paragraph analysis exploring main idea, supporting details, and grammatical structure in text. • Group discussion analyzing text paragraphs in terms of main idea and supporting details to derive meaning. • Students work collaboratively to engage in research and evaluate sources found on the Internet based on given criteria. • Students work in groups to formulate arguments and debate aspects of a topic. **Journal** • Students are encouraged to use inference in weekly journals to respond and react to readings on a continuing basis throughout the semester. **Portfolio** • Students engage in self-evaluation and self-reflection of performance portfolios.

Table 5 Course Assignments for ESL Reading Course (Brazda & Singhal, 2002).

Methods of Evaluation

Finally, no course design would be complete without an evaluation component. Teachers must consider the methods of evaluation, decide, and explain how student work will be evaluated. When designing the reading course, teachers should ensure that the methods evaluation demonstrate that students have met the expected outcomes for the course.

This process requires the re-visiting of course goals, which are then converted into statements that can be measured in some way through a measurement instrument or evaluative task. Such instruments and tasks might include tests, quizzes, homework, reports, and presentations. Chapter 8 deals with assessment and evaluation of reading in more detail. The following chart gives examples of the various methods of evaluation used in this reading course.

Methods of Evaluation

Essay Exams
- Student mastery of skills in analyzing, examining, critiquing, synthesizing, defining, discussing texts, and inherent issues and concepts is evaluated by comprehensive essay exams.

Exams and Quizzes
- Objective examinations, such as: multiple choice, true/ false, matching items, completion, etc.
- Student ability to select, connect, classify, and relate researched data following an organizational pattern is evaluated by achievement tests.
- Students' ability to summarize, organize, and analyze information presented in texts is assessed by classroom tests.
- Student retention of information in texts is assessed by discrete-point quizzes.
- Students are evaluated on their application of appropriate reading strategies to selected texts.

Written Homework
- Students' written assignments determine their ability to recognize author purpose for writing, to identify main ideas and major supporting details, to extrapolate information, to recognize writer and reader assumptions, identify rhetorical patterns and their markers.
- Written homework, judged on instructor established criteria, provides practice in further comprehending texts, analyzing and evaluating texts and implementing reading strategies and skills.

Reading Reports and Summaries
- Reading reports and summaries that are evaluated according to established rubrics and that assess student ability to research, organize notes, and assimilate information.

Organization of Information
- Student comprehension of the organization of information in academic texts is tested by their ability to reorganize prose into outline and graphic organizer formats.

Portfolio
- Students will collect samples of work over the semester and assess their own skills and select areas for improvement. Semester portfolio is evaluated on the basis of instructor-established criteria.

Table 6 Methods of Evaluation for ESL Reading Course

The design of a reading course is time-consuming but most essential as it creates a framework for the reading course and what takes place in the classroom. The well-thought out course serves as a guide for both teachers, as they introduce the goals of the course and implement the methods by which to achieve them, and students, as they embark on the journey of understanding the reading process, and the exploration of their experiences as readers.

Summary

The planning and design of a reading course requires teachers to make careful decisions, often taking up a great deal of time during the initial stages. Teachers must begin by conceptualizing the purpose of the course - that is to formulate a description of the course which explains what the course is about and what will be accomplished in the course. The next step is to think about the goals and objectives which should reflect the expected outcomes which are the reading abilities students should develop and achieve in the course. Appropriate materials must then be chosen to fulfill course goals. The course content is likely to involve the greatest amount of time in terms of planning and decision-making as teachers decide what is to be learned, the specific approaches through which course goals will be achieved, the time that will be spent on each aspect of the course, and the specific assignments that will help students achieve the identified learning objectives. Once that has been established, the methods of instruction, largely dependent on objectives and the teacher's view how reading is best taught need to be decided on. Finally, teachers must consider the methods of evaluation which demonstrate whether students have met the expected outcomes and the extent to which this has occurred.

Discussion Questions and Activities

1. Locate a syllabus or curriculum statement/course plan for a specific reading course. Identify and evaluate all of the elements discussed in this chapter.

2. Work in groups to design a reading lesson based on the course plan provided in this chapter. The reading lesson should contain objectives, materials, procedure and methods of instruction, and an assessment component.

3. Interview a reading teacher at a college and find out the process they went through to create a course plan. Record notes so they may be shared with others.

4. Locate a syllabus or course plan and take a look at the textbooks and assignments used in the course. Evaluate and justify the appropriateness of these materials used to meet the course goals and objectives.

Chapter 10
Teaching Reading: Professional Development and Reflective Teaching

This chapter begins by discussing the importance of reflective teaching and the ways in which this can occur in the reading classroom. The discussion also emphasizes the importance of professional development and the various opportunities that exist to allow for advancement of knowledge of the L2 reading field, including participating and presenting in conferences and carrying out classroom research to both contribute to the field of L2 reading and better understand the processes of L2 reading.

Learning and Reflecting

Effective teaching requires a willingness to carefully examine and reflect on one's own teaching practices and thoughts. Clearly, as educators we understand that teaching is in essence a lifelong learning process involving knowing and experimenting to bring about positive change. It is hoped that the readers of this book will realize that the intention of this book was not to provide reading teachers with prescribed curricula, activities, or classroom methods, but rather to focus on the needs of the reading teacher on a daily basis. If a teacher can read the preceding nine chapters and come away with some practical ideas, the book will have met one of its major objectives. A secondary purpose of the book was to assist teachers in reflecting on their own practices as reading teachers in the second language/foreign language classroom. As reading teachers in this context, we have a responsibility to further our knowledge and to contribute to a growing knowledge of L2 reading. Continuing education and professional development for reading teachers includes reading major journals, enrolling in relevant courses, participating in and offering workshops, and becoming involved with professional organizations. Teachers must learn from and join scholars and educators in the field of L2 reading to identify questions and methods of addressing those questions as they emerge in the field. Participating and presenting in local, national, and international professional conferences are valuable opportunities for professional teachers to contribute to the field of reading and further refine their understanding of the theoretical foundation of reading as it is further informed by research. Doing so allows us to apply theory to our own classrooms, in turn allowing us to formulate teaching philosophies about how the skill of reading is best acquired and most effectively taught. Reading teachers forming their own teaching philosophies and reflecting on their own practices might begin by considering the following questions:

Reflecting on Teaching
• What should happen in an L2/FL reading class? • What should not happen in such a class? • What should readers be learning in class? • What should readers be doing in class? • What forms of interaction are successful in the reading class? • What is my goal as a reading teacher? • What do I know about myself as a reading teacher now? • Do my lesson plans reflect what went on in reading class? • What changes did I make in the reading lesson plan during the class and why? • Was the reading lesson successful? Why or why not? • What changes can make the class more successful? • What did I learn about teaching reading today? • What did I learn about my students today?

Reflections can occur in the form of new ideas and insights during a class, or at the end of a class and can be noted on lesson plans, or in a teacher's journal. The important point here is that as reading teachers we take stock of what we do in our classrooms, the effect it has, and how we might improve on what we do. Stepping outside of ourselves in this manner allows us to assess the purposes and consequences of our intentions and actions in the classroom. The result of such reflection and reflective teaching is that classroom teachers are also researchers. By paying close attention to our students and effective ways of teaching and learning, we are able to improve the quality of student learning. As reading teachers it is, therefore, imperative that we continue to engage in classroom-based research in which we try out and implement new ideas in practice as a means of improvement and increased knowledge.

Conclusion

My own thoughts as an educator in the field of TESL and as a reading teacher is that while the reading process is complex and much more remains to be uncovered as we traverse through less explored areas, including the area of reading in the digital age, there are key factors emerging from the research in reading and effective classroom practices.

The following are some of the key issues that a reading teacher might wish to consider.

Principles for the Effective Teaching and Learning of Reading

- Effective reading is teachable and learnable and that flexibility and teacher and student commitment are necessary for both.
- Teachers should help students to value themselves as readers.
- Teachers should model the reading process.
- Students should read from a wide variety of genres.
- Students should have access to a wide variety of materials.
- Teachers should emphasize that reading has multiple purposes.
- Students should be given ample time to read.
- Students should be given opportunities to self-select texts.
- Extensive reading should be part of every classroom.
- Reading is a meaning-making process.
- Class and group discussion of texts facilitates reading comprehension.
- Successful reading involves effective use of strategies and schemata.
- Strategy lessons should be provided to all readers and such lessons should be contextualized, and be part of meaningful tasks and activities.
- Reading strategy instruction improves reading comprehension and proficiency.
- The teaching of effective reading strategies and skills is an ongoing process.
- Themes or topic units allow for the acquisition and development of academic concepts and linguistic proficiency.
- Teachers should provide meaningful activities and reading tasks that allow readers to develop critical-thinking and cognitively-demanding skills.
- Writing should be part of every reading class as the reading-writing connection is imperative to language development and critical thinking.
- Evaluation of student reading ability in an essential part of the reading class and reading assessment methods should be ongoing and methods should vary.
- The reading course curriculum should be planned from exit objectives that are based on what students will be able to do upon completion, and with consideration to the parameters of the program, duration of the course, and student needs.
- Because of the diversity of students and their differing proficiency levels, reading teachers must be aware of the factors that influence reading and of cross-cultural issues.
- Teachers themselves are classroom researchers, constantly investigating, reflecting upon, and interpreting information from their classroom to make their teaching, and in turn their students, more successful.

As teachers consider the issues in this book, it is hoped they keep in mind the context of the learning situation, their learners, and realize that the teaching of reading is both an art and a science. As teachers we bring to the classroom our creativity and originality, but in so doing, understand that such creativity and originality can be further informed by research and classroom practice, allowing us to recognize that the skill of reading can be developed in a coherent, meaningful and systematic way, be given continuity, and be taught.

Summary

Teaching is a lifelong process during which a great deal of experimentation and knowledge building occurs. Reflections on classroom experiences and teaching can allow teachers to grow personally and professionally. Professional development is also an essential part of this growth and includes reading journals, enrolling in courses, presenting at and attending relevant conferences, participating and offering workshops, and becoming involved with professional organizations. Engaging in the above allows teachers to evaluate what they do in the classroom, consider the effect it has on learning, and take steps to improve what they do and how they do it.

Discussion Questions and Activities

1. Choose an article dealing with reading research published in the past one year. Write a brief journal response to the article commenting on the content and what you learned.

2. Do an Internet search to determine upcoming reading related conferences in your areas.

3. Observe an ESL reading class as an action-researcher. Before you enter the class, do some reading on one of the topics below. Write two questions about the topic. Collect data about your research topic by taking notes, audio-taping, video-taping, or other methods). Write an essay describing what you found out about your topic. Topics - You might consider the sequencing of tasks, modeling of reading strategies, making text and input more comprehensible, teaching students of varying proficiency levels, types of feedback given during an ESL reading class, amount of student time on task, etc.

4. This book has focused on both the theoretical aspects of teaching reading and the practical application of those theories. Using this text and at least three other sources, write a 4-6 page paper formulating your philosophy of teaching reading to second language learners.

Appendix A – List of Reading Journals and Organizations

International Reading Association
http://www.ira.org/
The International Reading Association is a professional membership organization dedicated to promoting high levels of literacy for all by improving the quality of reading instruction, disseminating research and information about reading, and encouraging the lifetime reading habit.

The Reading Matrix
http://www.readingmatrix.com
This site serves as a source of information for researchers and educators interested in current issues and information surrounding reading in both first and second language contexts. Sections include Online Articles, Reviews, Organizations and Journals, Reading Disabilities, Reading Improvement, Research and Ethics, and others. The site also contains links to online reading activities and reading resources. This site also allows users to input their own suggestions.

Reading Online
http://www.readingonline.org/
This online journal focuses on literacy practice and research in K-12. "Literacy" is broadly defined to include traditional print literacy, as well as visual literacy, critical literacy, media literacy, digital literacy, and so on. A special mission of the journal is to support professionals as they integrate technology in the classroom, preparing students for a future in which literacy's meaning will continue to evolve and expand.

The Reading Matrix: An International Online Journal
http://www.readingmatrix.com/journal.html
The Reading Matrix: An International Online Journal is a peer-reviewed professional journal with an editorial of scholars in the fields of second language acquisition and applied linguistics. The journal seeks to disseminate research to educators around the world. It is interested in exploring issues related to L2 reading, L2 literacy in a broader sense, and other issues related to second language learning and teaching.

Reading Research Quarterly
Reading Research Quarterly (RRQ) is the leading peer-reviewed professional research journal for those committed to scholarship on questions of literacy among learners of all ages. RRQ supports the spirit of inquiry that is essential to the ongoing development of literacy research, and provides a forum for multidisciplinary research, alternative modes of investigation, and variant viewpoints about the nature of literacy practices and policies of diverse groups of persons around the world.

The Reading Teacher

The Reading Teacher (RT) is the choice for those involved with literacy education of children to the age of 12. A peer-reviewed, professional journal published eight times yearly, RT gives thoughtful consideration to practices, research, and trends in literacy education and related fields. It takes an active stance on issues affecting education today: appraising and extending the profession, promoting literacy worldwide, embracing pluralism, transforming teaching, owning technology, and connecting with the community. The journal is available to individuals as a benefit of IRA membership and to institutions by subscription.

Reading in a Foreign Language

http://nflrc.hawaii.edu/rfl/October2002/reviews/hood.html

A refereed online journal dealing with issues in foreign language reading and literacy. This fully-refereed journal is published twice a year. The journal focuses on both the practice and theory of learning to read and the teaching of reading in any foreign or second language. Reviews of scholarly books and teaching materials are also included.

Appendix B - Internet Sites – Online Interactive Reading Activities

Interactive Reading Exercises – Full Database	http://www.readingmatrix.com/directory/pages/
Reading Exercises	http://web2.uvcs.uvic.ca/elc/studyzone/330/reading/index.htm
Vocabulary Levels Tests Online	http://www.er.uqam.ca/nobel/r21270/levels/
Pulp Friction	http://web2.uvcs.uvic.ca/elc/studyzone/570/pulp/index.htm
Wild Children	http://web2.uvcs.uvic.ca/elc/studyzone/490/wchild/index.htm
Reading Exercises	http://web2.uvcs.uvic.ca/elc/studyzone/200/reading/index.htm
Reading Exercises-Short Stories	http://web2.uvcs.uvic.ca/elc/studyzone/410/reading/index.htm
Vocabulary-Internet TESL Journal Listings	http://iteslj.org/quizzes/vocabulary.html
CNN SF-Learning Resources-Articles	http://literacynet.org/cnnsf/archives.html
CNN-SF Learning Resources	http://literacynet.org/cnnsf/archives.html
EViews-Listening and Reading Activities	http://www.eviews.net/
Vocabulary Cloze Tests	http://yunus.hacettepe.edu.tr/~hoz/cloze/advanced/index.htm
Scrambled Word Quizzes	http://iteslj.org/quizzes/sw.html
Beginner ESL-Vocabulary	http://a4esl.org/a/v.html
Intermediate ESL-Vocabulary	http://a4esl.org/a/v5.html
Scholastic Interactive Storybooks-Early Readers	http://teacher.scholastic.com/clifford1/
Aesop's Fables	http://www.umass.edu/aesop/
Looking for the Freed Whales	http://www.geocities.com/frankie_meehan/WhalesQuiz3.htm
Trapped Whales Set Free	http://www.geocities.com/frankie_meehan/WhalesQuiz2.htm
Three Gray Whales Trapped in Alaskan Ice	http://www.geocities.com/frankie_meehan/WhalesQuiz1.htm
Gray Whales-Cloze Exercise	http://www.geocities.com/frankie_meehan/GrayWhales.htm
Who's Who and What's What	http://www.nytimes.com/learning/students/quiz/index.html
News Stories	http://www.cdlponline.org/news.html
Articles on Healthcare	http://www.litcracynet.org/vtd/articles.html
Story Plus	http://www.storyplus.com/FreeStoriesList.asp
The Moonlit Road-Ghost Stories	http://www.themoonlitroad.com/featurestories001.asp
Vocabulary Exercises	http://www.smic.be/smic5022/Onlineexercises.htm#Vocabulary
Linguarama-Business Vocabulary	http://www.linguarama.com/ps/vocab.htm
Beginner-level exercises	http://web2.uvcs.uvic.ca/elc/studyzone/200/vocab/index.htm
English Club.Com Vocabulary	http://quizzes.englishclub.com/vocabulary.htm
Advanced Level-Vocabulary	http://cctc2.commnet.edu/grammar/vocabulary.htm#quizzes
More Advanced Level Words	http://cctc2.commnet.edu/grammar/definition_list.htm

SAT Vocabulary Quizzes	http://www.seldeen.com/sat/index.html
Reading and Writing Activities-The Writing Den	http://www2.actden.com/writ_den/menu.htm
Quiz on Short Story Elements	http://www.quia.com/tq/212071.html
Vocabulary Test-Intermediate	http://www.forumeducation.net/servlet/pages/vi/show/static_vocabulary2.html
Word Formation Test	http://www.forumeducation.net/servlet/pages/vi/mat/w001.htm
Halloween Short Story	http://www.neko.ca/halloween/historyquiz.htm
High-Frequency Words-Cloze-Tests	http://132.208.224.131/ListLearn/2000_quiz_menu.htm
Vocabulary Quiz	http://www.readingmatrix.com/interactive_exercises/matching/matching.html
Latin Roots in English Words (Authorware)	http://www.readingmatrix.com/interactive_exercises/lessons/lesson11/chap11.html
Vocabulary-Fill-in the-Blank (Authorware)	http://www.readingmatrix.com/interactive_exercises/lessons/lesson3/lesson3.html
Multiple-Choice Vocabulary Quiz	http://www.readingmatrix.com/interactive_exercises/lessons/lesson7/chap7.html
Multiple-Choice Vocabulary Quiz	http://www.readingmatrix.com/interactive_exercises/lessons/lesson9/lesson9.html
Multiple-Choice Vocabulary Quiz (Authorware)	http://www.readingmatrix.com/interactive_exercises/lessons/lesson8/chap8.html
Vocabulary Exercise-Intermediate	http://www.readingmatrix.com/cgi-bin/ezmatch/quiz.cgi?q=chapter5
Identifying Tone	http://www.readingmatrix.com/cgi-bin/ezquiz/main.cgi?q=Tone
Vocabulary Exercises-Bob's Page.Com	http://www.robertoamorim.com/pages/sb_voc.htm
English Zone-Reading Exercises	http://www.english-zone.com/reading/
English Works-Reading Exercises	http://depts.gallaudet.edu/englishworks/exercises/main/reading.html
Watershed Game	http://www.bellmuseum.org/mnideals/watershed/watershed2.html
On the Prairie-Minnesota Ideals	http://www.bellmuseum.org/mnideals/prairie/index.html
Vocabulary Matching Exericse	http://www.readingmatrix.com/cgi-bin/ezmatch/quiz.cgi?q=chapter5
Vocabulary Multiple Choice	http://www.readingmatrix.com/cgi-bin/ezquiz/quiz.cgi?q=chapter9
Reading Exercises -English Works	http://depts.gallaudet.edu/englishworks/exercises/main/reading.html
Vocabulary - Matching Quiz	http://www.readingmatrix.com/cgi-bin/ezmatch/main.cgi?q=chapter8esl63
Vocabulary-Beginner Level	http://www.geocities.com/pccprep/qz.htm#vocab
Illustrated Vocabulary-Beginners	http://users.skynet.be/providence/vocabulaire/anglais/menu.htm
Reading-Doug Jones' Stories	http://www.eslbears.homestead.com/Map_and_Directions.html
Sight Word Books	http://www.netrover.com/~kingskid/dolch_store/indexstore.html
Room 108-Animated Books	http://www.netrover.com/~kingskid/108b.html
Stories to Read Online	http://www.beenleigss.qld.edu.au/requested_sites/storiesontheweb/storiesontheweb.html
Audio-Stories - Read On Site	http://www.beenleigss.qld.edu.au/requested_sites/audiostories/index.html
Kidspace-Internet Public Library	http://www.ipl.org/div/kidspace/storyhour/
Medical English reading exercises	http://www.englishmed.com

California Distance Learning Project	http://www.cdlponline.org/news.html
Vocabulary Exercises	http://www.fis.edu/eslweb/esl/vocab/index.htm
Proofreading	http://www.penandpage.com/EngMenu/prfread.htm
Proofreading	http://www.penandpage.com/EngMenu/prfread2.htm
Reading-ACE Practice Tests	http://college.hmco.com/devenglish/resources/reading_ace/students/index.html
South China Morning Post	http://vlc.polyu.edu.hk/SCMP/
Reading Comprehension Tests	http://218.103.45.154/vlc/comp/readcomp.htm
Synonyms-VLC	http://218.103.45.154/vlc/vocabsyn/vocabsyn.htm
Cloze Exercises-VLC	http://218.103.45.154/vlc/cloze/cloze.htm
Gap-Fill Exercises – VLC	http://218.103.45.154/vlc/vocab/vocab.htm
Aesop's Fables	http://www.pacificnet.net/~johnr/aesop/aesopsel.html

(*Links active at time of publication)

Appendix C - Glossary of Reading Terms

Academic Language Proficiency - Ability in language skills needed for mastering academic material; pertains to both written and oral language.

Accuracy - The ability to recognize words correctly.

Affixes - Affixes are word parts that are attached to either the beginnings of words (prefixes) or the ending of words (suffixes). The word *disrespectful* has two affixes, a prefix (dis-) and a suffix (-ful).

Alphabetic Principle - The idea that all letters have corresponding sounds and that letters and sounds can be put together to build words.

Analogy-Based Phonics - In this approach, children are taught to use parts of words they have already learned to read and decode words they don't know. They apply this strategy when the words share similar parts in their spellings, for example, reading "screen" by analogy to "green." Children may be taught a large set of key words for use in reading new words.

Analytic Phonics - In this approach, children learn to analyze letter-sound relationships in previously learned words. They do not pronounce sounds in isolation.

Answering Questions - Effective question-answering instruction shows students how to recognize what kinds of information is needed to answer questions. For example, students might learn that some questions require the synthesis of information from across a text.

Automaticity - Automaticity is a general term that refers to any skilled and complex behavior that can be performed rather easily with little attention, effort, or conscious awareness. These skills become automatic after extended periods of training. Examples of automatic skills include driving a car through traffic while listening to the radio, sight reading music for the piano, and reading orally with comprehension. With practice and good instruction, students become automatic at word recognition, that is, retrieving words from memory, and are able to focus attention on constructing meaning from the text, rather than decoding.

Balanced Approach/Balanced Literacy Instruction - A way of teaching reading that features different kinds of instruction. It usually means a combination of phonics and whole language instruction. Using this approach, readers learn to read through daily exposure to literature as well as instruction on the basic how-to skills of reading and writing.

Basal Reading Program - An approach to reading instruction that uses textbooks to guide the teaching of reading skills and strategies.

Base Words - Base words are words from which many other words are formed. For example, many words can be formed from the base word *migrate: migration, migrant, immigration, immigrant, migrating, migratory.*

Big Book - An oversized book used by a teacher for reading to a group that allows the children to more easily look at pictures, words, letters and sounds, and/or read along with the teacher.

Blending - Combining parts of a spoken word into a whole representation of the word. For example, /p/ /oo/ /l/ can be blended together to form the word POOL.

Bottom-Up Processing - Bottom-up models claim that the reader perceives every letter, organizes the perceived letters into words, and then organizes the words into phrases, clauses, and sentences. Meaning, at any level (e.g. word or phrase), is accessed only once processing at previous (i.e. lower) levels has been completed. Thus the reader will process all the letters in a word before the meaning of the word is accessed; likewise, the reader will process all the words in a phrase or a clause before constructing its meaning. The reader focuses exclusively on what is in the text itself, and especially on the words and sentences in the text. Also called text-based or data-driven reading.

Cloze - This is a method of assessment wherein a word is eliminated from a passage, and the reader's task is to use the context of the passage to fill in the blank with an appropriate word. Different cloze tasks focus on different skills; a cloze assessment can be used to test reading comprehension, language comprehension, vocabulary, syntax, and semantics.

Comprehension -The ability to pull meaning from spoken and written words.

Comprehension Strategies - Comprehension strategies are conscious plans or sets of steps that good readers use to make sense of text. There are six strategies that have been found to have a solid scientific basis for improving text comprehension. (See text comprehension.)

Comprehension Strategy Instruction - Comprehensive strategy instruction is the explicit teaching of techniques that are particularly effective for comprehension strategy instruction. The steps of explicit instruction include direct explanation, teacher modeling ("think aloud"), guided practice, and application. Some strategies include *direct explanation* (the teacher explains to students why the strategy helps comprehension and when to apply the strategy), *modeling* (the teacher models, or demonstrates, how to apply the strategy, usually by "thinking aloud" while reading the text that the students are using), *guided practice* (the teacher guides and assists students as they learn how and when to apply the strategy) and *application* (the teacher helps students practice the strategy until they can apply it independently).

Concepts of Print - Ideas about how print conveys meaning that readers need to have before they can learn to read, such as the left-to-right direction of text, the difference between letters and words, and the parts of a book.

Context Clues - Context clues are sources of information outside of words that readers may use to predict the identities and meanings of unknown words. Context clues may be drawn from the immediate sentence containing the word, from text already read, from pictures accompanying the text, or from definitions, restatements, examples, or descriptions in the text.

Cooperative Learning - Cooperative learning involves students working together as partners or in small groups on clearly defined tasks. It has been used successfully to teach comprehension strategies in content-area subjects.

Decodable Texts - Books for beginning readers that contain words with the same vowel sounds and similar spellings, such as, "The fat cat sat on the mat."

Decode - The ability to sound out letters and words.

Deep Orthography - A writing system that does not have consistent or one-to-one correspondence between the phonemes in speech and the written code. English is an example of a deep orthography -- no phoneme is consistently represented by the same letter in all words, and only one letter (the letter v) consistently corresponds to a specific phoneme. Examples of shallow orthographies would include Spanish and Finnish.

Developmental (Invented) Spelling - Spelling that results when young children use what they know about letters and sounds to write, for example, "I can read" spelled as "i kn rd."

Developmental Lag - When a reader's development in a particular area is behind most readers of the same age.

Direct Vocabulary Learning - Direct vocabulary learning is when students learn vocabulary through explicit instruction in both the meanings of individual words and word-learning strategies. Direct vocabulary instruction aids reading comprehension.

Duet Reading - An activity where a skilled reader sits next to a learner and the two read a text simultaneously.

Dyslexia - Difficulty in reading, spelling, writing, and related language skills that results from impairment in the way the brain processes information.

Early Reader - An early reader can read and sound out words and is able to extract meaning from what they read. Whereas an emergent reader may look to pictures to predict what will happen in a story, an early reader will use the pictures to check their understanding of what they read.

Embedded Phonics -In this approach, readers learn vocabulary through explicit instruction on the letter-sound relationships during the reading of connected text, usually when the teacher notices that a reader is struggling to read a particular word. Letter-sound relationships are taught as part of sight word reading. If the sequence of letter-sounds is not prescribed and sequenced, but is determined by whatever words are encountered in text, then the program is not systematic or explicit.

Emergent (Early) Literacy - The belief that literacy learning is an ongoing process that begins at birth and takes place when children have meaningful interactions with adults, including that they are read to, encouraged to talk about stories and events, and given opportunities to explore books on their own.

Emergent Reader - A child in the beginning stages of learning to read. This child knows the letters of the alphabet and can begin to match them with the sounds they make. The child also knows how to handle a book and interpret pictures.

Environmental Print - Words and symbols encountered outside of books in everyday life, such as product labels, logos, and traffic signs.

Fluency - Fluency is the ability to read a text accurately, quickly, and with proper expression and comprehension. Because fluent readers do not have to concentrate on decoding words, they can focus their attention on what the text means.

Fluent Reader - A fluent reader reads most words and phrases and is able to use varying strategies to figure out the pronunciation and meaning of unknown words and phrases. A fluent reader is able to question the meaning of what is being read.

Functional Print - Writing used for a specified purpose, such as signs, directions, lists, and personal messages.

Generating Questions - Generating questions involves teaching students to ask their own questions. This strategy improves students' active processing of text and comprehension.

Grapheme - A unit (a letter or letters) of a writing system that represents one phoneme; a single symbol that has one phonemic correspondent within any particular word.

Graphophonemic - Refers to the sound relationship between the orthography (symbols) and phonology (sounds) of a language.

Graphic and Semantic Organizers - Graphic and semantic organizers summarize and illustrate concepts and interrelationships among concepts in a text, using diagrams or other pictorial devices. Graphic organizers are often known as maps, webs, graphs, charts, frames, or clusters. Semantic organizers are graphic organizers that look somewhat like a spider web where lines connect a central concept to a variety of related ideas and events.

Indirect Vocabulary Learning - Indirect vocabulary learning refers to students learning the meaning of words indirectly when they hear or see the words used in many different contexts - for example, through conversations with adults, through being read to, and through reading extensively on their own.

Language Experience Approach (LEA) – This is a method of promoting reading in which the teacher begins with the experiences of the students bring to class (or experience together), and then develops oral and written activities around these experiences. The teacher uses the students' own words to write stories, which are then used in a variety of ways.

Letter Knowledge - The ability to identify letters of the alphabet.

Letter Recognition - The ability to name a letter that is displayed or find a letter in a group.

Letter-Sound Correspondence - The ability to say or write the letter that corresponds to a speech sound.

Lexical - Refers to the words or the vocabulary of a language as distinguished from its grammar and construction.

Lexicon - Often called the "mental dictionary," the lexicon is a representation of all knowledge a person has about individual words.

Literature Circles - In literature circles, small groups of students gather together to discuss a piece of literature in depth. The discussion is guided by students' response to what they have read. Literature circles provide a way for students to engage in critical thinking and reflection as they read, discuss, and respond to books. Collaboration is key in this approach. Literature circles guide students to deeper understanding of what they read through structured discussion and extended written and artistic response.

Logograph - A writing system wherein each spoken word in the language is represented by a unique symbol. Chinese is an example of a logographic writing system.

Metacognition - Metacognition is the process of "thinking about thinking." For example, good readers use metacognition before reading when they clarify their purpose for reading and preview the text.

Metalinguistic — Language and terminology used to describe language and the component parts of language.

Miscue Analysis – A miscue is defined as the difference between the oral response of a reader and the actual words printed on the page. Miscue Analysis is a method of evaluating reading comprehension using a detailed analysis of the types of errors made when reading aloud. Particular strategies are then used to help the reader correct his comprehension errors.

Monitoring Comprehension - Readers who monitor their comprehension know when they understand what they read and when they do not. Students are able to use appropriate correction strategies to resolve problems in comprehension.

Onset - All of the sounds in a word that come before the first vowel, for example /str-/ in "string."

Onset-Rime Phonics Instruction - In this approach, young readers learn to break monosyllabic words into their onsets (consonants preceding the vowel) and rimes (vowel and following consonants). They read each part separately and then blend the parts to say the whole word.

Orthography - A complete writing system for a language or languages. Orthographies include the representation of word boundaries, stops and pauses in speech, and tonal inflections.

Phoneme - The smallest units of sound that may be used to form words. For example, p-ea-k (peak) has three phonemes.

Phonemic Awareness - The awareness that spoken words are made of sounds, and the ability to identify individual sounds in spoken words.

Phonemic Blending - Blending individual sounds together to make words, for example c-a-t to "cat."

Phonemic Segmentation - The opposite of phonemic blending, separating a word into sounds, for example "cat" to c-a-t.

Phonics - The relationship between letters and the sounds they make.

Phonics Instruction - An approach to reading instruction that focuses on the sounds and spellings of written words.

Phonological Awareness - The ability to understand the relationships of sounds in spoken words. At a simple level, readers can identify rhyming words. At a more complex level, readers can identify similarities in sounds and spellings.

Picture Cues - Story illustrations that are closely matched to the words so that a reader can refer to the picture for help if he or she has difficulty with an unknown word.

Primary Language - The first language a child learns to speak.

Print Awareness - Awareness of the rules of written language, such as knowing that letters and numbers convey meaning and that words are separated by spaces.

Read Actively – To mark a text and take notes about important ideas as one reads.

Read Aloud - During a read aloud, a book that is too advanced for a beginning reader to read aloud to himself or herself is read aloud by an adult or more proficient reader. The purpose of a read aloud is to expose readers to a variety of books and to inspire a love for reading.

Reading Comprehension - The ability to understand written language. Comprehension includes both getting the gist of the meaning and interpreting the meaning by relating it to other ideas, drawing inferences, making comparisons and asking questions about it.

Reading Strategies - Approaches a reader uses to help discover the meaning of words and phrases, such as studying illustrations and making predictions.

Reading Study System - A systematic way in which to read and make sense of a text. P2R refers to Preview, Read, and Review. SQ3R refers to Survey, Question, Read, Recite, and Review, while S-RUN refers to Survey, Read, Underline, Notetaking. Students can be taught how to utilize these systems.

Reciprocal Teaching -Reciprocal teaching is a multiple-strategy instructional approach for teaching comprehension skills to students. Teachers teach students four strategies: asking questions about the text they are reading, summarizing parts of the text, clarifying words and sentences they don't understand, and predicting what might occur next in the text.

Repeated and Monitored Oral Reading - In this instructional activity, students read and reread a text a certain number of times or until a certain level of fluency is reached. This technique has been shown to improve reading fluency and overall reading achievement. Four re-readings are usually sufficient for most students. Students may also practice reading orally through the use of audiotapes, tutors, peer guidance, or other means.

Retelling - Summary of events in a story as told by a reader that helps an instructor or researcher gauge the reader's understanding of the story and ability to use language.

Rime - The first vowel in a word along with all of the sounds that follow, for example, /-utterfly/ in "butterfly."

Running Record - A method of observing, scoring, and analyzing a person's reading.

Scaffolding - A teaching strategy in which instruction begins at a level encouraging students' success and provides the right amount of support to move students to a higher level of understanding.

Scanning - A technique which involves moving the eyes quickly down the page to locate specific words and phrases. In most cases, the reader knows what he/she is looking for, so they are concentrating on finding a particular answer. Scanning is also used when one first finds a resource to determine whether it will answer their questions.

Schemata – Conventional knowledge structures that are activated as we collect and interpret experience; analogous to computer files into which data is constantly being placed.

Schema Theory - This theory is based on the belief that every act of comprehension involves one's knowledge of the world as well. Thus, readers develop a coherent interpretation of text through the interactive process of combining textual information with the information a reader brings to a text. Readers' mental stores are termed 'schemata' and are divided into three main types: content schemata (background knowledge of the world) and formal schemata (background knowledge of rhetorical structure) and linguistic schemata (knowledge of language structure).

Second Language - The second language a student has learned or is in the process of learning after a first language has already been learned.

Self-Monitoring - The mental act of knowing when one does and does not understand what one is reading.

Semantics - The study of the development and changes of the meanings of speech forms. Semantics is also a study of the process by which meaning is derived from symbols, signs, text, and other meaning-bearing forms.

Shared Reading - During shared reading, teacher and students read a familiar poem or story together. Shared reading gives students opportunities to read, gain confidence as readers, and appreciate reading as a social activity.

Sight Word - A word in a reading lesson containing parts that have not yet been taught, but that is highly predictable from the context of the story or which the reader has memorized. It is a word that a reader recognizes and reads without having to sound it out.

Skimming - A method of quickly identifying the main ideas of a text. Often this means reading the first and last sentences of paragraphs to obtain a gist of the text.

Story Structure - In story structure, a reader sees the way the content and events of a story are organized into a plot. Students learn to identify the categories of content (setting, characters, initiating events, internal reactions, goals, attempts, and outcomes) and how this content is organized into a plot. Often students recognize the way the story is organized by developing a story map. This strategy improves students' comprehension and memory of story content and meaning.

Summarizing - Summarizing is a process in which a reader synthesizes the important ideas in a text. Teaching students to summarize helps them generate main ideas, connect central ideas, eliminate redundant and unnecessary information, and remember what they read.

Survey – To go through a reading quickly to look at headings and the final paragraph before one reads.

Syllable - The smallest part that a spoken word can be broken into that includes a vowel, for example, "watermelon" has four syllables: wa-ter-mel-on.

Syllabication - Breaking words into syllables.

Synthetic Phonics - In this instructional approach, readers learn how to convert letters or letter combinations into a sequence of sounds, and then how to blend the sounds together to form recognizable words.

Systematic and Explicit Phonics Instruction – This is a method of teaching phonics. A program is systematic if the plan of instruction includes a carefully selected set of letter-sound relationships that are organized into a logical sequence. Explicit means the programs provide teachers with precise directions for the teaching of these relationships.

Text Comprehension - Text comprehension is the reason for reading: understanding what is read, with readers reading actively (engaging in the complex process of making sense from text) and with purpose (for learning, understanding, or enjoyment).

Think Aloud Protocol – This is a technique in which readers are asked to speak their thoughts as they perform a task/read a text aloud. While the focus in user testing is primarily on how effectively a user performs the required tasks, it is also on how users believe they are performing;

Verbalizations, therefore, are quite useful in understanding mistakes that are made and getting ideas for what the causes might be and how the interface could be improved to avoid those problems.

Top-Down Processing - Top down theories posit a non-linear view of the process in which comprehension begins with the readers contribution, i.e. from higher levels of processing and use of background knowledge, and proceeds to use the lower levels selectively. This type of reading involves approaching a text on the basis of prior content, language, or textual schemata that the reader might have with regard to that particular text.

Whole Language Instruction - An approach to reading instruction that focuses on learning the meaning and messages of the written words through exposure to poetry and literature. Readers are encouraged to use language creatively and expressively. It is also a philosophy of language instruction emphasizing integration of all language skills (reading, writing, speaking, and listening); reading for meaning; and contextualized language learning and use.

Word Attack - An aspect of reading instruction that includes intentional strategies for learning to decode, sight read, and recognize written words.

Word parts - Word parts include affixes (prefixes and suffixes), base words, and word roots.

Word roots - Word roots are words from other languages that are the origin of many English words. About 60% of all English words have Latin or Greek origins.

Word Wall - A tool to help young readers learn to recognize and read specific words. Words are listed alphabetically on a chart and displayed in the classroom for readers to refer to while reading.

Wordless Books - Picture storybooks containing no words, used to encourage storytelling and language skills.

-Adapted from: Every Child Reading: A Professional Development Guide. (November, 2000). Learning First Alliance. (*www.learningfirst.org*)
-The Language of Literacy – Some Commonly Used Terms. The Partnership for Reading. (*www.nifl.gov/partnershipforreading*)
-Glossary – Ballard and Tighe - (https://www.ballard-tighe.com/Ballard-Tighe/source/CommunityHTML/glossary.htm)

References

Adams, M. J. (1990). *Beginning to read: Thinking and learning about print*. Cambridge, MA: MIT Press.

Adler-Kassner, L. & Reynolds, T. (1996). Computers, reading and basic writers. Online strategies for helping students with academic texts. *Teaching English in the Two Year College, 23*(3), 170-178.

Aebersold, J. & Field, M. (1997). *From reader to reading teacher: Issues and strategies for second language classrooms.* Cambridge: Cambridge University Press.

Afflerbach, P.P., & Johnston, P.H. (1986). What do expert readers do when the main idea is not explicit? In J.F. Baumann (Ed.), *Teaching main idea comprehension* (pp. 49-72). Newark International Reading Association.

Agathocleous, T. and Dean, A. (2003). *Teaching literature: A companion.* New York: Palgrave Macmillan.

Ahmed, M.O. (1989). Vocabulary learning techniques. In P.Meara (Ed.), *Beyond words* (pp. 3-14). London: CILT.

Al-Seghayer, K. (2003). Technological and pedagogical considerations for a more effective electronic glossary. *The Reading Matrix: An International Online Journal.* http://www.readingmatrix.com/articles/al-seghayer/article.pdf

Alderson, J. C. (2000). *Assessing reading*. Cambridge, UK: Cambridge University Press.

Altman, R. (1997). Oral production of vocabulary: A case study. In J. Coady and T. Huckin (Eds.), *Second language vocabulary acquisition* (pp. 69-97). Cambridge: Cambridge University Press.

Ammon, M.S. (1987). Patterns of performance among bilingual children who score low in reading. In S.R. Goldman & H.T. Trueba (Eds*.). Becoming literate in English as a second language* (pp. 71-105). Norwood, NJ: Ablex.

Anderson, N. (1991). Individual differences in strategy use in second language reading and testing. *Modern Language Journal, 75,* 460-472.

Anderson, N. (1999). *Exploring second language reading: Issues and strategies.* Boston: Heinle and Heinle.

Anderson, N. (2002). The role of metacognition in second/foreign language teaching and learning. ERIC Digest. Washington, DC: ERIC Clearinghouse on Languages and Linguistics. Retrieved December 10, 2002 from http://www.cal.org/ericcll/digest/0110anderson.html

Anderson, N. (2003). Scrolling, clicking, and reading English: Online reading strategies in a second/foreign language. *The Reading Matrix: An International Online Journal, 3,*(3), 1-3. Retrieved December 2, 2003 from http://www.readingmatrix.com/articles/anderson/article.pdf

Anderson, R.C. (1984). Role of the reader's schema in comprehension, learning, and memory. In R.C. Anderson, J. Osborn, & R.J. Tierney, *Learning to read in American Schools: Basal readers and knowledge texts* (pp. 243-258). Hilldale, NJ: Erlbaum.

Arroyo, C. (1992). *What is the effect of extensive use of computers on the reading achievement scores of seventh grade students?* (ERIC Document Reproduction Service No. ED 353544).

Baker, L. & Brown. A. (1984). Metacognitive skills and reading. In D. Pearson (Ed.) *Handbook of reading research* (pp. 353-394). New York: Longman.

Barr, R., Pearson, P.D., Mosenthal, P.B., & Kamil, M.L. (Eds.). (1991). *Handbook of reading research: Volume II.* White Plains, NY: Longman.

Beach, R., & Hynds, S. (1991). Research on response to literature. In R.Barr, M.L. Kamil, P.B. Mosenthal, & P.D. Pearson (Eds.), *Handbook of reading research* (Vol. 2, pp. 453-489). New York: Longman.

Barnett, M. (1988a). Reading through context: How real and perceived strategy use affects L2 comprehension. *Modern Language Journal, 72*, 150-162.

Barnett, M. (1988b). Teaching reading strategies: How methodology affects language course articulation. *Foreign Language Annals, 21*(2), 109-119.

Barnett, M.A. (1989). *More than meets the eye: Foreign language reading theory and practice.* Englewood Cliffs, NJ: CAL & Prentice Hall.

Baumann, J.F., Jones, L.A., & Seifert-Kessell, N. (1993). Using think alouds to enhance children's comprehension monitoring abilities. *The Reading Teacher, 47*(3), 184-193.

Bean, T.W., Potter, T.C., & Clark, C. (1980). Selected semantic features of ESL materials and their effect on bilingual students' comprehension. In M. Kamil & A. Moe (Eds.) *Perspectives on reading research and instruction.* Twenty-ninth yearbook of the National Reading Conference, pp. 1-5. Washington, DC: National Reading Conference.

Beauvillain, C. (1992). Orthographic and lexical constraints in bilingual word recognition. In R. J. Harris (Ed.), *Cognitive processing in bilinguals* (pp. 221-235). North Holland: Elsevier Science Publishers.

Bernhardt, E.B. (1983a). Three approaches to reading comprehension in German. *The Modern Language Journal, 67*(2), 110-115.

Bernhardt, E.B. (1983b). Testing foreign language reading comprehension: The immediate recall protocol. *Die Unterrichtspraxis, 16*(1), 27-33.

Bernhardt, E.B. (1986). Reading in a foreign language. In B. Wing (Ed.), Listening, Reading and Writing: Analysis and Application. Northeast Conference on the Teaching of Foreign Language. Middlebury, VT: Northeast Conference.

Bernhardt, E. (1987). Cognitive processes in L2: An examination of reading behaviors. In J.P. Lantolf & A. Labarca (Eds.), *Research in second language learning: Focus on the classroom* (pp. 35-50). Norwood, NJ: Ablex Publishing Corporation.

Bernhardt, E. (1991a). *Reading development in a second language: Theoretical, empirical, & classroom perspectives.* NJ: Ablex Publishing.

Bernhardt, E.B. (1991b). Proficient texts for proficient readers? *ADFL Bulletin, 21*, 25-28.

Biederman I.& Tsao, Y.C. (1979). On processing Chinese ideographs and English words: Some implications from Stroop-test results. *Cognitive Psychology, 11*, 125-132.

Blake, R. (1992). Second language reading on the computer. *ADFL Bulletin,24*(1), 17-22.

Block, E.(1986). The comprehension strategies of second language readers. *TESOL Quarterly, 20*(3), 463-494.

Block, E. (1992). See how they read: Comprehension monitoring of L1 and L2 readers. *TESOL Quarterly, 26* (2), 319-341.

Bloom, B.S. (Ed.). (1956). *Taxonomy of educational objectives: Classification of educational goals. Handbook I: Cognitive domain.* New York: Longman, Green & Co.

Brazda, W. & Singhal, M. (2002). *Course Review for ESL 63.* Long Beach, CA: Institutional Research and Academic Services (Curriculum): Long Beach City College.

Brett, P.A. (1996). Multimedia applications for language learning – what are they and how effective are they? In Dangerfield, M. et.al *East to West,* 171-180. Bulgaria.

Brown, A. (1981). Metacognition in reading and writing: The development and facilitation of selective attention strategies for learning from texts. In M. Kamil (Ed.) *Directions in Reading research and instruction.* (pp. 21-43). Washington, D.C. National Reading Conference.

Brown, A. L. (1987). Metacognition, executive control, self-regulation, and other more mysterious mechanisms. In F. E. Weinert & R. H. Kluwe (Eds.), *Metacognition, motivation, and understanding* (pp. 65-116). Hillsdale, New Jersey: Lawrence Erlbaum Associates.

Brown, A, Armbruster, B, & Baker, L. (1983). The role of metacognition in reading and studying. In J. Orsany (Ed.) *Reading comprehension: From research to practice.* (pp. 49-75), Hillsdale, NJ: Lawrence Erlbaum.

Brown, A., & Palincsar, A. (1985). Reciprocal teaching of comprehension strategies: A natural history of one program for enhancing learning (Tech. Rep. No. 334). Urbana: University of Illinois, Center for the Study of Reading.

Canale, M. (1984). Considerations in the testing of reading and listening proficiency. *Foreign Language Annals, 17*(4), 349-357.

Carlson, P.A., & Larralde, V. (1995). R-WISE: A learning environment for teaching reading comprehension. *Journal of Computing in Higher Education, 6*(2), 74-98.

Carrasquillo, A., & Nunez, D. (1988). Computer–assisted metacognitive strategies and the reading comprehension skills of ESL elementary school students. (ERIC Document Reproduction Service No. ED 301838).

Carrell, P.L. (1981). Culture-specific schemata in L2 comprehension. In R. Orem & J. Haskell. (Eds.). *Selected papers from the Ninth Illinois TESOL/BE Annual Convention, First Midwest TESOL Conference,* pp 123-132. Chicago: Illinois TESOL/BE.

Carrell, P.L. (1984). The effects of rhetorical organization on ESL readers. *TESOL Quarterly, 18,* 441-469.

Carrell, P.L. (1987). Content and formal schemata in ESL reading. *TESOL Quarterly, 21,* 461-481.

Carrell, P.L. (1988). Some causes of text-boundedness and schema interference in ESL reading. In P.L. Carrell, J. Devine, and D.E. Eskey (Eds). *Interactive approaches to second language reading.* Cambridge: Cambridge University Press.

Carrell, P.L. (1989). Metacognitive awareness and second language reading. *Modern Language Journal, 73,* 121-134.

Carrell, P. & Eisterhold. J.C. (1983). Schema theory and ESL reading pedagogy. *TESOL Quarterly, 17*(4), 553-573.

Carrell, P.L, B. Pharis, & J. Liberto. (1989). Metacognitive strategy training for ESL reading. *TESOL Quarterly, 23*(4), 647-678.

Carter, R., & Long, M.N. (1991). *Teaching literature*. New York: Longman.

Chalhoub-Deville, M. (2001). Language testing and technology: Past and future. *Language Learning and Technology, 5*(2), 95-98.

Chalhoub-Deville, M., Ed. (1999). *Issues in computer-adaptive testing of reading proficiency.* Cambridge, UK: Cambridge University Press.

Chalhoub-Deville, M. & Deville, C.W. (1999). Computer-adaptive testing in second language contexts. *Annual Review of Applied Linguistics, 19*, 273-299.

Chamot, A. U., Barnhardt, S., El-Dinary, P.B., & Robbins, J. (1999). *The learning strategies handbook*. New York: Longman.

Chamot, A. U., & O'Malley, J. M. (1994). *The CALLA handbook: Implementing the cognitive academic language learning approach.* New York: Addison-Wesley.

Chou Hare, V. & Smith, D. (1982). Reading to remember: Studies of metacognitive reading skills in elementary school aged children. *Journal of Educational Research, 75,* 157-164.

Chun, D.M., & Plass, J.L. (1996). Effects of multimedia annotations on vocabulary acquisition. *The Modern Language Journal, 80*(2), 183-198.

Chun, D. M. & Plass, J.L. (1997, July). Research on text comprehension in multimedia environments. Language Learning & Technology, 1(1), 60-81. Retrieved December 21, 2002 from http://llt.msu.edu/vol1num1/chun_plass/default.html .

Clarke, M.A. (1988). The short circuit hypothesis of ESL reading - or when language Competence interferes with reading performance. In P. Carrell, J. Devine, & D. Eskey (Eds.), *Interactive approaches to second language reading.* Cambridge: Cambridge University Press.

Cloud, N., Genesee, F. & Hamayan, E. (2000). *Dual language instruction.* Boston, MA: Heinle and Heinle.

Coady, J. (1993). Research on ESL/EFL vocabulary acquisition. Putting it all in context. In T. Huckin, M. Haynes, and J. Coady (Eds.), *Second language reading and vocabulary learning* (pp. 3-23). Norwood, NJ: Ablex.

Coady, J. (1997). L2 vocabulary acquisition through extensive reading. In J. Coady and T. Huckin (Eds.), Second language vocabulary acquisition (pp. 225-237). Cambridge: Cambridge University Press.

Coady J. & Huckin, T. (1997). *Second language vocabulary acquisition.* Cambridge: Cambridge University Press.

Cohen, A.D. (1994). *Assessing language ability in the classroom.* Boston, MA: Heinle and Heinle.

Coiro, J. (2003). Reading comprehension on the Internet: Expanding our understanding of reading comprehension to encompass new literacies. Reading Online. Retrieved December 17, 2003 from http://www.readingonline.ortg/electronic/elec_index.asp?HREF=/electroni c/rt/2-03_Column/index.htm

Collie, J. & Slater, S. (1987). *Literature in the language classroom.* Cambridge, Cambridge University Press.

Connor, U. & Kaplan, R.B. (Eds.). (1987). *Writing across languages: Analysis of L2 text.* Reading, MA: Addison Wesley.

Connor, U. (1996*). Contrastive rhetoric: Cross-cultural aspects of second language writing. Cambridge:* Cambridge University Press.

Cook, G. (1989). *Discourse in language teaching: A scheme for teacher education.* Oxford: Oxford University Press.

Cook, V. (2001) *Second language learning and language teaching.* London: Edward Arnold.

Coxhead, A.J. (1998). *An Academic Word List.* English Language Institute Occasional Publication Number 18. Wellington: Victoria University of Wellington

Coxhead, A. (2000) A New Academic Word List. *TESOL Quarterly, 34*(2): 213-238

Coxhead, A. (2002). *The Academic Word List: A Corpus-based Word List for Academic Purposes in Teaching and Language Corpora* (TALC) 2000 Conference Proceedings Rodopi: Atlanta.

Coxhead, A. and Nation, P. (2001) The Specialized Vocabulary of English for Academic Purposes. In Flowerdew, J. and Peacock, M. *Research Perspectives on English for Academic Purposes*. Cambridge University Press: Cambridge.

Cummins, J. (1979). Linguistic interdependence and the educational development of bilingual children. *Review of Educational Research, 49*, 222-251.

Cummins, J. (1985). *Bilingualism and special education: Issues in assessment and pedagogy.* Clevedon, England: Multilingual Matters.

Cummins, J. (1998): e-Lective Language Learning: Design of a Computer - Assisted Text- Based ESL/EFL Learning System. *TESOL Journal*, Spring, 18-21.

Davis, J.N., & Lyman-Hager, M. (1997). Computers and L2 reading: student performance, student attitudes. *Foreign Language Annals, 30*(1), 58-72

Day, R.R. (ed.) (1993). *New ways of teaching reading*. Alexandria, VA: TESOL.

Day, R.R. & Bamford, J. (2002). Top ten principles for teaching extensive reading. *Reading in a Foreign Language,* 14(2), 136-141. Retrieved December 23, 2003 from http://nflrc.hawaii.edu/rfl/October2002/day/day.html

Devine, J. (1983). ESL readers internalized models of the reading process. On TESOL' 83 In J. Handscombe, R. Orem & B. Taylor (Eds.), Washington: *TESOL*, 95-108.

Devine, J. (1987). General language competence and adult second language reading. In J. Devine, P.L. Carrell, and D.E. Eskey (Eds.), *Research in reading English as a second language* (pp. 73-86). Washington, DC: TESOL.

Devine, J. (1993). The role of metacognition in second language reading and writing. In J.G. Carson & I. Leki (Eds.), *Reading in the composition classroom: Second language perspectives* (pp. 105-127). Boston: Heinle & Heinle.

Dole, J.A., Brown, K., & Trathen, W. (1996). The effects of strategy instruction on the comprehension performance of at-risk students. *Reading Research Quarterly, 31*(1), 62-87.

Draper, C.G. (1993). *Great American short stories 1: An ESL/EFL reader.* Englewood Cliffs. NJ: Regents/Prentice Hall.

Duff, A., & Maley, A. (1990). *Literature.* Oxford: Oxford University Press.

Ekwall, E. (1979). *Ekwall Reading Inventory Manual,* Boston: Allyn and Bacon.

Ericsson, K., & Simon, H.J. (1980). Verbal reports as data. *Psychological Review, 87,* 215-251

Esky, D. (2002). Reading and the teaching of L2 reading. *TESOL Journal, 11*(1), 5-9.

Flavell, J. H. (1987). Speculations about the nature and development of metacognition. In F. E. Weinert & R. H. Kluwe (Eds.), *Metacognition, motivation and understanding* (pp. 21-29). Hillside, New Jersey: Lawrence Erlbaum Associates.

Fletcher, J.D., & Atkinson, R.C. (1972). Evaluation of the Stanford CAI program in initial reading. *Journal of Educational Psychology, 63,* 597-602.

Fletcher, J.D. & Suppes, P. (1972). Computer assisted instruction in reading. Grades 4-6. *Educational Technology*, 45-49.

Garner, R. & Kraus, K. (1981-82). Good and poor comprehender differences in knowing and regulating reading behaviors. *Educational Research Quarterly, 6,* 5-12.

Gairns, B. (1992). *Cognitive processing in ESL reading.* Master's thesis, Ohio University, Athens. OH.

Garner, R. (1987). *Metacognition and reading comprehension.* Norwood, NJ: Ablex.

Geva, E. (1983). Facilitating reading comprehension through flow charting. *Reading Research Quarterly, 18,* 384-405.

Goodman, K.S. (1992). *Reading, writing, and written texts: A transactional socio-psycholinguistic view.* Tucson, AZ: Literacy and Learning Center, University of Arizona.

Goodman, K. (1996). *On reading: A common-sense look at the nature of language and the science of reading.* Portsmouth, NH: Heinemann.

Gough, P.B. (1972). One second of reading. In J. F. Kavanagh and I.G. Mattingly (Eds). *Language by ear and by eye.* Cambridge, MA: MIT Press.

Gower, R., & Pearson, M. (1987). *Reading literature.* Burnt Mill, UK: Longman.

Grabe, W. (1988). Reassessing the term 'interactive'. In P.L. Carrell, J. Devine, and D.E. Eskey (Eds). *Interactive approaches to second language reading.* Cambridge: Cambridge University Press.

Grabe, W. (1991). Current developments in second language reading research. *TESOL Quarterly, 25*(3), 375-406.

Grabe, W. & F.Stoller (2002). *Teaching and researching reading.* London: Pearson Education Longman.

Grainger, J. & Beauvillain, C. (1987). Language blocking and lexical access in bilinguals. *Quarterly Journal of Experimental Psychology, Human Experimental Psychology, 39*(2), 295-319.

Grainger, J. & Dijkstra, T. (1992). On the representation and use of language information in bilinguals. In R. J. Harris (Ed.). *Cognitive processing in bilinguals* (pp. 207-220). North Holland: Elsevier Science Publishers.

Hansen, J. (1981). The effects of inference training and practice on young children's reading comprehension. *Reading Research Quarterly, 16,* 391-417.

Hansen, J., & Pearson, P.D. (1983). An instructional study: Improving the inferential comprehension of good and poor fourth grade readers. *Journal of Educational Psychology, 75,* 821-829.

Hanson-Smith, E. (2002). *A brief history of CALL theory*. Retrieved December 21, 2002 from http://www.geocities.com/ehansonsmi/call_history.html.

Hanson-Smith, E. (2003). Reading electronically: Challenges and responses to the reading puzzle in technologically-enhanced environments. *The Reading Matrix: An International Online Journal*. Retrieved November 15, 2003 from http://www.readingmatrix.com/articles/hanson-smith/index.html

Hinds, J. (1983). Linguistics and written discourse in particular languages: Contrastive studies: English and Japanese. In R. B. Kaplan (Ed.), *Annual Review of Applied Linguistics, III* (pp. 75-84). Rowley, MA: Newbury House.

Holmes, B.C., and Roser, N. (1987). Five ways to assist readers' prior knowledge. *The Reading Teacher, 40,* 646-649.

Hong, C.S. (1997). The reader response approach to the teaching of literature. *REACT* (1). Retrieved October 2, 2002 from http://eduweb.nie.edu.sg/REACTOld/1997/1/6.html.

Hosenfeld, C . (1977). A preliminary investigation of the reading strategies of successful and nonsuccessful second language learners. *System 5,* 110-123.

Hudson, T. (1982). The effects of induced schemata on the short circuit in L2 reading: Non-decoding factors in L2 reading performance. In P.L.

Carrell, J. Devine, and D.E. Eskey (Eds). *Interactive approaches to second language reading.* Cambridge: Cambridge University Press.

Hulstijn, J.H. (1997). Mnemonic methods in foreign language vocabulary learning: Theoretical considerations and pedagogical implications. In J. Coady and T. Huckin (Eds.), *Second language vocabulary acquisition* (pp. 203-224). Cambridge: Cambridge University Press.

Janzen, J. (1996). Teaching strategic reading. *TESOL Journal, 6*(1), 6-9.

Janzen, J. (2001). Strategic reading on a sustained content theme. In J. Murphy & P. Byrd (Eds.), *Understanding the courses we teach. Logical perspectives on English language teaching.* Ann Arbor, MI: The University of Michigan Press.

Jimenez, R., Gamez, A. Literature-based cognitive strategy instruction for middle school Latina/o students. *Journal of Adolescent and Adult Literacy, 40*(2), 84-91.

Johnson, P. (1981). Effects on reading comprehension of language complexity and cultural background of a text. *TESOL Quarterly, 15*(2), 169-181.

Johnson, P. (1982). Effects on reading comprehension of building background knowledge. *TESOL Quarterly, 16*(4), 503-516.

Kamil, M.L., Mosenthal, P.B., Pearson, P.D., & Barr, R. (Eds.). (2000). *Handbook of reading research: Volume III.* Mahwah, NJ: Lawrence Erlbaum.

Kang, H. (1992). The effects of culture-specific knowledge upon ESL reading comprehension. *School of Education Review, 4,* 93-105.

Kaplan, R.B. (1966). Cultural thought patterns in inter-cultural education. *Language Learning,16,* 1-20.

Karlesen, B., R. Madden, & E.F. Gardener. (1966). *Stanford Diagnostic Reading Test.* New York: Harcourt, Brace & World.

Karolides, N. (Ed). (2000). *Reader response in secondary and college classrooms* (2nd Edition). Mahway, NJ: Lawrence Erlbaum Associates.

Kern, R. (1989). Second language reading strategy instruction: It's effects on comprehension and word inference ability. *Modern Language Journal, 73*, 135-146.

Kintsch, W. (1988). The use of knowledge in discourse processing. A construction-integration model. *Psychological Review, 95*, 163-182.

Kline, D. (2002). *Teaching literature online*. New York: Longman.

Knight, S., Padron, Y. & Waxman, H.C. (1985). The cognitive reading strategies of ESL students. *TESOL Quarterly, 19*, 789-792.

Koda, K. (1993). The role of phonemic awareness in L2 reading. Paper presented at the meeting of AAAL, Atlanta, April.

Koda, K. (1997). Orthographic knowledge in L2 lexical processing: A cross linguistic perspective. In J. Coady and T. Huckin (Eds.). *Second language vocabulary acquisition,* Cambridge University Press, Cambridge, UK.

Kramsch, C., A'Ness, F., Lam, Wan Shun Eva. (2000). Authenticity and authorship in the computer-mediated acquisition of L2 literacy. *Language Learning & Technology, 2*(4), pp. 78-104. Retrieved December 2, 2003 from http://llt.msu.edu/vol4num2/kramsch/default.html

Krashen, S. (1989). We acquire vocabulary and spelling by reading. Additional evidence for the input hypothesis. *Modern Language Journal, 73*(4), 440-464.

Krasilnikov, B.A. (1989). *Computers and reading skills development.* (ERIC Document Reproduction Service No. ED 312900.

Kurniawan, S.H., & Zaphiris, P. (2001). *Reading online or on paper: Which is faster?* In Proceedings of the 9th International Conference on Human Computer Interaction, August 5-10. New Orleans, LA.

Langer, J.A., Bartolome, L., Vasquez, O, & Lucas T. (1990). Meaning construction in school literacy tasks: A study of bilingual students. *American Educational Research Journal, 27*(4), 427-471.

Laufer, B. (1997). The Lexical plight in second language reading: Words you don't know, words you think you know, and words you can't guess. In J. Coady and T. Huckin (Eds.), *Second language vocabulary acquisition* (pp. 69-97). Cambridge: Cambridge University Press.

Leu, D.J.,Jr. (2002). The new literacies: Research on reading instruction with the Internet. In A.E. Farstrup & S.J. Samuels (Eds.), *What research has to say about reading instruction* (3rd ed.) (pp. 310-336). Newark, DE: International Reading Association.

Lindeberg, A.C. (1988). Cohesion, coherence, and coherence patterns in expository and Argumentative student essays in EFL: An Exploratory Study. Licenciate thesis, Department of English, Abo Akademi University, Turku, Finland.

Liontas, J. (1999). *Developing a pragmatic methodology of idiomaticity: The comprehension and interpretation of SL vivid phrasal idioms during reading* (Doctoral dissertation, The University of Arizona, 1999).

Lomicka, L. (1998). To gloss or not to gloss: An investigation of reading comprehension on-line. *Language Learning and Technology, 1*(2), 41-50. Retrieved September 15, 2003 from http://llt.msu.edu/vol1num2/article2/default.html.

Loranger, A.L. (1997). Comprehension strategies instruction: Does it make a difference? *Reading Psychology: An International Quarterly, 18*, 31-68.

Lyman-Hager, M., Davis, J. (1996). The case for the computer-mediated reading: Une Vie de Boy. *The French Review, 69*(5), 775-790.

Macaro, E. (2001). Learning strategies in foreign and second language classrooms. London: Continuum.

Martínez-Lage, A. & Herren, D. (1998). Challenges and opportunities: Curriculum pressures in the technological present. In J. Harper, M. Lively & M. Williams (Eds), *The coming of age of the profession: Issues and emerging ideas for the teaching of foreign languages* (pp. 141-167). Boston: Heinle & Heinle Publishers.

Mauranen, A. (1993). Contrastive ESP rhetoric: Metatext in Finnish-English economic texts. *English for Specific Purposes, 12*, 3-22.

McConkie, G. W., Zola, D., Blanchard, H. E. and Wolverton, G. S. (1982). Perceiving words during reading: Lack of facilitation from prior peripheral exposure. *Perception & Psychophysics, 32,* 271-281.

McLaughlin, B. (1984). *Second language acquisition in childhood: School age children.* Hillsdale, NJ: Lawrence Erlbaum.

Miller, G.E. (1985). The effects of general and specific self-instruction training on children's comprehension monitoring performances during reading. *Reading Research Quarterly, 20,* 616-628.

Miller, G., Giovenco, A., & Rentiers, K.A. (1987). Fostering comprehension monitoring in below average readers through self-instruction training. *Journal of Reading Behavior, 19*(4), 379-393.

Mills, D. & Salzmann, A. (2002, July 12). Grammar Safari. DEIL/IEI Lingua Center, University of Illinois at Urbana. Retrieved December 8, 2002 from http://www.iei.uiuc.edu/web.pages/grammarsafari.html.

Minsky, M. (1975). A framework for representing knowledge. In P.H. Winston (Ed.), *The psychology of computer vision* (pp. 211-277). New York: McGraw Hill.

Mokhtari, K., & Sheorey R. (2002). Measuring ESL students' awareness of reading strategies. *Journal of Developmental Education, 25*(3), 2-10.

Muter, P., & Maurutto, P. (1991). Reading and skimming from computer screens and books: The paperless office revisited? *Behavior & Information Technology, 10,* 257-266.

Nagy, W.E., and Anderson, R.C. (1984). How many words are there in printed school English? *Reading Research Quarterly, 19*(3), 304-330.

Nagy, W.E., Herman, P.A., and Anderson, R.C. (1985). Learning words from context. *Reading Research Quarterly, 20*(2), 233-253.

Nation, P. (1990). *Teaching and learning vocabulary.* Rowley, MA: Newbury House.

Nation, P. (2001). *Learning vocabulary in another language*. Cambridge, Cambridge University Press.

Nunan, D. (1995). *Language teaching methodology: A textbook for teachers*. New York: Phoenix ELT.

Nuttall, C. (1982). *Teaching reading skills in a foreign language*. London: Heinemann.

Olshavsky, J. (1977). Reading as problem solving: An investigation of strategies. *Reading Research Quarterly, 4*, 654-674.

O'Malley, J.M., & Chamot, A.U. (1990). *Learning strategies in second language acquisition*. New York: Cambridge University Press.

Omaggio, A.C. (1986). *Teaching language in context: Proficiency-oriented instruction*. Boston, MA: Heinle and Heinle.

Orndorrf, J. (1987). Using computers and original texts to teach critical reading and thinking. Paper presented at the meeting of the conference on Critical Thinking (Newport News, VA, April 9-12, 1987. (ERIC Document Reproduction Service No. ED 283137).

Oxford, R.L. (2001). Language learning strategies. In R. Carter & D. Nunan (Eds.), *The Cambridge guide to teaching English to speakers of other languages* (pp. 166-172). New York: Cambridge University Press.

Oxford, R.L., & Crookall, D. (1989). Research on language learning strategies: Methods, findings, and instructional issues. *Modern Language Journal, 73*, 404-419.

Oxford, R.L., & Crookall, D. (1990). Vocabulary learning: A critical analysis of techniques. *TESL Canada Journal, 7*, 9-30.

Oxford, R.L., & Scarcella, R.C. (1994). Second language vocabulary learning among adults: State of the art in vocabulary instruction. *System, 22*(2), 231-243.

Palincsar, A. & Brown, A.L. (1984). Reciprocal teaching of comprehension-fostering and monitoring activities. *Cognition and Instruction, 1,* 117-175.

Parkinson, B. & Reid Thomas, H. (2001). *Teaching Literature in a Second Language.* Edinburgh: Edinburgh University Press.

Paribakht, T.S. & Wesche, M. (1997). Vocabulary enhancement activities and reading for meaning in second language vocabulary acquisition. In J. Coady and T. Huckin (Eds.), *Second language vocabulary acquisition* (pp. 174-200). Cambridge: Cambridge University Press.

Paris, S.G., Meyers, M.. (1981). Comprehension monitoring, memory and study strategies of good and poor readers. *Journal of Reading Behavior, 13,* 5-22.

Parry, K. (1997). Vocabulary and comprehension: Two portraits. In J. Coady and T. Huckin (Eds.), *Second language vocabulary acquisition* (pp. 55-68). Cambridge: Cambridge University Press.

Pearson, P.D., Barr, R., Kamil, M.L., & Mosenthal, P.B. (Eds.). (1984). *Handbook of reading research: Volume I.* White Plains, NY: Longman.

Pederson, K. (1986). An experiment in computer-assisted second-language reading. *Modern Language Journal, 70,* 36-41.

Peregoy, S. & Boyle, O.F. (2001). *Reading, Writing, and Learning in ESL. A Resource Book for K-12 Teachers.* New York, NY: Addison Wesley Longman Inc.

Pritchard, R. (1990). The effects of cultural schemata on reading processing strategies. *Reading Research Quarterly, 25,* 273-295.

Pressley, M., Borkowski, J.G., & Schneider, W. (1987). Cognitive strategies: Good strategy users coordinate meta-cognition and knowledge. In R. Vasta & G. Whitehurst (Eds.), *Annals of Child Development* (Vol, 4, pp. 89-129). Greenwich, CT: JAI.

Pressley, M., Goodchild, F, Fleet, J., Zajchowski, R, & Evans, E.D. (1989). The challenges of classroom strategy instruction. *Elementary School Journal, 89,* 301-342.

Pressley, M. (1994). Embracing complexity: Studying good information processing and how it might develop. *Learning and Individual Differences.*

Pressley, M., & Afflerbach, P. (1995). *Verbal protocols of reading: The nature of constructively responsive reading.* Hillsdale, NJ: Lawrence Erlbaum Associates Inc.

Pressley, M. & Ghatala, E. S. (1990). Self-regulated learning: Monitoring learning from text. *Educational Psychologist*, 25, 19-33

Price, E. & Driscoll, M. (1997). An inquiry into the spontaneous transfer to problem-solving skill. *Contemporary Educational Psychology, 22,* 472-494.

Purves, A. (1993). *Towards a revaluation of reader response and school literature.* NRCLTL, Report Series 1.8. Albany, New York.

Rayner, K. (1975). The perceptual span and peripheral cues in reading. *Cognitive Psychology, 7,* 65-81.

Read, J. (2000). *Assessing vocabulary.* Cambridge, UK: Cambridge University Press.

Rigney, J.W. (1978). Learning strategies a theoretical perspective. In H.F. O'Neil (Ed.), *Learning strategies.* New York: Academic Press.

Rosenblatt, L. (1938). *Literature as exploration.* New York: Modern Language Association.

Rosenblatt, L. (1978). *The reader, the text, the poem: The transactional theory of the literary work.* Carbondale: Southern Illinois University Press.

Rosenblatt. L. (1990). *Retrospect transactions with literature: A fifty-year perspective.* (Eds.), Farrell, E. and Squire, J. (pp. 97-107). NCTE. Urbana, IL.

Rosenblatt, L. (1994), "The transactional theory of reading and writing." In R.B. Ruddell, M.R. Ruddell, & H. Singer (eds.), *Theoretical models and processes of reading, 4th edition*. Newark, DE: International Reading Association.

Royer, J.M. & Carlo, M.S. (1991). Transfer of comprehension skills from native to second Language. *Journal of Reading, 34*(6), 450-455.

Rumelhart, D.E. (1977). Toward an interactive model of reading. In S. Dornic (Ed.), *Attention and performance VI* (pp. 575-603). Hillsdale, NJ: Lawrence Erlbaum.

Scarry, S., & Scarry, J. (1999). *The writer's workplace with readings*. Orlando: Harcourt Brace & Company.

Schank, R.C., & Abelson, R.P.(1977). *Scripts, plans, goals and understanding*. Hillsdale, NJ: Lawrence Erlbaum Associates.

Schmitt, N. (2000). *Vocabulary in language teaching*. Cambridge: Cambridge University Press.

Segalowitz, N. (1986). Skilled reading in the second language. In J. Vaid (Ed.), *Language processing in bilinguals: Psycholinguistic and neuropsychological perspectives* (pp.3-19). Hillsdale, NJ: Lawrence Erlbaum.

Sheorey, R.,& Mokhtari, K. (2001). Differences in the metacognitive awareness of reading strategies among native and non-native readers. *System, 29*, 431-449.

Shimoda, T. (1989). The Effects of interesting examples and topic familiarity on text comprehension, attention, and reading speed. *Journal of Experimental Education, 61*(2), 93-103.

Shohamy, E., and Reves, T. (1985). Authentic language tests: Where from and where to? *Language Testing, 2*(1), 48-59.

Silberstein, S. (1994). *Techniques and resources in teaching reading*. New York: Oxford University Press.

Singer, H., & Donlan, D. (1982). Active comprehension problem solving schema with question generation for comprehension of complex short stories. *Reading Research Quarterly, 17,* 166-186.

Singhal, M. (1999). *The effects of reading strategy instruction on the reading comprehension, reading process, and strategy use of adult ESL readers* (Doctoral dissertation, The University of Arizona, 1999).

Singhal, M. (2001). *CALL for reading skills in English: An interactive web program for college-level ESL students.* Proceedings of the Information Technology & Multimedia in English Language Teaching Conference, June 1-2, 2001, The English Language Center of The Hong Kong Polytechnic University.

Singhal, M. (2002). Essay Genres: Personal Exploratory, Reader Response, and Language Autobiography Assignments. *WIRE-Writing Instructors' Resource.* Tucson, AZ: The University of Arizona Composition Program.

Smith, F. (1986). *Understanding reading: A psycholinguistic analysis of reading and learning read.* Hillsdale, NJ: Erlbaum.

Steffensen M.S., & Joag-Dev, C.(1984). Cultural knowledge and reading. In J.C. Alderson & A. H. Urquhart (Eds.), *Reading in a Foreign Language* (pp. 48-61). New York: Longman.

Stone, R. (1985). Effects of English/Spanish language pattern differences on ESL learners' Comprehension of English text. (ERIC Document Reproduction Service No. ED 266434).

Swaffar, J.K., Arens, K.M., & Byrnes, H. (1991). *Reading for meaning: An integrated approach to language learning.* Englewood Cliffs, NJ: Prentice Hall.

Tomlinson, C., & McGraw, R. (1997). Children's literature in adult EFL classes: Learning through response. *The Journal of the Imagination in Language Learning IV,* 50-57.

Van Dijk, T.A., & Kintsch, W. (1983). *Strategies of discourse comprehension.* New York: Academic Press.

Vandergrift, L. (2002). It was nice to see that our predictions were right: Developing metacognition in L2 listening comprehension. *The Canadian Modern Language Review, 58*, 555-575.

Wade, S.E. (1990). Using think alouds to assess comprehension. *The Reading Teacher, 43,7*, 442-451.

Wainer, H., Dorans, N., Flaughter, R. Green, B., Mislevy, R., Steinberg, L. & Thissen, D. (1990) *Computerized adaptive testing: A primer.* Hillsdale, NJ: Lawrence Erlbaum Associates.

Warschauer, M. (1999). *Electronic literacies. Language, culture, and power in online education.* Mahwah, NJ: Lawrence Erlbaum.

Warschauer, M. (2002). Networking into academic discourse. *Journal of English for Academic Purposes, 1*-45-58.

Warschauer, M. & Healey, D. (1998). Computers and language learning: An Overview. *Language Teaching, 31*, 57-71. Retrieved December 2, 2003 from http://www.gse.uci.edu/markw/overview.html.

Warschauer, M., & Kern, R. (Eds.). (2000). *Network-based language teaching: Concepts and practice.* New York: Cambridge University Press.

Warren, B.& Rosebery, A.S. (1988). Theory and practice: Uses of the computer in reading. *Remedial and Special Education, 9*(2), 29-38.

Waxman, H.C, & Padron, Y. (1987). *The effect of ESL students' perceptions of their cognitive strategies on reading achievement.* Presented at the Annual Meeting of the Southwest Educational Research Association, Dallas.

Weaver, S., & Cohen, A.D. (1997a). Strategies-based instruction: A teacher training manual. CARLA Working Papers Series #7. Minneapolis, MN: University of Minnesota, The Center for Advanced Research on Language Acquisition.

Weaver, S., & Cohen, A.D. (1997b). Strategies-based instruction: A teacher training video. CARLA Working Papers Series #8. Minneapolis, MN: University of Minnesota, The Center for Advanced Research on Language Acquisition.

Weaver, C.A. & Kintsch, W. (1991). Expository text. In R. Barr, M.L. Kamil, P.B. Mosenthal, & P.D. Pearson (Eds.), *Handbook of reading research* (Vol. 2, pp. 230-245). New York: Longman.

Wepner, S., Feeley, J.T., & Wilde, S. (1989). Using computers in college reading courses. *Journal of Developmental Education, 13*(1), 6-8, 24.

West, M. (1953). *A General Service List of English Words*. London: Longman, Green and Company.

Widdowson, H.G. (1983). *Learning purpose and language use.* Oxford: Oxford University Press.

Wong, C.J. *Integrating CALL into an ESL reading and writing class.* Retrieved September 15, 2003 from http://www.coe.missouri.edu/~cjw/call/intern.htm

Wurr, A., Eroz, B., and Singh-Corcoran, N. (Eds.), (2000). *A student's guide to first year composition.* Boston: MA, Pearson Custom Publishing.

Xue Guoyi and Nation, I.S.P, 1984, A University Word List, Language Learning and Communication 3, 215-229.

Zimmerman, C.B. (1994). *Self-selected reading and interactive vocabulary instruction: Knowledge and perceptions of word learning among L2 learners.* (Doctoral dissertation, University of Southern California, Los Angeles).

Zinn, A. & Poole, C. (1996). *Instructor's manual and test bank to accompany strategies for interactive reading.* New York: Harcourt Brace & Company.

Index

methods of evaluation, 200, 203
methods of instruction, 198, 203, 204
multimedia, 64, 68, 76, 85, 87, 88, 89
    multiple-choice, 42, 46, 47, 70, 72, 86,
    148, 172, 181, 183, 186, 187, 188, 190,
    191, 215

O

orthographic knowledge, 94, 97

P

portfolios, 172, 175, 176, 189, 191, 200
post-reading, 65, 103, 113, 115, 120, 121,
    171
pre-reading, 12, 44, 70, 98, 103, 106, 109,
    110, 112, 113, 120, 121, 171
prior knowledge, 10, 11, 12, 15, 21, 22, 28,
    39, 43, 44, 54, 65, 91, 92, 96, 98, 99,
    102, 105, 107, 112, 236
professional development, 6, 205
protocol analysis, 39, 40

R

reading strategies, 5, 13, 21, 25, 29, 30, 33,
    35, 37, 38, 39, 41, 42, 43, 44, 45, 54, 57,
    63, 68, 72, 92, 93, 95, 103, 104, 109,
    110, 113, 119, 120, 121, 142, 143, 157,
    159, 170, 183, 192, 194, 196, 198, 202,
    207, 208,
reflective teaching, 205, 206

S

scanning, 30, 51, 61, 70, 107, 119, 163, 173
schema theory, 11, 12, 20
schemata, 11, 12, 18, 19, 21, 25, 26, 46, 48,
    49, 57, 62, 81, 95, 96, 98, 99, 100, 104,
    125, 150, 151, 159, 172, 191
skills-driven approach, 23
skimming, 30, 61, 70, 86, 106, 119, 173,
    240
sociotransactional, 23
strategy training studies, 29, 41
summarizing, 21, 39, 44, 45, 62, 119, 155,
    198, 222

T

text-driven, 9
top-down, 7, 9, 10, 12, 20, 22, 23, 27, 30,
    37, 41, 61, 112

V

vocabulary acquisition, 64, 89, 154, 156,
    168, 170, 171, 226

W

web-based, 59, 60, 85, 89
word structure analysis, 161, 162, 163, 170